Godly People

From My Book The Ugly Side Of Pleasure

By
Lee Charles

Art: Marlen Boga
Cover Design: Lee Charles

Airleaf
Publishing

airleaf.com

ISBN: 1-59453-582-5

This novel contains adult themes, which may
not be suitable for some readers.

Get ready for Casey Park, and it's gossiping
wine tree. Where all the Ungodly, Godly people
reside. Where news travels faster than the speed
of light and where lust is more important than
nourishment, sleeping, even breathing.

From beginning to end God is in their mouths,
but is he really in their hearts? You be the
judge. Godly people just might remind you of
someone, maybe many people.

Chapter 1

BREAKFAST BETWEEN FRIENDS

"Bert! Girl! You sho' can make some good catfish 'n' grits!"

"It should be good, Selma. I been standin ova yo' stove since six this monin'...! You wont some mo' coffee?"

"Naw. Um about tuh burst, Bert. But you go ahead don't let me stop you from enjoyin' anotha one."

"Nigh you know that sometimes I like more than just coffee with my coffee, girl! A little brown liquor with it takes me a long, long way, takes the edge off, that's why I keeps me some in my purse, so you know I'll be enjoyin this one!"

"Girl! You somethin' else...Ooh, Bert, look what time it is! Let's git downstairs and open the sto' it's afta nine o'clock! We gotta stock them shelves! Baby Fatina probably outside the do' waitin fuh us tuh open up!"

"But I haven't finished my special coffee, Selma!"

"Bring it witcha, Bert! Ain't goan be nobody in the sto' fuh a while yet but you me and maybe Baby Fatina if she here. Come oan. Let's git goin'. I don't wont tuh make huh stand outside too long if she is here."

"Okay chil' just let me git my thangs togetha. I don't wont Clark findin nothin uh mine all thrown across y'all apartment. He don't seem too fond of a mess, Selma!"

"I don't know how you know it, Bert, but he sho' nuff ain't! Nigh come oan, we late!"

TROUBLED BORDERS

"There they go again. Them college kids, they parents, and teachers all lined up downtown carryin signs, marchin, shoutin, and demonstratin fuh black rights! They make so much noise and get oan my nerves so bad! Sometimes I hate that me and Selma bought this sto' downtown! I'd lack tuh git away from this foolishness, but they be doin the same thang at work! They contradictin theyself with that mess! Maybe we ain't, wonted in high payin jobs! But ain't nobody keepin us out of um but us! We be the only one's tellin oan each otha, and every time I pick up a paper all I see is some black person done killed anotha! They ain't nothin but a bunch uh hypocrites! That's why I do what I wont with who I wont and how I wont tuh do it! Them hypocrites cain't tell me nothin...

"Hey, Clark! Watchoo leanin up ginst that pole watchin so contented with yo' arms folded?"

"Hey, Anita! Um just watchin these fool protesters put oan a show, that's all! They just seem pointless tuh me! They ain't nothin but a bunch uh hypocrites! How you doin, Nita?"

"Um fine, Clark. How you doin?"

"Um okay, Nita I just told you, um okay."

"I ain't seen you in a while, Clark. That make you look better than okay! Tuh me, you look extra fine!

2

I lack that white straw hat with that black band and the way you got that white silk shirt rolled up tuh yo' elbows. You 'bout the only man I know who can wear his shirts lack that and look good in um. Clark. You built good and you look good. You just one fine man tuh me!"

"Stop it, Nita, stop talkin lack that...! Watchoo doin in town anyway? You come tuh pick up Tina? You know you don't hafta do that. We'll bring huh home. You know that ain't no problem...

"No, Clark, no. I didn't come fuh Tina. Um doin a little shoppin. I need me some new night clothes, undergarments—stuff lack that...

"Nita. I really gots tuh go—

"Why you rushin off, Clark?"

"Um tryin tuh slip in fo' Selma see me. She always find somethin fuh me tuh do if—

"Clark. Why you don't come 'round tuh see me no mo'? What I do? Did I do somethin wrong?"

"Naw, Nita, naw. You and yo' husband doin good nigh. I didn't wont him tuh catch us doin nothin wrong."

"We *was*, doin good, Clark. He been spendin most his time with Tina. He be takin huh tuh the racetrack, his job, basketball games, and anywhere else he go. He even be takin huh shoppin. He be buyin huh all sorts uh stuff. He spoilin that chil' rotten. I knew we shoulda had mo' chil'ren."

"Um sorry, Nita. I didn't know."

3

"Now that you do. You goan start comin 'round again, Clark?"

"You know 'bout me, Nita. You know once I drop one woman I get me anotha."

"Clark. I know all about you and that yella gal. You don't need huh or them otha women who be followin you 'round all the time. You done just about taught me everythang I need tuh know tuh please you—

"Nita! If you knew everythang. You'd know that I cain't leave that yella gal rat now. She'd tell Selma 'bout what me and huh been doin. I cain't let huh do that!"

"CLARK! YOU TRYIN TUH TELL ME THAT SELMA DON'T KNOW 'BOUT YOU AND THAT GAL! SINCE WHEN YOU GOT SO MODEST! OTHA THAN ME, OR SOMEBODY ELSE SELMA CLOSE TUH, SINCE WHEN YOU TRIED HIDEN YO' WOMEN FROM HUH!"

"Anita! Quiet down nigh! People walkin by! They all know you got a husband! You don't wont him and Selma tuh find out 'bout us! Odell damn near killed you when he found out 'bout you and Celdrin Brown!"

"Clark, please, nigh! Come tuh see me! Um buyin all these new thangs, fuh you, baby...!"

"How you buyin all them thangs fuh me, Nita! 'Til today you ain't seen me since I don't know when!"

"Please, Clark, please, nigh! Stop by tonight, Clark, pleeease! Odell goan be at work

'til in the monin. When you brang Tina home I'll
send huh rat tuh bed and me and you can be
tuhgetha fuh a couple hours lack befo'. Odell
won't nevva know."

"Okay, Nita. I'll see."

"You promise, Clark, you promise?"

"Nita! I tol' you, I'll see what I can do!"

"Please, don't dissapoint me, Clark. I need
tuh be with yah real bad tonight."

"I tol' you I'd see, Nita. Nigh let go uh my
arm fo' the wrong people see yah and start
talkin."

"Okay, Clark. I'll see you later. Please try
not tuh stand me up."

"I knew I shouldn'tna nevva messed 'round with no Nita,
but she so damned shapely and pretty. And I loves women with
long hair. I know she can please me, but I cain't mess with
huh no mo'. Odell kinda crazy. He don't need tuh be findin
out 'bout me and no, Nita. Naw, I betta not. Bad as I wont to
I don't thank um goan mess with Nita no mo'...

"Clark?"

"Gina! How you doin?"

"The question is, how you doin, Clark? You
sho' look lack you thankin hard. Did I scare yah?
Did I surprise yah?"

"Yeah, yeah, well, well—

"Clark, stop stutterin and talk tuh me. You
done fuhgot where I live?"

"Naw, Gina! Naw!"

"Then why ain'tchoo been by in ova two
weeks?"

"Girl. I been busy."

"You don't be doin nothin but sittin under that wine tree every day you come from work and all day long every weekend. Ain't nothin busy 'bout that."

"Gina, can we talk later? Um tryin tuh sneak in and git me some sleep fo' Selma see me and try tuh put me tuh work."

"You goan call me later, Clark?"

"Yeah. I'll call you soon as I wake up."

"Give me a kiss tuh seal yo' promise."

"Woman, you crazy? Don't you see all these people walkin by? They can talk all they wont about me messin 'round! I ain't goan let um see me do it!"

"Calm down, Clark. Calm down. Um just playin 'round!"

"Don't even play lack that, Gina! You know I done whooped you befo' fuh playin too much!"

"Okay, Clark! Okay! Um sorry!"

"Put yo' hands down, Gina! I ain't goan hitcha out in public! And move oan out my way! I'll call you when I git up!"

"Fuh real, Clark?"

"I said I would! Didn't I! And if I don't you know I was lyin! Nigh move oan out my way! If Selma catch me fo' I git my rest you might see me sooner than you wont to and the visit wont be a good one!"

THE STORE INCIDENT

"WHOA! WHOA! WHOA! A-A-A-A-H! I GOT IT!"

"FATINA! YOU OKAY BACK THERE?"
"YES, MA'AM! I JUST DROPPED SOMETHIN THAT'S
ALL. A BOX UH CEREAL ALMOST FELL OVA WHILE I WAS
TRYIN TUH STOCK THE CAN GOODS!"
"OKAY NIGH! JUST BE CAREFUL!"
"YES, MA'AM...!"

"Look, Selma, there's Daizell stealin again."
"You sho'-right, Bert...PUT THAT BACK,
DAIZELL! WHY YOU STEALIN! GIMME THAT STUFF, NOW!
I thought you was s'pposed tuh be a good Psychic!
Why ain't you somewhere readin palms tuh make you
some money tuh buy what you wont instead uh
stealin from me?"

"SELMA, JEAN, PORTER! HOW DARE YOU TRY TUH
EMBARRASS ME IN FRONT UH THIS BIG FAT HEFFA,
BERTHA MAE...

"DAIZELLE! YOU KEEP MY NAME OUT YO' MOUTH!"

"SHUT UP, YOU BIG FAT COW! I AIN'T TALKIN TUH
YOU! UM TALKIN TUH SELMA! WHEN UM DONE WITH HUH!
THEN IT'LL BE YO' TURN—

"Mommy Selma? What's goin' oan? Why ya'll
arguin—

"Fatina, these grown folks matters. You go
oan back in the storeroom and finish unpackin
them boxes. Me and yo' Auntie Bert'll handle
this."

"Auntie Bert! Auntie Bert! Hmph! Some aunt...
NIGH, SELMA! NIGH THAT THE CHIL' GOAN LET ME
FINISH TELLIN YOU SOMETHIN! JUST 'CAUSE YOU SEE
ME WITH SOMETHIN IN MY HAND DON'T MEAN UM STEALIN
IT JUST 'CAUSE YOU GOTS A LITTLE BIT MORE UH
SOMETHIN THAN OTHA FOLKS IN THIS TOWN! I DON'T
HAFTA STEAL NOTHIN FROM YOU! I MIGHT NOT MAKE THE
MONEY YOU DO! AND I MAY NOT HAVE AS MANY FRIENDS!
BUT ONE THANG FUH SHO'! UM A GOOD PSYCHIC! THE
BEST THERE EVVA WAS AND I DON'T HAVE TUH STEAL
FROM NOBODY! DON'T YOU FUHGIT THAT MISS, HIGH AND
MIGHTY!"

"Then what's in yo' pocket, Daizelle? Looks
like somethin' outta my sto' tuh me! Nigh, if you
gotta steal tuh feed yo'self, yo' fortune tellin
skills fall short!"

"I can tell you this, Selma, Jean, Porter!
That ugly, sorry ass man uh yo's is cheatin oan
you!"

"Daizelle! I don't need no fortunetella tuh
tell me that! Everybody 'round here that got eyes
knows that! And watch yo' dirty mouth 'til you
outta my sto'."

"Oh yeah? Well, they eyes ain't the first
thang that made um notice that sorry dog's trash,
I tol' um 'bout it first! And my mouth cain't be
nearly as dirty as Clark Porter!"

"Daizelle. Just put the items back and leave
my sto'."

"I'll put um back and I'll leave! Befo' I do, I gotta letcha know somethin I know yah don't know. That sorry, good fuh nothin yah married tuh is sexually abusin this chil'... Mm-hm, you heard me right, he messin with a chil'. She got long wavy black hair, 'n' she bright skin. She tall, 'n' got a pretty shape fuh huh age and she ain't but foeteen. Huh looks ain't goan last long though, 'cause he done got huh strung out oan drugs and stands under the wine-tree every day braggin 'bout it 'n' how if you knew you couldn't do a damned thang about it...!

Oh! So you and everybody 'round here who got eyes didn't know 'bout that, now did ya'll? Is that why you standin there with yo' mouth gaped wide-open lack you ready tuh catch flies and ain't sayin nothin, Selma? Well, it's true and you goan know it's true when he eitha dead, uh in prison! Now here yo' shit—

"DAIZELLE! I TOLD YOU TUH WATCH YO' MOUTH WHILE YOU IN MY STO'!"

"AAAAH JUST SHUT UP, 'CAUSE UM LEAVIN'! Ms. Daizelle don't need nothin from you, but um takin my time I ain't in no hurry!"

"GIT OUTTA MY STO' YOU OLD WITCH BEFORE I FUHGIT UM A CHRISTIAN 'N' KILL YOU!"

"Hee, Hee, Hee! I knew I could git tuh you, Selma, 'cause you weak! You cain't even let go of a sorry man lack Clark!

9

Why you stayin with a man lack that, anyway,
Selma? What he doin...hm? He doin them wicked
thangs tuh yah in the bed, ain't he? Them same
thangs he be doin tuh all his women...! Look
atcha, caint even say nothin, but I knows he is,
'cause he brags 'bout that too under the wine-
tree!"

"I WARNED YOU, DAIZELLE!"

"No, Selma, No!"

"Bertha, let me go!"

"No, they don't call me big Bert fuh nothin!
I'll sit oan you if I have tuh."

"Why you takin huh side, Bert?"

"Um not; um keepin you outta trouble! You
don't need tuh be goin no jail fuh that old
sorry, dirty mouthed, gossipin woman. She don't
know no betta, but you got mo' sense than that."

"Let huh go, Big Bert! I'll whip that bitch's
ass but good!"

"Okay Daizelle, whoop huh!"

"E-e-e-e-e-e-y, goan fo' I hurt you, Selma!"

"COME OAN BACK HERE DAIZELLE! WHY YOU
RUNNIN?"

"LACK I SAID, I DON'T WONNA HURT YOU! AND
YOU, BIG BERT, MISS NOW IT ALL, FAT BEHIND,
CONTROLIN BUSYBODY! I'LL TELL SELMA 'BOUT YOU,
LATER...!"

"What she done goan and got oan you, Bert?"

"Girl, you know how that crazy, dirty mouthed bird is. She might say anythang."

"That's fuh sho', Bert!"

"It sho' is! There's two thangs we can always count oan 'round here, Selma. Stories 'bout Clark bein who'eish and gittin a good laugh outta Daizelle."

"Um sorry, Bert, but the stories 'bout Clark have just about woe me out. And Daizelle, she just ain't funny tuh me no mo'."

"I noticed that. It just ain't like you. I ain't nevva seen you git that angry with huh befo', Selma. It ain't worth it. She just a crazy woman with a dirty mouth who goes 'round peepin in folks windows gitten dirt oan um, claims she can see what's happenin in they life, then she turns rat back 'round and throw it in they faces."

"I know that, Bert. The funny thang is, she always be tellin the truth. Even about me and Clark in the bed."

"Selma, you don't have tuh explain yo' sex life tuh me uh nobody else."

"I know that, but what Clark been doin tuh me fuh years been makin me feel dirty lately."

"That's nonsense, Selma, he's yo' husband!"

"He's also sleepin 'round, Bert! He probably is doin all them little nasty thangs he do tuh me, tuh all them otha women, just lack Daizelle

11

said. That's probably why they so crazy 'bout him."

"Come oan, Selma, don't talk lack that."

"It's gotta be the truth, Bert, 'cause women always be afta my husband. He won't as much as look at a woman when he with me, but everybody knows he who'eish. It makes me shame.

Afta sex with Clark, it's lack he done raped me in my own bed! But, I just caint help but lack it!"

"Girl, some women would do anythang tuh git a man lack that and you complainin."

"Bert, you just don't understand. It feel dirty tuh be messin with a man who mess 'round with all them women. I been blessed so far, but a man lack Clark can brang anythang home tuh me. Any old disease. It's just lack Daizelle said. Um too weak tuh let him go even though I know that. Um his fool, Bert! His fool! And it's gittin tuh me!

Bert, you suppose tuh love somebody enough tuh let um leave and too much tuh stay if they don't wontcha 'round. You shouldn't feel obligated tuh die fuh um but feel privileged tuh do it. When you see that person comin it should make yah feel happy and alive, and sex with um shouldn't feel lack somethin you done got paid tuh give, but somethin' you mo' then happy tuh fulfill. But, Bert. I don't feel lack that with

Clark. Every time we have sex I feel lack a who'e he done paid. I feel guilty 'bout sleepin with my own husband —lack God don't approve uh how um lettin Clark use me.

Sometimes Bert, I do thank that um cursed because uh that. All my sustas and brothas have chil'ren. Um already thirty-seven. Why don't I have any? WHY, BERT? Is it 'cause uh that? Am I sinnin fo' the Lord? Am I doin wrong? See, Bert, I just cain't thank straight no mo'. He killin me, mentally and physically. I gotta leave him fo' he finish me off."

"You tried that befo', Selma. Remember? You couldn't leave him."

"That's 'cause he caught me. He tol' me how much he loved me and went into that old mess uh his."

"I remember you tellin me 'bout it, Selma, but you never really tol' me what exactly happened that day."

"Oh, girl, it was somethin else. He pushed me ginst the 'frigerator and I tried tuh fight him off. He lifted my blouse, bra and put my breasts in his mouth. I screamed and scratched his face up but good. He wouldn't stop until he had me moanin and beggin him tuh finish what he'd started and thought I didn't wont, and agreed tuh stay. That same night, he slipped off and went down tuh Clarrietta's house."

"Selma. You ain't talkin 'bout that yella gal that stay in the slums oan Old Alm drive?"

"Wait a minute, Bert. Let me go check and see where Fatina is."

"Hurry back, Selma, this gitten good."

"She okay, Bert. She still unpackin, it's goan take huh a while tuh finish. But yeah, Bert! That's the Clarrietta. The one that stay in them slums."

"But, she lay up with anybody and anythang!"

"I know that, Bert. But he was there in huh dirty kitchen with just the light of a candle. He was sittin in one uh huh old raggedy dirty kitchen chairs and she was kneelin in front of him with huh head down in his lap. I thought that was all he was there fuh 'cause everybody knows how nasty that gal is. It shocked me when he stood up befo' she was done, grabbed a hand full of huh dirty-brown-red hair in his fist and pushed huh, face first 'ginst the wall. She had this confused, scared look oan huh face that I'll nevva fuhgit.

He pulled up that filthy gown uh huh's and put hisself inside huh rear. She screamed lack what she is, "a pig," and she started strugglin tuh git free from Clark. Huh nose had started bleedin from him slammin huh face into the wall so hard, and huh face was beet red. Huh feet was slippin 'n' slidin. She was clawin up the wall

lack a cat, tryin tuh find a way tuh git a grip
oan somethin so she could git him off huh. That
gal was strugglin and squealin so, I could even
see the veins in huh forehead and neck stickin
out.

That musta been the only thang that dirty sow
hadn't done. I done heard mo' stories 'bout huh."
"Most everybody in Casey Park done heard them
stories, Selma."
"Um Sho' they have, Bert."

"Selma, how'd you know he was at
Clarrietta's?"
"I'd followed him befo', Bert, but I'd nevva
had the nerve tuh look inside. I'd just go tuh
make sho' that's where he was, in case I evva got
up enough nerve tuh confront him 'bout it, and
God knows, Bert, after what I saw, I was sorry
that I'd chose that night outta all the othas I'd
followed him tuh git bold. Blood was runnin down
huh legs, too it was sickenin, Bert. Clarrietta
was tremblin and moanin as if she'd goan in shock
uh somethin. She was limp and gaspin fuh breath,
but that nasty, husband uh mine didn't let up oan
huh. The mo' she tried tuh struggle with the
little strength she had, the tighter Clark's hold
got. He had one arm 'round huh waist 'n' was
pushin huh head 'ginst the wall with the otha
one. She could barely breathe. She so skinny and
frail, I thought he was goan break huh neck the

way she was strugglin tuh git free. That scared
me tuh death, Bert, 'cause see, ya'll don't know
how strong Clark is fuh a man his size but I do.
He could break a person in half if he wont to.
That's all I could thank about and I wonted tuh
turn 'n' run, but I felt stiff and before I could
he'd turned his head and seen me lookin in the
window. All he did was turn his head the otha way
'til he was done.

He let Clarrietta drop tuh the flo' lack
somethin he was goan throw 'way later. She laid
there curled up with one hand holdin huh nose the
otha oan huh stomach lack huh guts had been
ripped out.

He stared at me while he zipped his pants. I
knew he was goan come afta me, but I couldn't
move.

I snapped back tuh reality, turned tuh run,
and fell. Befo' I could git up he was standin ova
me. He picked me up, snatched my car keys, threw
me in my car, and took me home."

"How did he git tuh Clarietta's house?"

"He'd drove his truck there, but he left it.
You know how bold he is. He didn't care nothin
'bout no truck rat then. His mind was oan teachin
me a lesson.

That was a gruesome night, Bert. That was the first time I'd ever seen him silent.

All the way home I begged that man not tuh do tuh me what he'd done tuh Clarrietta, but he wouldn't say nothin. Bert, he's been overly blessed and I didn't wont tuh feel the pain Clarrietta had...

"Selma. Maybe Clarietta had experienced what Clark had done to huh. Law'd knows she dirty! I heard that chil' will do anythang! Maybe she just nevva let him do it 'cause uh that—'cause uh his blessin!"

"I don't know, Bert. But I didn't wont no parts of it. So when we pulled up tuh the do' I tried tuh jump out the car so that I could run and lock myself inside the house. He grabbed my wrists and pulled me out the car oan the driver's side. He took me straight tuh the bedroom and threw me down oan the bed so hard I had tuh grab oan tuh the mattress tuh stop rollin 'n' bouncin and tuh keep myself from fallin off the side of it.

I knew I was goan have tuh fight that man, 'cause the look oan his face tol' me I was in big trouble so I started swangin and kickin lack crazy. I knocked that stupid lookin white hat off his head. He grinned that evil sarcastic grin uh his at me, grabbed my ankles while I was still kickin, and kneeled down oan the bed. I tried tuh crawl away from him but I couldn't. He grabbed me with one arm 'round my waist, and flipped me upside down. My skirt flew ova my head and Clark went tuh takin off my under clothes. I couldn't see a thang, but my mind was still workin. I knew he was goan touch me and he'd just been with that filthy—h-heffa! I went tuh strugglin and that, I thought, loosened his hold oan me. But befo' I could straighten up, he put both arms 'round the backs uh my knees, pushed them into my chest so I'd stay upside down and curled up, pulled me tuh him and did somethin so indecent tuh me it made me sick. He let me up, but he didn't let go uh me 'til afta he squeezed my checks tuhgetha so that he could stick his tongue in my mouth."

"Oh my God, Selma; Clark's a dog! Only a dog would put his face someplace lack that! Suppose you woulda passed gas!"

"Bert, that ain't even funny! He reeked of cigarettes, alcohol, Clarietta, and me! That shamed me fuh 'bout six months! He made me sick! It just wadn't funny!"

"I know, sweetnin. That Clark ain't worth a dime!"

"You tellin me, Bert!"

"Naw, Selma! 'Cause we both know he impure, vile, disgustin, and insensitive! Ain't nothin sacred tuh him or about him! He just one uh these real nasty people that's all!"

"I know how he is, Bertha Mae, but he ain't all that bad! He was just upset 'cause I followed

him! I didn't have no right tuh do it and he was
just lettin me know that! He even asked me if I
was goan follow him again! I tol' him that I
wouldn't and girl, I made sho' I didn't!

At the time we'd only been married two years
and he'd already been messin with mo' women than
I had teeth. I was glad he'd hurt Clarrietta
though. I kept hopin she'd die. It wadn't two
weeks befo' she was up tuh huh old tricks again
and probably willingly doin what Clark had taught
huh that night."

"You mean if Clark the one who taught huh,
Selma!"

"Well, yeah, I guess that's what I mean,
Bert. Anyway, bein young and silly; I tried
reasonin with Clark. You know. 'Bout his
lustfulness 'n' all? I asked him why he needed so
many women. He tol' me 'cause he loved me too
much tuh do them thangs with me. I tol' him the
same thang you tol' me. That um his wife and what
we did in our bedroom was between us. He started
doin them thangs tuh me little by little, except
fuh what he did tuh Clarietta that night, and he
tried not tuh hurt me. Bert, that man was so
gentle you wouldn't believe it. He still real
gentle with me. The only time he wadn't, was the
night I followed him, and I done jumped oan him
many times since then 'bout women I done caught
him with, uh heard about and he ain't nevva done

as much as raise a hand tuh me. And his paycheck always mine.

He always tellin' me how he love me so much he'd die fuh me and it would kill him if I left him, but Bert, why do his sex habits and his cheatin make me feel so dirty now? Why is it afta twelve years uh marriage I wonna leave him? I feel lack I caint put up with his cheatin or his evil habits no mo'. I know this sound funny, but when I kiss him all I can thank about is how um kissin every gal's butt in Casey Park, except fuh yours and old crazy Daizelle's."

"It is funny, Selma, but do you thank bein in the church has anythang tuh do with what you feelin? I don't mean the kissin every gal's butt in town, but ya'll's sexual ways?"

"I don't know, Bert. Do you thank it does? Why would it just start botherin me now? I been in the church fuh years."

"Selma, the only place you goan find an answer that's goan satisfy you is within yo'self. I don't thank nobody can give you a comfortable answer."

"I suppose you right, Bert. But I gotta do somethin! I might end up killin Clark."

"Naw, baby, don't do that."

"I won't, Bert—um just talkin foolish, but I gotta do somethin befo' he push me ova the edge!"

"Bert, do you thank he done had white women too?"

"I don't know, suga. Why you thankin 'bout that foolishness?"

"'Cause, he seem tuh love light women. He seem tuh thank they special —I mean, um light, but that don't seem tuh be good enough no mo'. You done seen Clarietta, she look almost white...

"Selma, baby—

"Naw, Bert, I know what I know, and I know what I see and hear. Us black women be who'es if we have mo' then one man or date a white one. Them black men accept anythang them light skinned gals and white gals do."

"They just silly, Selma, that's all. Cain't nobody be clean and dirty at the same time."

"I know, Bert, but if you say somethin lack that to um they start contradictin theyself, sayin, God made everybody the same, we all alike."

"Selma, we all different. Even if we the same color, we different. If God woulda wonted all of us tuh act alike, walk alike, talk alike, and look alike he wouldn'tna separated us at the tower of Babel. He wont us tuh thank fuh ourselves, Selma. Lack reverend told us. We thank we in these different towns cities and states 'cause we took us there. He said, God will send yah where he need yah. But no matter where he send yah he cain't use yah if you ain't capable of thankin fuh yo'self."

21

Lee Charles

"Bert, you remembered that sermon! It did make a lot uh sense! I just wish mo' people saw it that way! Thanks fuh makin thangs so clear, Bert. Thanks fuh tryin tuh make me feel better. You the best friend I evva had. I hope we don't nevva lose each otha. Life just wouldn't be the same without you."

"What the hell goin oan down here...!"
"Clark, I didn't know you was home!"
"I know yah didn't! I snuck in and got me a nap! I gotta work tonight!"
"What? Ovatime, Clark? They ain't gave you no ovatime since, I don't know when!"
"Well, they short, Selma. They need people tuh work. I might as well drop Fatina off oan my way. I saw huh mamma earlier today. I tol' huh I would...FATINA, GIRL, STOP STOCKIN THEM SHELVES AND COME OAN! UM GOAN RUN YAH HOME OAN MY WAY TUH WORK!"
"YES, SIR! UM COMIN!"

"Um goan ride with y'all, Clark. Bert can watch the sto'—
"Naw, naw, naw! That don't make no sense! I'll just have tuh come back here tuh drop you off!"
"You gotta come back this way tuh get tuh work, Clark!"

22

"Selma! I'd planned oan stopin by Big Freddy's and doin a little gamblin fo' I went in!"

"Oh, all right. Then go ahead, Clark. I just thought you might uh wanted some company oan the way back. It's a two hour ride yah know."

"Selma, um well aware of how long the ride is. We done been out there ova a hundred times, back and forth with Fatina! Now stop talkin or I ain't goan nevva get this chil' home ...Fatina! Get in the back seat so you can lay down if you wont to. You know how you always fall asleep...See you when I git from work tonight, Selma."

"Clark, you should at least let Selma ride witcha...

"BERT! WHY YOU MINDIN MY BUSINESS, HUH? WHY YOU MINDIN MY-Y-Y-Y, BUSINESS!"

"I just thought—

"JUST SHUT UP, BERT. AND STAY OUTTA ME AND MY WIFE BUSINESS!"

"Okay, Clark. Okay. Um sorry."

"Clark Porter! There ain't no 'cause fuh you tuh talk that way tuh Bert!"

"Not as long as she stay out my business there ain't, Selma! Besides! She'll be dealt with later! Come oan, Fatina! Let's go!"

"I wonder what Clark meant by that? What did he mean, "I'll be dealt with later"? Uh-oh. I done talked too much.

23

Lee Charles

Ain't no tellin what that man might do tuh me. He gave me a
dirty stare fo' he left. He just might stop by my house when
he drop that gal off. Heaven help me if he do...

"What's the matter, Bert? What you thankin
'bout?"

"Nothin, Nothin, Selma. Um just wonderin what
he meant by that."

"Bert. You know how crazy that man is. He
'bout foolish as that old Daizelle. Don't pay him
no mind."

"Selma. You trust Clark with that baby?"

"He ain't goan do nothin with her, Bert. She
lack his own chil'. Besides that, she too young."

"You probably right, Selma. Um just bein
silly...jealous is mo' lack it. I know how Clark is. Selma
just don't know. At least she pretend she don't. But Clark a
dirty somethin. He might get a notion tuh mess with that
chil'. She developed fuh huh age. It hurts me every time he
be with another woman. I don't care if she is a chil' it
makes me jealous! I mean, I love Selma lack a sister, but um
even jealous of huh and he know that, too. That's why he be
comin in here sometimes puttin his mouth oan huh breasts
through huh blouse gittin it wet in front uh me so she'll
hafta go upstairs lack she goan change it. He follow huh.
They be up there fuh hours and um left down here thankin
'bout what they doin! Then when they do come back down, he be
rubbin and kissin all oan huh! That day he picked huh up and
sat huh up oan that counter lack they was goan have sex in
front uh me and he was lookin ova huh shoulda grinnin at me
and she was gigglin and sayin, "Stop Clark, stop. You see
Bertha Mae still here...!" Ooh-ooh! I wonted tuh stab him
with that knife I was peelin them sweet potatoes with! Um
glad I just got my thangs and left. Of course it didn't do no

24

good. Selma gave me all the details the next day! He knew she was goan do that!

I need tuh leave Clark alone, that's what I need tuh do! And um goan do that, but I need some time tuh find somebody else. Um a big woman. It's hard fuh me tuh find a man, single or married that wonts tuh be with me.

I wish Selma hadn't nevva talked about huh and Clark's lovemakin. That's what made me wont tuh experience first hand what Clarrietta had tuh contend with the night Selma said Clark took full advantage of Clarrietta. I wonted him tuh make love tuh me. Instead, he did me lack he did Clarrietta. I was sick fuh a while just lack Clarrietta the first time he did me lack he done huh. But every since that day he messed me up, I lack that kinda sex. It's better than what I was gittin—nothin! Now, Clark always oan my mind and I caint stay 'way from him no matter what he do.

I hope Selma don't find out I been with him. Um plannin oan lettin Clark go, anyway. Selma ain't nevva got tuh know nothin evva went oan between us. Besides, he mess 'round with so many women in Casey Park, she ain't goan nevva find out 'bout me..."

"Bert. You through packin them preserve jars?"

"...Oh, yeah, yeah, Selma. Here. They all done."

"Thanks, Bert. I appreciate yo' help...Dear God, thank you fuh a friend lack, Bert. She concerned 'bout me and Fatina. But um tryin tuh give Fatina what I nevva had, a childhood. At least Clark pay huh some attention and treat huh lack she his chil'. I ain't nevva been treated lack a chil' and I ain't nevva felt lack one. From the time I was five I had tuh be a mother tuh somebody's chil'. First my siblins, then they children. That's why I chose tuh marry Clark, a man almost ten years olda than me. If somethin was tuh happen tuh Clark I don't nevva wont no man younga than me. God knows I don't thank I evva wonna do that. It only takes me back tuh my childhood. One thang fuh sho'. Afta all these years, I finally realize that yah hafta work out the pain from yo' youth with God. Cain't nobody love it outcha shove it outcha or talk it outcha. It take time tuh heal, a lot uh time and don't nobody but you know when you okay."

WAKING UP TO REALITY

"Daddy Porter! Daddy Porter! Watchoo doin...EEEY...!

"Lay back down, Fatina. Um not goan hurtcha...

"Where we at? What you doin this for? You my goddaddy."

"Fatina. Um use tuh gittin what I wont. I ain't got time tuh argue with you and I ain't goan argue with you...

"Just tell me why, Daddy Porter. Why you doin this tuh me? What did I do tuh—

"You runnin 'round in these little skirts and tight blouses without a bra with yo' stomach showin, that's what, Fatina!"

"But, all the girls be wearin this stuff, Daddy Porter!"

"You the only one be in my sto' almost everyday reachin and bendin ova in my face temptin me, Fatina. Nigh. Lay back down oan the seat. When um done witcha I'll take yah home."

"Daddy Porter—

"LAY DOWN, FATINA!"

"Okay! Okay!"

"That's a good girl."

"Fatina. Yo' belly so smooth. Yo' thighs so soft. Ain't none uh them old women I got lack you."

"No, daddy Porter! DON'T!"

"Um not hurtin you, Fatina! Um just kissin yo' thighs!"

"Daddy Porter. It just don't feel right. You lack my daddy uh somethin."

"Stop cryin, Fatina. It's better than them little boys bein under yo' clothes."

"I—ain't—had—no—boys—daddy Porter! F-f-f-fuh real! DON'T! DON'T! DON'T! D—UUUUUH —EEEY...!"

"See? Nigh that felt good, didn't it, Fatina? Nigh. Take that little blouse off."

"Daddy Porter. Just take me home. You done made my stomach hurt."

"Take it off, Fatina. I don't wont tuh git it wet and dirty. Yo' parents goan ask you 'bout it."

"Daddy P—

"TAKE IT OFF, GIRL!"

"Okay, Daddy Porter, okay!"

"And stop cryin, Fatina!"

"But you rapin me! I know what you doin!"

"Better me than them boys, Fatina. They ain't goan treat you nowhere this good."

"No, Daddy Porter! No! This ain't right! It don't feel good! You hurtin me! You bitin me!"

"CAUSE, YOU WON'T SHUT UP, FATINA! SHUT UP, FATINA! SHUT UP!"

"Okay! Okay!"

"Nigh, it's time fuh me tuh make you a real woman. Them little clothes you be wearin only part of it.

Selma tol' me you done started yo' periods. I meant tuh git tuh yah befo' that happened so I wouldn't have tuh worry 'bout nothin. But, if you git pregnant—

"PREGNANT! UM JUST A LITTLE GIRL! Whatchoo talkin 'bout! Whatchoo mean! WHAT? WHY YOU UNZIPPIN YO' PANTS, DADDY PORTER?"

"Fatina. You know what um talkin 'bout and you know what's about tuh happen. Nigh. Lack I said. If you git pregnant. Call me so I can git rid of it. You big fuh yo' age, but I don't need my eleven year old god daughter pregnant with my chil'."

"How um goan know um pregnant, God-daddy? I don't wont tuh git pregnant! I don't wont no baby! I don't wont tuh do this!"

"Fatina. Quiet down, nigh. Ain't no need fuh you tuh be gitten all upset. Um goan explain it all tuh yah. You remember havin the flu, dontcha?"

"Yeah."

"Well, afta tonight you might feel lack that again. It might not be nothin, but you call me anyway, you hear?"

"Please, don't, Daddy P! Please! Don't hurt me! I'll be good! I won't wear no more grown clothes! I swear tuh God! I won't wear um no mo'! No Daddy P! No—

"You use tuh call me daddy P when you was little whenever you got in trouble. Remember...?"

"Daddy P, stop! YOU HURTIN ME! YOU HURTIN ME! IT'S BURNIN! IT'S HURTIN! AAAAH...

GODDADDY KNOWS WHAT'S BEST

"Um burnin! Um hurtin! I need tuh go tuh the doctor!"

"Naw, Fatina. It's always lack that the first time. Just git out the car and walk around."

"No! Um naked!"

"Ain't nobody goan see you. Ain't nobody out here but me and you. Now go oan. Let goddaddy see how you done grow'd up."

"No! Please! Just take me home tuh my mamma and daddy! Please!"

"I cain't take you home actin lack this, Fatina! If you wont tuh go home you goan hafta correct yo' attitude!"

"But um hurtin!"

"I don't care if you dyin, Fatina! Nigh! You listen tuh me! If you wont tuh git home you do what I say! If you don't wont me tuh git you again you goan keep this tuh yo'self! If I even thank you done tol' somebody um goan come back fuh yah! And you know I can find yah! Nigh, do lack I said and git out the car and walk around.

29

I got some stuff in the trunk tuh clean you up real good with afta that so I can take you home...

"I can clean myself up! I DON'T WONTCHOO TOUCHIN ME NO MO'! MY MAMMA DON'T EVEN LACK MY DADDY TOUCHIN ME, AND YOU TOUCHIN ME!"

"What yo' daddy doin tuh you that yo' mamma don't lack, Tina? She tol' me earlier today he take you everywhere with him. He touchin you wrong?"

"My mamma and daddy ain't lack that! They—

"Tina, um goan tell you somethin. Yo' mamma lack that. So you can talk tuh me."

"NO SHE AIN'T! NO SHE AIN'T!"

"Ain't yo' daddy workin late tonight?"

"SO WHAT!"

"So. How would I know that if yo' mamma didn't tell me?"

"You been knowin us a long time! You know when my daddy work! So what if she tol' you that! It don't mean nothin no way!"

"Okay then. Tell me this. How do I know yo' mamma got a tattoo of cherries oan huh behind?"

"I HATECHOO DADDY PORTER! I HATECHOO! YOU RAPED MY MAMMA JUST LACK YOU DOIN ME! SHE LOVE MY DADDY! SHE WOULDN'T MESS AROUND WITH YOU!"

"I can see you real upset 'bout what just happened, Fatina, and you don't wont tuh believe me. I guess um goan hafta prove it tuh yah. I see um goan hafta go inside with yah anyway tuh keep yah from runnin yo' mouth. Um goan hafta see tuh

it that you do what she say you goan do. She say
she goan send you rat upstairs tuh bed and that's
what you goan do so that I kin make sho' you keep
yo' mouth shut and so that me and huh can be
tuhgetha lack she wont us tuh be. If you don't
believe she wont me tuh be with huh, you come
back down a little later and watch what go oan.
We goan be doin everythang me and you done
tonight. So ain't no real need fuh you tuh be
shame or tell huh 'bout what happened out here
tonight between me and you. She so in love with
goddaddy, she probably won't believe yah no way
and git real made at you fuh you sayin somethin
'bout it."

"WHY YOU GOT TUH BE MESSIN WITH ME AND MY
MAMA! JUST DON'T TOUCH ME NO MO', DADDY PORTER.
JUST DON'T TOUCH ME! LET ME CLEAN MYSELF UP!"

"Fatina. Um goan do it. I hafta make sho' you
real clean befo' I kiss them pretty thighs uh
yours and make you shiver and shake again...

SATISFIED

"Clark. You home early."

"I thought you was sleep, Selma."

"I was, but Anita called tuh check oan
Fatina. I told huh you'd taken huh home, that
y'all shoulda been there—

"I had a flat tire, Selma. It took me almost
two hours tuh get them nuts loose and Fatina
quieted down. She woke up while I was changin the

tire and got restless and whiney! You know how she is!"

"So, you didn't go tuh work?"

"Naw. And I didn't git a chance tuh gamble either. My whole night was ruined. I didn't git no ova time and no fun."

"Clark, what's the matter? Why you sittin oan the bed rubbin yo'self lack that? You okay?"

"Yeah, Selma, yeah! Um okay! I thank I pulled a groin muscle changin that tire that's all. I'll be alright. Um just a little sore and tired."

"Aw, Clark. You must be hungry, too. You didn't have yo' dinner. You wont me tuh warm it up and fix you somethin tuh eat?"

"Naw, baby. Fuh some reason I feel full and satisfied. Um goan take me a shower and fall out. All that work I done oan that tire done wore me out. Shoot. I might sleep fuh two or three days. Nigh you just lay oan back down. And don't worry about me I'll be fine, just, fine."

"Why he still sittin oan the side uh this bed grinnin and rubbin oan hisself lack that? I believe Clark done gone plum fool."

Chapter 2

CHURCH DAY

"Clark? You goin tuh church today?"

"Yeah! Is somethin wrong with that? Is somethin wrong with a man wontin tuh be with his wife in the house of the Lord oan Sunday?"

"Naw, but you ain't been in a while."

"Well, um goin today. Nigh git yo' purse and let's go fo' we be late."

THE SERMON

"It's nice to see Diamond Prescott sitting out there as part of my congregation. After all those years of living the wild life in Trinston and having to travel all this way for service, this is the last place I thought I'd see Brother Prescott. He said he wanted to see me after service today. I hope he hasn't planned to leave the church after only two years. He's really been a blessing to the church and its ministry...

"Mornin reverend!"

"Good morning, Sister Porter. You broke my chain of thought!

"Um sorry, reverend."

"That's okay, Sister."

"Brother Porter? I Haven't seen you in church for a while! Good to see you!"

"Mornin, reverend. I know you haven't. I felt lack bein with Selma this mornin. It sho' feels good bein in the house of the Lord with her—with my wife...

"Oh my God! Daddy Porter in church! I cain't let him see me! He done seen me! He goan sit next tuh me...!"

"Mornin, Fatina baby."

"Mornin, Daddy Porter."

"What's wrong, Fatina? I ain't nevva seen you look so shy and talk so low."

"Nothin, Mommy Selma. I just don't feel too good."

"Well, just don't move too much. You'll probably be okay...nigh be quiet. The sermon 'bout tuh start...

"Good morning, congregation! Today's sermon is on sexuality, discrimination, murder, lying and cheating...

"He feelin oan my leg and mommy Selma don't even see em. Um goin tuh the bathroom...

"Fatina! You okay?"

"Yes, ma'am. Um just goin tuh the bathroom."

"Um goan go see 'bout huh, Clark. She don't look too good."

"Naw, Selma. You stay here and enjoy the sermon. I'll go downstairs and tend to huh...

"Fatina! Fatina!"

"Go 'way, Daddy Porter! I don't wont you messin with me no mo'!"

"GIRL! HAVE YOU GOAN CRAZY! I tol' you not tuh mention nothin and I meant it...Nigh lower yo' voice. We don't wont the whole congregation down here! You understand me, Fatina!"

"Yes, sir."

"Nigh, open that do'...

"Please, daddy Porter. Don't mess with me no mo'."

"Only a little bit, Fatina. I knew I wouldn't have a lot uh time withca, but I come tuh church just fuh you. All I wont you tuh do is sit down oan the toilet and pull up yo' bra and blouse fuh God-daddy 'til he finished. Soon as um done you can go back upstairs. Um goan leave so you won't hafta look at me no mo' today. You tell Selma you okay and I had tuh go home and git my wallet...

"But, daddy Porter! We in church, in front of God —a-a-a-and I ain't dressed bad today!"

"Whatchoo call that short skirt you wearin? And yo' breasts real big, Fatina. A man cain't help from messin with breasts lack yours no matter where he at. All I did was thank about you since the last time we was tugetha!"

"But, I cain't help what size they are! It ain't my fault! And um wearin a pleated skirt, it ain't tight uh nothin!"

"Naw, it ain't tight. But it's short enough fuh a man tuh see all between yo' thighs just lack he wont to, and yo' breasts is real noticeable, Fatina. A man cain't help hisself but wont tuh mess with um...

"Daddy Porter—

"Fatina! The sooner you do what I tell you tuh do the sooner you can git rid uh me and back upstairs."

"Daddy Porter—

"Do you wont tuh leave this church with me, Fatina?"

"No, sir."

"Then stop cryin and do lack I tell yah, or um goan hafta do it. 'Cause either way, um goan git what I wont from you fo' I leave here today...

THE SERMON CONTINUES

...There are too many Christians who are afraid to speak on these subjects. They lock them away as if not talking about them will solve the problem. Christians are beginning to conform to the world, instead of renewing the mind. As Romans 12:2 Says, and I quote; "And be not conformed to this world, but be ye transformed by the renewing of your mind, that ye may prove what is that good, and acceptable, and perfect, will of God...

"Amen Pastor, amen...Fatina, you okay?"

"Yes, ma'am, Mommy Selma."

"Where Clark?"

"He say he got tuh go home tuh git his wallet."

"His wallet? Maybe he didn't have no money fuh the collection dish."

"Maybe, Mommy Selma. I'on know."

"What's wrong with that chil'? She been actin different—wait a minute! Ain't no way Clark messed with this baby. I know she developed, but—naw, naw. Clark wouldn't do nothin lack that. She like his own."

"...Congregation! We find it convenient to reject those who make us feel uncomfortable if they seem to be different, and there are those of

36

us who lie, cheat, steal, rape, and even kill out of pride and lust...!

> "Selma, girl, that man can preach a sermon, cain't he?"
> "Yes, sister Smith, he sure can...

"...As Proverbs 6:16-19 states; "God hates a proud look, a lying tongue, hands that shed innocent blood, a heart that devises wicked plans, feet that are swift in running to evil, a false witness who speaks lies, and one who sows discord among brethren. These are the seven deadly sins. The sins which cause instant punishment from God. Sins that may cause your death, or the death of a loved one.

Some of us who are here today also refuse to acknowledge Exodus 20:1-7 and Deuteronomy 5:6-21, the Ten commandments, which come strictly from our leader, God! When a leader commands you to do something, either you follow that command or suffer the punishment. Yet and still, instead of taking these commands seriously, some of us continue on the same sinful paths hoping to get by each time without serious punishment, just because we're in church every Sunday. Sometimes, by the grace of God they do! But congregation! I'm warning you! If you think that church covers your sins you're wrong! You're playing Russian Roulette with your lives by being disobedient. You must not only read and hear God's word, but live it, and there are many of us who are not!

Infidelity is so common, that there are husbands with more girlfriends than single men. Married men and women who are more sexually promiscuous, heavier drinkers, and bigger partygoers than the single ones. There's nothing wrong with having a good time, but the bible speaks of doing everything in moderation and without bringing sin upon your household. Cheating and sexual promiscuity should be avoided all together. Anyone; and I mean anyone, who believes that they are benefiting from cheating and sexual misconduct, should be aware of the many dangers involved in this type of behavior. There are sexually transmitted diseases! There are babies being born with birth defects if a disease is passed on to the mother! There's sterility in males and females caused by disease! Divorce, abuse, even, crimes of passion brought on by cheating and sexual misconduct! There are perversions and lustful passions that become so strong that they develop into rape, and this does not exclude the rape of your children or them being raped by someone you may know very well! And the ugly, ugly list goes on!

Instant sex, is reckless, people! There's nothing to profit from it but pain! If someone thinks you're special enough to sleep with then they should feel that you're special enough to marry because they don't want some other person all over what they love, at any time! They'll want to continue to treat you with respect, honor, and kindness 'til death do you part! And a strong foundation is needed to keep a relationship like that together! Sex, is not enough!

Never base relationships on sex, money, looks, or any of the worldly values. These are lustful, vain reasons to form any union. They can wear on a relationship with time and usually end them on a distasteful note because there is no real bond.

There are many lessons in scripture. They help us to build friendships, partnerships, and relationships. They teach us or talk about kindness, forgiveness, responsibility, and respect, etc. They tell us how we should treat others and what we should expect in return. They also lessen your suffering here on earth and help you through them. For example, if you see someone in trouble, hungry, sick, or in need, help them out if it is spirit led to do so. Do these things so that you may get these in return and prosper from your prayers, and never let someone else's opinion override your spirit of doing good.

When you pray, do so believing, and don't ever think that God has said no if your prayers aren't answered right away. It's just not the right time. He's teaching us while we are waiting and showing us who we are. God already knows what you want. He wants you to be sure of your request. But, no matter what the prayer, God has a way to make it work for good.

I want all of you to go home today and be a blessing to someone. The only way that we can please God, is by being obedient to him and by being a blessing to one another."

Chapter 3

AFTER THE SERMON

"Hello, Brother Prescott. How's the family doing?"

"They're wonderful, reverend, but I'm not here to discuss family problems, it's me."

"What's troubling you, brother?"

"A woman who insulted me made me angry."

"Brother, that's normal."

"No, pastor, you don't understand. I have a really big problem with anger. In a rage I raped and forced her into sodomy as a repercussion for speaking negatively about my family. Reverend, I become blinded when anyone says negative things about my wife and children. I go into these mad rages. At other times, I'm a giving, loving, caring person. I know that I need to get help for this monstrous characteristic that's controlling my unity with the father, but—

"Brother Prescott, it's called pride. We all let it control us one way or another. The only way we can begin to handle it is to realize what we're trying to be so proud about. For example, are we becoming upset over a truth or a lie? If it's truth, accept it, but believe that whatever it is the person is saying about us can be remedied through our Lord and savior Jesus Christ. If it's a lie, he will reveal that, too.

41

You should always remember that each time we take matters into our own hands and hurt one of God's children, with or without cause, we not only hurt God, but we have consequences to pay for those actions."

"Believe me reverend, my conscience and other things that are going on in my life right now are making me pay."

"Count it all as a blessing, and thank God for the lessons he'll be teaching you throughout your suffering. But Brother Prescott. We all take steps backwards. It's all a part of strengthening our spirituality and learning who God is."

"But, Reverend—

"Diamond, some would say that what you did to that woman is worse than any sin they've ever committed. If you're asking me to measure your sin because I'm a minister, even I can't do that. God is the highest priest of all. Even he sees sin as sin.

Ask God's forgiveness Brother Prescott. You know he forgives us each time if we're sincere."

"Thank you reverend, I've already done that, thank you."

"Oh, and Diamond!"

"Yes, Reverend."

"Pray for the woman, yourself, and battle with your flesh to refrain from repeating that or any other coarse action.

If you are unable to control your temper, and take a step backwards, talk it over with someone, do not be ashamed. Shame is almost like pride, it can keep you from growing in the Lord, and from doing what's right."

"Thank you, reverend, I'll never shut myself out to you again. I promised God that I'd be a leader and it's a promise that I'm going to keep."

"I know that you will, Brother Prescott. Sometimes we have more faith in others than we have in ourselves, but God knows exactly what each of us is capable of contributing."

BERT TALKS TO FATINA

"Fatina! Wait up! I wonna talk tuh you!"

"Yes, ma'am, Miss Bert?"

"Girl! What was you doin down in that toilet so long with, CLARK!"

"M-m-miss B-B-Bert, p-p-p-p-please—aaaaah! Aaaaah!"

"Fatina? Baby? Don't cry. Did he hurt you against yo' will?"

"Yes, ma'am and he goan kill me nigh. He done tol' me not tuh say nothin."

"You mean tuh tell me. He messed with you in the basement uh the church?"

"Mm-hm. He was puttin his mouth oan my breasts fuh a real long time and puttin his hands up in me 'til my panties got wet. Then he made me put some paper towel in um so it wouldn't git oan my skirt."

43

"Why he do that, baby? Why he messin with you?"

"He say I dress bad and my breasts big. So he had tuh do it. He couldn't control hisself. Do I look bad, Miss Bert?"

"Lord, have mercy, Jesus—no baby—no—Did he do somethin tuh you the night he took you home and wouldn't let Selma ride with y'all?"

"Miss Bert, please. I couldn't help from tellin you that but don't tell him. Um goan git in trouble. He goan hurt me some more. He goan—"

"Naw he ain't! Um goan let him whoop me. Just tell me what he done, Fatina!"

"You sho', Miss Bert?"

"Um sho', Fatina."

"Miss Bert. I always fall asleep oan the way home. I was dreamin that my mamma was undressin me. When I woke up it was real dark and Daddy Porter was kissin and lickin my thighs and between my legs. I screamed, but befo' I could really say somethin he put his tongue inside uh me and made me feel full and I holl'd real loud. He put his mouth oan the top of my private stuff again and made me lay down 'til he made me feel real funny and tremblin and scream and made water come outta me. Then—then—then—then, he sucked oan my breasts and stuck his thang in me. It hurt me, Miss Bert. It hurt me real bad. I was burnin, but he wouldn't take me to the doctor lack I asked him. He just took some stuff out his trunk, cleaned me up again and put his mouth down there some mo'."

"I knew it! I knew he was goan try somethin with you! I knew he was actin strange! I knew he was goan do it! I told Selma that!"

"Don't tell, Miss Bert! He goan git me if you tell!"

"No he won't. I'll tell him Daizelle seen him. He'll beat me, but he'll stay 'way from you."

"Miss Bert. My daddy kiss me there sometimes, but he say it's okay, 'cause a daddy can kiss his daughter, but—

"Fatina, No! Yo' daddy been kissin you down there?"

"Yes, ma'am, but he my daddy. He buy me everythang and take me everywhere! He don't even let mamma follow us! It's okay fuh him tuh do that! My daddy said so! Goddaddy Porter the one made it bad!"

"Fatina! Ain't nobody got the right tuh do that tuh you, even yo' daddy. When relatives do thangs lack that tuh each otha, it's called incest. In the bible that's a sin."

"But, I cain't stop my daddy from kissin me!"

"He can kiss you, Fatina. But not in a private way. In none uh the places where Clark touched you. That's sexual."

"You goan tell my mamma now, Miss Bert?"

"Fatina. Somebody gotta help you. It might as well be me."

"But, he say he messin with my mamma, too."

"HE, SAID, WHAT, FATINA?"

"That he messin with my mamma."

"He probably just said that tuh make sho' you wouldn't tell huh."

"Naw, Miss Bert that wadn't the only reason why he said that. In the car he tol' me that my

mamma had asked him tuh be with huh afta he
dropped me off that night. He tol' me if I didn't
believe him tuh come back down later and I'd see
he wadn't lyin. Almost as soon as we got through
the do' mamma tol' me to go oan upstairs tuh bed.
Daddy Porter said, "Do lack yo' mamma say" and I
went upstairs. I listened tuh see if Daddy Porter
was goan leave. I didn't hear the do' open and
close again. I looked out the window. His car was
still parked in front of our house.

I was scared, but I did it. I came back
downstairs lack he tol' me. They was in the dark,
but the light oan our big fish tank made it so
that I could see what was goin oan. He was sittin
oan the sofa and my mamma was kneelin in front uh
him. I sat oan the steps and watched my mamma do
the same thang tuh Daddy Porter he'd done tuh me.
He saw me watchin and started grinnin at me. I
sat oan the steps and cried real quiet. He got
up. He was still grinnin. He winked his eye at
me, put his two fingers to his lips, and blew me
a kiss.

My mamma tol' him she wadn't finished. He
tol' huh he'd had enough. My mamma wrapped huh
arms 'round his legs and begged him tuh let huh
finish. He sat back down and let her do it.
Knowin that I was oan them stairs, he kept oan
sayin, "Don't let Fatina hear us, Nita! Don't let
my Baby Tina hear. God knows that would kill me
if she evva found out." He was starin at me the

46

whole time. The only time he wadn't was when she
made that thing happen tuh him. He closed his
eyes and made loud noises lack I did and tried
tuh push mamma away from him, but he couldn't.

When mamma did let him go, he got up and
zipped his pants. She was beggin him fuh sex. He
patted huh oan the head lack a dog and tol' huh
maybe some otha time he had tuh git home. I ain't
nevva seen my mamma the way she was that night.
She was beggin goddaddy tuh be with huh.

She took off huh new negligee that I thought
she'd bought tuh wear fuh daddy. When Daddy
Porter saw huh naked he stopped lookin at me. He
picked my mamma up, put his mouth oan huh breasts
and carried huh back tuh the sofa. He told mamma
tuh wait a minute he had tuh use the bathroom. He
came up them steps and tol' me tuh go tuh bed. I
went in my room and came back out when I thought
he was back downstairs. I thought he was rapin my
mamma. He was doin the same thangs tuh huh, he'd
done tuh me, but she liked it. When he put
hisself inside her, she didn't scream, it didn't
hurt her. They had sex a long time.

Daddy Porter fell asleep oan the sofa with
mamma in his arms. I went tuh sleep oan the
steps. It was a good thing the phone rang. It was
daddy. He told mamma he had tuh work a double
shift. Afta the phone call, Daddy Porter, and

47

mamma did stuff to each otha again and had sex
some more. I went tuh bed befo' he left.

Miss Bert. My mamma looked real upset this
mornin, and my daddy wadn't home. So I come tuh
church oan the bus all by myself hopin that God
would cleanse me from what goddaddy had done tuh
me and my mamma, and that my daddy would love my
mamma again and just stop touchin and bein with
me so much. The only thang that happened is that
goddaddy hurt me again right in church right in
front uh God. Why he let that happen tuh me, Miss
Bert? Why'd God let that happen?"

"Tina, God can only show us thangs. Parents
got tuh teach they kids tuh tell when thangs lack
that happen no matter who doin um and the kids
need tuh know that they parents goan protect um."

"But, my parents didn't know goddaddy was
lack that."

"But, yo' daddy know'd he was doin wrong by
kissin you in the wrong places. Yo' Mamma had tuh
know that yo' daddy wadn't takin you all around
with him and ignorin huh fuh nothin! She just
didn't wont tuh know.

Fatina. Cheatin people cain't be trusted.
Everybody in Casey Park know how Clark messin
'round with any and everybody, and young girls
ain't excused. Yo' mamma had tuh know 'bout that
too. And she still messed with Clark, a man who
don't care who he take tuh bed, knowin she got a

young daughter he might decide he wont at any time. How many signs God got tuh give huh?"

"But, my mamma ain't bad! She just need my daddy tuh love huh! I done heard huh ask him tuh love huh! SHE NEED MY DADDY TUH LOVE HUH, MISS BERT!"

"Don't cry, Tina. Don't cry. Um goan do everythang I can tuh help yah through this ugly situation."

THE LESSON

"Who is it!"

"OPEN THE DAMN, DO'!"

"Oh my God! It's Clark...! Good evenin Clark—

"Is yo' chilr'en home, Bertha?"

"Naw, Clark. They ain't here. I sent um 'way I figured you'd be comin—

"YOU FIGURED RIGHT! URRRRRGH...!

"OH MY GOD, CLARK! YOU DONE BROKE MY JAW! YOU DONE—

"FO' I LEAVE HERE! THAT AIN'T ALL GOAN BE WRONG WITH YOU! NIGH! YOU LAY DOWN THERE AND DON'T MOVE! YOU HEAR ME, BERT! YOU HEAR ME!"

"Yeah, Clark—I hear yah! I hear yah!"

"Um goan teach you, Bert. Um goan teach you 'bout tryin tuh stop me from doin what I wont tuh do with who I wont tuh do it with if I hafta kill you...!"

"Don't kill me, Clark! Please, don't kill me! My chil'ren need me! DON'T CLARK! DON'T! PLEASE! DON'T TWIST MY ARM NO MO'! YOU GOAN BREAK IT AGAIN! EEEEEY...YOU DONE BROKE MY HAND! YOU DONE BROKE IT!"

"GOOD! Nigh! Maybe that'll teach you 'bout tryin tuh defend Fatina! Afta all the plannin I done tuh git huh, you almost messed that up fuh me, Bert!"

"She just a baby, Clark! A baby! That's all!"

"It ain't none uh yo' business what she is! She *my* Goddaughter! And you ain't concerned 'bout Tina! You jealous! You don't wont me messin with nobody but you! Ain't that right, Bert! Ain't that right...!

...YOU DON'T HEAR ME TALKIN TUH YOU, BERT...! UH—UH—UH—UH—

"EEEEY! STOP, CLARK! DON'T HIT ME NO MO'!"

"THEN YOU ANSWER ME...!"

"YEAH, CLARK! YEAH! IT'S TRUE!"

"Bert! You and me both know that ain't goan come tuh pass! 'Cause you already know that I ain't nevva really wonted you! I keep oan usin you fuh what you come tuh me fuh that first time and when I cain't make Selma or them otha gals do lack I wont! I done tol' you that! And anotha thang! Keep yo' mouth shut 'bout me!

All the while you and Selma was down them stairs talkin 'bout how no good I am, I was thankin 'bout how and when I was goan git even with you!"

"But, Clark! Selma was talkin 'bout you too! Why you—

"BABY FATINA WAS MY WAY UH GITTIN' BACK AT HUH FUH THAT! BUT I COME TUH YOU DIRECTLY, 'CAUSE YO' MOUTH TOO BIG FUH YO' OWN GOOD, THAT'S WHY! AND YOU AIN'T NOTHIN TUH ME! Selma my wife! She done earned some right tuh talk 'bout me! You just thank you betta than me 'cause you got that college degree tuh counsel people, that's why you do it! What you goan counsel people oan, Bert? How tuh be a backstabbin low-lifed who'e lack yo' self?

Look atcha, Bert! Look at what you done helped me turn you into! A big, fat, blonde, black who'e fuh Clark!"

"Clark! I had long, pretty, jet-black hair befo'! You made me cut and die my hair lack this! You the one got me wearin this blonde afro!"

"Sho' you right, Bert! It's yo' trademark! Any woman mess with me the wrong way gits one. Yours make you look ridiculous just lack I wonted! Every time I see you comin' with that fat, light, bald head uh yours I go tuh laughin tuh myself or start grinnin 'bout how messed up you look. It's payback Bert, payback! You embarrassed me that day I was drunk and couldn't git you off me and now it's yo' turn, Bert! It's yo' turn tuh git me, off you!"

"Clark, please, don't keep oan beatin and mistreatin me fuh that. I swear, I wadn't tryin tuh embarrass you that day. All I wonted was a man tuh be with me from time tuh time. Most men lack what I done tuh you. I didn't thank you was goan take it lack that. I was just tryin tuh make you feel good so you'd come tuh me sometime."

"And that's what um doin, Bert! Comin to yah from time, tuh time!"

"But, it ain't the right way, Clark!"

"Um yo' best friend husband, Bert! Ain't no right uh wrong way tuh treat a nasty who'e!"

"SO WHAT, CLARK! YOU MESSED WITH BABY TINA! AND HUH MAMMA!"

"WHAT! YOU MUST BE DONE LOST YO' MIND! I KNOW YOU AIN'T RAISIN YO' VOICE AND TALKIN TUH ME LACK THAT! A MAN, BERT? YOU TRYIN TUH REMIND ME, A MAN, UH WHAT HE DONE? YOU MUST WONT ME TUH KILL YOU...!"

"NAW! NAW, CLARK...CLARK! Take yah arm from 'round my neck! You goan kill me! Yah chokin me tuh death! I cain't breathe...

"GIT YO' HANDS OFF MY ARM, BERT OR I'LL CRUSH YO' WINDPIPE FUH SHO'! YOU DONE BEEN MESSIN 'ROUND WITH JUNIOR WINTERS' FIFTEEN YEAR OLD SON, AND GOAN TRY 'N' TALK 'BOUT ME? I'LL KILL YOU, B—

"Okay, Clark! Okay! Oh my God! Oh my God! You almost killed me...I didn't have no sex with that boy, Clark!"

"THAT'S 'CAUSE I WHOOPED YOU FO' YOU COULD! BUT YOU'D DONE EVERYTHANG ELSE WITH HIM! I

SHOULDA KILLED YOU THE FIRST TIME I WHOOPED YOU
'BOUT JUNIOR'S BOY!"

"That was last year, Clark! You tol' me you didn't wont
me!"

"AND I STILL DON'T! BUT YOU'D BETTA ACT LACK
I DO WHILE UM MESSIN WITCHA! I AIN'T SLEEPIN AFTA
NO OTHA MAN! NO MATTER WHAT WE DOIN, YAH NASTY
COW!"

"Hu-hu-hu-hu-hu! Clark! I cain't catch my breath! You
done—

"Where yo' mirror at, Bert? WHERE IS IT! YOU
AIN'T THAT WEAK! YOU CAN TALK!"

"It's oan my dresser, Clark! Oan my dresser!"

"GO GIT IT...!"

"Here, here it is, Clark. Here it is. I caint stand no
longer—

"JUST GIVE IT HERE! LOOK...HOLD UP YAH HEAD
AND LOOK! SEE HOW STUPID YOU LOOK, BERT! SEE! YA
KNEELIN DOWN OAN THE FLO' LACK A DOG! HOLDIN YO'
THROAT, COUGHIN, CHOKIN, BREATHIN HARD, AND TRYIN
TUH CATCH YO' BREATH! How somebody lack you goan
be a counselor? Who you think goan listen tuh
you—git yo' stupid, fat behind up off that flo'!
You ain't no counselor, you ain't nothin, and you
ain't goan nevva be nothin! You know what else,
Bert? You was steady talkin 'bout me bein a
nasty, low, disgustin man with no morals uh
decency 'bout myself, but you just lack me. You
come tuh my room that night while I was drunk,
and did thangs tuh me only them lil' junkies and

who'es do tuh me fuh pocket change. Only you did um fuh free and yah still doin um fuh free. Um goan keep oan makin yah do um free 'til I git tired uh seein that big, fat, pig lookin, ugly, double chinned face uh yours!"

"Why you gotta tear me down lack that, Clark? I try so hard tuh make up tuh yah fuh what I done that day. Why cain't we just—

"Bert, there ain't nothin in this world goan make me do right by you. You keep oan tryin tuh rule me and make me be with yah knowin I don't love me no big women! Plus, yo' mouth too big! It's almost big as you! If you had just kept yo' big fat mouth shut I wouldn't be here tonight whoopin oan yah and havin tuh put you in yo' place. If you had waited I wouldn't be here havin tuh stomp yah and puttin my foot in yo' behind 'bout runnin yo' mouth so much. If you and Selma hadn't been runnin y'all mouths so, I wouldn'tna messed with baby Tina, either. I'd been noticin huh, I was tempted, but you didn't have tuh do uh say nothin! I wadn't goan mess with huh! When you and Selma talked about me downstairs in my own sto', that's when I made up my mind tuh git hold of huh, but I did it mostly fuh spite. I wadn't goan mess 'round with Fatina long. She got you and Selma tuh thank fuh what happened tuh huh that night. Y'all mouths caused me tuh take Baby Tina. TAKE YO' HANDS FROM OVA YO' EARS BERT! YOU GOAN HEAR WHAT I GOT TUH SAY!"

"*Clark, please—*

"WOMAN! DON'T TRY BEGGIN ME FUH NOTHIN! DON'T
EVEN TALK 'TIL UM DONE...I was already tempted,
Bert! I was already tempted by Tina's looks!
Y'all made me mad with that mess y'all was puttin
down! Y'all pushed me tuh huh, Bert! Thanks tuh
you and Selma's mouths and the fact that she was
convenient at a time when I needed somethin young
'cause my young yella gal wadn't around, I messed
huh up. Maybe I wouldn'tna even messed with huh
again afta' that, but I'd also been noticin how
she was gittin a figure and developin through
them skimpy clothes she was wearin. She got
huhself tuh thank fuh that one. Them clothes
showed me what she had and what I'd be gittin,
and that's when I started gittin ideas of bein
with huh; and how and when I was goan git with
huh befo' anybody else did if I decided tuh do
it. Until then, I thought of huh as my baby and
only my baby. I wadn't goan mess with huh, at
least not that soon, 'cause I still hadn't made
up my mind 'bout Fatina. I was goan try tuh see
what was goan happen with huh when she got about
sixteen, maybe I wadn't goan wont huh then, maybe
them urges was goan go away. I kinda wonted um to
go. She was too close tuh me and I really don't
believe in no dog eat dog. I'd reasoned about
that a lot, but Tina ain't really mine uh no kin,
and once I got started oan huh and didn't feel
guilty uh nothin I knew what me and huh was doin
was okay. Thanks tuh you and Selma y'all helped
me tuh make up my mind that night and I was

55

hungry fuh huh too, Bert, and I got greedy when I
finally got with huh and I took what I needed. I
went further than I'd planned oan 'cause she felt
good. She made me feel good, Bert. Even betta
than the one I call my young, yella gal. Yeah,
Bert, I was cravin huh, but I'd already made up
my mind that I wadn't goan mess with huh no mo'
afta church that day. I wonted tuh mess with huh
some mo'—I wont huh now, but I ain't goan mess
with huh no mo', she too dangerous. Young as she
is, I knew huh parents was goan find out so I had
tuh back away, but I still wonna mess with huh
again, but I cain't! Huh mind ain't able tuh take
what um doin to huh. If I quit nigh she probably
just goan leave it 'lone. She don't wont nobody
tuh know I been messin with huh, she too shame
tuh tell it...AND YOU, BERT! You betta pray tuh
God that she do, leave it 'lone! If that come
back oan me! Um comin tuh git you fo' they git me
and you know I mean what I say!

Nigh, Bert, um hopin afta I finish witchoo
tonight you goan stay out my way—out my business.
I need me somethin young every nigh and then and
there ain't nothin you can do 'bout the way I am.
If I didn't change fuh Selma. Ain't no way in
hell um goan do nothin different fuh you. Um goan
be this way 'til um dead and gone. You should
know that by nigh."

"You ain't goan mess with huh no mo'?"

"Naw! But you ain't so lucky and maybe that lil' daughter uh yours won't be, either! Maybe she'll like some uh what I done tuh Baby Tina the otha night, and what I done tuh git that young yella gal so close tuh me...! Shoulda been mindin yo' *own*, business, Bert! You shoulda minded yo' *own*, business...What time yo' kids comin home?"

"You wouldn't mess with my baby, would yah, Clark! Lashella ain't got nothin tuh do with this. This between me and you...

"I COULDA SWORE I ASKED YOU WHAT TIME YO' CHIL'REN WAS GOAN GIT HOME! NOT WHO THIS BETWEEN!"

"Not 'til in the monin, Clark...!

"GIT UPSTAIRS, BERT!"

"Clark. Don't mess with my baby. Pl—

"UH—UH—UH—UH—UH! I SAID! GIT OAN UPSTAIRS...!"

"OH, CLARK, OH-H-H...PLEASE! DON'T RAM ME NO MO' IN MY BACK WITH YOU FEET AND ELBOW...

"YOU WONT SOME MO', BERT!"

"NAW, CLARK! NAW!"

"THEN GIT UP OFF THAT FLO', AND GIT OAN UP THEM STEPS OR UM GOAN WHOOP YAH DOWN HERE AND MAKE SHO', YO' CHIL'REN FIND YOU OAN THE FLO', BEAT UP, AND BUTT NAKED IN THE MONIN!"

"Okay, Clark! Um goin! But—

"WHAT YOU MEAN, "YOU GOIN" LACK YOU GOT A CHOICE! HAH, WHAT YOU MEAN!"

"Naw, Clark, naw! I don't mean it lack that! I just wont tuh know what you goan do tuh me? You ain't goan hurt me too bad is yah? You done

already broke my hand. What else you goan do? WHAT ELSE! I GOT TUH BE ABLE TUH TAKE CARE UH MY KIDS WHEN THEY GIT HOME, CLARK! YOU AIN'T GOAN MAKE ME SO I CAIN'T WALK LACK BEFO'! IS YAH CLARK! IS YAH!"

"You'll see when we git upstairs! You wadn't thankin 'bout what I was goan do tuh you and yo' chil'ren fo' you went tuh cuttin yo' best friend throat and mindin my business! NIGH GIT YO' FAT—

"OKAY, CLARK! OKAY! JUST DON'T HIT ME NO MO'! PLEASE...I done been through this befo'. I don't know why um cryin so hard. I already know he ain't goan have no pity oan me. He goan beat me and abuse me 'til he tired and I ain't goan be no good when he done. How um goan take care uh my chil'ren when they git home? Um goan just hafta tell um I fell down the stairs again and tell um how tuh fix they food and serve me...NAW CLARK! NAW! PLEEEEEEEASE...!"

"KEEP OAN BEGGIN ME, BERT! MAYBE YOU'LL THANK TWICE THE NEXT TIME YOU FUHGIT WHICH ONE UH US THE MAN!"

Chapter 4

SELMA & DAIZELLE

"Uh-oh. Here come Daizelle again this mornin. Um sho not in the mood tuh fight with huh today...Good mornin' Daizelle."

"Humph! I don't need yo' good mornin'! I didn't come here tuh socialize! And I didn't come tuh steal! See here! I gots money! I wouldn't even be spendin it here if Bodell's opened up earlier! And if you try tuh put me out yo' sto' um goan report you—maybe even sue ya!"

"Why do you hate me so much, Daizelle? What have I done tuh you? We both Christians, cain't we work out our differences?"

"Naw! You thank you better than all of us just 'cause you got this sto' and that old no good husband tuh take care you."

"No I don't, Daizelle."

"Yes you do, you thank this sto', yo' husband, and that pitiful fat friend uh yo's is everythang!"

"So, you tellin me you thank I be wavin what I got and my friendship with Bert under people's noses? That's why you hate me? You jealous uh that, Daizelle? You jealous uh me and Bert friendship and what I got?"

"Hah! Jealous uh yo' friend! With friends lack huh, don't nobody need enemies! I tol' huh I was goan tell yah, and I am!"

"Tell me what, Daizelle, tell me, what?"

"I saw huh! I saw that pitiful, big fat heffa and yo' husband."

"YOU LYIN, DAIZELLE!"

"Naw, I ain't lyin and you know I ain't lyin' and you know I kin prove that I ain't lyin' by tellin yah what I seen! He started off by just messin with huh. He had his mouth all over huh bosoms. Squeezin um and carryin on. She was moanin lack a dog in heat. She acted lack she was tryin tuh push him 'way. He had that big gal so wound up he made huh fall tuh huh knees..."

"DAIZELLE, I DON'T WONT TUH HEAR NO MO'—

"She was callin his name. "*Clark, Clark, Clark.*" Then he asked huh if she wonted some mo' uh did she wont him tuh stop. She begged him fuh it. He tol' huh that he wouldn't 'til she pleased him and pushed huh tuh huh knees again. When she was done, he had sex with that big fat heffa, rat where you standin, and I don't believe he had it normal."

"Uh-h-h-h!"

"Ain't no sense uh you jumpin 'round and hollin nigh, Selma! He done already huh there! He had huh oan huh knees and he was smackin huh rump! She was hollin and I could see the tears rollin down huh cheeks. When he got finished with that big fat gal, he pushed huh, and she feel ova

oan huh side. She lay there cryin lack a big ol'
elephant fuh a while. Then she got huhself
tugetha and ran outta yo' sto' half-naked, 'cause
Clark had tow huh clothes off huh. He thought he
was bein funny."

"THAT NEVVA HAPPENED DAIZELLE AND YOU KNOW IT
DIDN'T!"

"You know Ms. Daizelle ain't lyin, 'cause it
happened that week you was outta town and had
Bert watchin yo' sto' fuh yah.

See; they didn't know I was in the sto' and
was watchin from one uh them grocery aisles. I
left soon as I saw Clark go upstairs and heard
him close y'all apartment do'."

"He hurt my friend and she didn't tell me?"
"She didn't tell you, Selma, 'cause she
lacked it. She been messin with yo' husband every
since then. Maybe, befo'! I still see him 'round
tuh huh house all the time. She be cookin fuh
him, bathin him and anythang else he wont huh tuh
do tuh please him.

One time I heard him threaten tuh leave huh.
She begged him tuh stay. She tol' him that she
was a big woman and it was hard fuh a big woman
tuh git a man, married or sangle. Then she got
oan huh knees and satisfied him. When she was
done, she asked him if he'd change his mind. He
tol' huh he'd thank about it.

I know you ain't seen huh in a while. She probably with him nigh. See, Selma, yo' friend ain't worth SH—

"Git out my sto', Daizelle! GIT OUT MY STO'! ALWAYS TIPPIN 'ROUND OTHER PEOPLE'S PROPERTY SPYIN OAN UM. ONE DAY SOMEBODY GOAN FIND YO' OLD ASS DEAD!"

"It ain't my fault, Selma! You ain't got no business tellin no woman 'bout yo' husband body parts and y'all personal business no way, not even yo' supposed tuh be best friend! And why you cussin at me, you s'pposed tuh be a Christian—

"GIT OUT, DAIZELLE, GET OUT!"

"Um leavin, um leavin...damn, fool!"

"OH MY GOD...SWEET JESUS! HOW COULD SHE DO IT! HOW CAN SOMEBODY GRIN IN YO' FACE EVERYDAY AND BE MESSIN 'ROUND WITH YO' MAN!

WHAT AM I GOAN DO? HELP ME FATHER! I WONNA KILL BERT SO HELP ME LORD!

FATHER, I KNOW UM A CHRISTIAN, BUT THERE'S A LIMIT FATHER, AND I THANK THIS IS MINE."

"M-m-m. Um glad I ain't married. Listen tuh that fool hollerin and yellin tuh huhself 'cause uh that no good fool husband uh huhs. Ain't no one man goan nevva take my mind lack that! Naw, naw, naw. Ain't no one man, goan nevva mess up Miss Daizelle mind and I mean that! 'Cause ain't none of um worth it!"

Chapter 5

DAIZELLE & THE REVEREND

"Sister Washington, how are you?"

"Um doin fine, Reverend, just fine, but I need tuh talk tuh yah 'bout somethin that's troublin me."

"What is it, sister?"

"Reverend, I've always had a big dirty mouth, even you knows that. But yesterday, I thank my big mouth went too far with its filth."

"What did you say, sister?"

"Reverend, you know how I've been needlin Selma all the while 'cause I always been jealous of huh? Well, lack I said, I went too far yesterday. I tol' huh 'bout huh husband messin 'round with huh best friend. I even went in tuh detail 'bout em."

"Daizelle, Daizelle, Daizelle...do you remember when you first told me how you felt about Selma?"

"Yes, reverend."

"What did I tell you to do about those feelings then?"

"You tol' me tuh come tuh you fuh counselin 'cause I needed tuh let go uh the frustration and find the reason why I envied huh."

"Exactly, Daizelle...

"Now I feel bad 'bout what I done did, reverend. She may kill that woman and it'll be all my fault."

"Tell me Daizelle, why are you so jealous of Selma?"

"'Cause, I ain't nevva had nothin and she got everythang. Even that sick-ass—

"Daizelle. Watch your mouth. You're not only in the presence of one of God's servants, but you're also in the house of the Lord."

"I'm sorry, reverend. Um sorry fuh cussin, but it's true that huh husband sick, and even he look out fuh huh lack she somethin special, and he done messed 'round with all the women here in Casey Park, 'cept me!"

"Come here and sit down with me Ms. Daizelle.

Now you listen to what I'm about to say to you. I've known Selma since she was a baby. Her parents treated her different than they did the other children. Despite that she's a kindhearted and giving person who's always worked hard to get what she wanted. I've never seen her pick on anyone, and I've never heard her talk about anyone no matter how much they might have deserved it or what her friends did—

"She talks about me with Bert when I go in huh sto'."

"Don't you take items form her to irritate her, Daizelle?"

"Yes, reverend."

"Then how do you think she should act when you constantly and purposely agitate her?"

"Lack a Christian, reverend."

"Oh, I see. You mean the way you act, Daizelle?"

"Naw, reverend, but—

"But what, Daizelle? Selma's a person too. Everyone has their breaking point and Selma has one too. And instead of taunting her you should be helping her. I remember the times you've gone to her store and she's given you free food. Do you remember those times, Sister Washington?"

"Yes, reverend, I remember."

"Then you must realize by now that Selma doesn't deserve the treatment you've been giving her. Am I right?"

"Yes, reverend, you right."

"As far as her husband not choosing you to be one of his concubines, that's a blessing to you. What he and those other women are doing will definitely get them a good seat in hell if they continue, and I'm sure you don't want to join them."

"Naw, suh!"

"Sister Daizelle, you go to Selma and apologize."

"Okay, reverend."

"One more thing before you leave."

"Yes, reverend."

"Try to stop gossiping, cursing, and spying on people, Daizelle. People don't like it and God definitely hates it."

"It's a habit, pastor. I don't thank I can evva stop."

"Yes you can, Daizelle. Pray every day and night if you have to and ask God to remove the habits."

"Yes, pastor, I'll do that, pastor."

"Good, Daizelle. The next time I see you, I'll expect to have heard from the streets and yourself how you've changed, and to see a change in you. You're one of my most devoted members and I need to know that you're getting something positive from my sermons."

"Um goan change, pastor, you'll see."

"I believe you, Daizelle, and remember; God is with you on that rough journey."

"I love you, pastor."

"And I love you too, Sister Washington."

Chapter 6

SELMA JUMPS ON BERT IN THE STORE

"A-H-H-H-H-H, WHAT'S WRONG WITH YOU, SELMA? YOU DONE GOAN FOOL JUMPIN OAN ME LACK THAT, UM GOAN KILL YOU!"

"COME OAN AND KILL ME THEN YOU FAT, RAUNCHY BITCH! 'CAUSE UM SHO' GOAN BE TRYIN TUH KILL YO' BIG ASS EVERY TIME I SWANG MY BAT!"

"COME OAN NIGH, SELMA! CAIN'T WE TALK ABOUT WHAT'S WRONG?"

"NAW! ALL I WONT YOU TUH DO IS STAND UP TUH ME LACK A WOMAN—COME OAN, BERT! STAND UP TUH ME THE WAY A BIG WOMAN LACK YOU SHOULD!"

"NAW, SELMA! I AIN'T COMIN NEAR YOU WHILE YOU HOLDIN THAT BAT!"

"YOU KIN RUN, BERT, BUT YOU CAIN'T HIDE! YOU ALMOST IN THE CORNER NIGH, BERT, WHAT YOU GOAN DO?"

"A-H-H-H-H-H, SELMA, PLEASE, DON'T HIT ME NO MO'!"

"NAW, YOU S'PPOSED TUH KILL ME, REMEMBER!"

"I THANK YOU DONE BROKE MY HAND, SELMA, THAT'S ENOUGH!"

"WHEN I BREAK THE REST UH YAH, THEN, IT'S ENOUGH!"

"SELMA, JUST TELL ME WHY YOU JUMPIN OAN ME!"

"NAW, YOU TELL ME WHY YOU TRYIN TUH PRETEND YOU MY FRIEND ALL THE WHILE YOU SLEEPIN WITH MY HUSBAND BEHIND MY BACK!"

"HE RAPED ME SELMA, HE RAPED ME!"

"IT MUSTA BEEN A MIGHTY GOOD RAPE, 'CAUSE YOU STILL SLEEPIN WITH HIM!"

"NAW, SELMA, IT WADN'T LACK THAT!"

"WHAT YOU MEAN, IT WADN'T LACK THAT, BERT! DAIZELLE SAW THE WHOLE THANG!"

"IF SHE SAW THE WHOLE THANG, THEN WHY DIDN'T SHE CALL THE POLICE WHILE HE WAS BEATIN ME? YOU EVEN SEEN THE BRUISES WHEN YOU CAME BACK! YOU SAW MY BLACK EYE, BUSTED LIP, AND I STILL HAD MY ARM IN A SLANG FROM THE DISLOCATED SHOULDER AND BROKE ARM! I TOLD YOU I FELL DOWN THE STAIRS, SELMA, BUT IT WAS CLARK, SELMA! CLARK HAD BEAT AND RAPED ME SO BAD I WAS IN THE HOSPITAL! HE STILL MISTREATIN AND BEATIN OAN ME! PLEASE, SELMA, DON'T YOU BEAT ME TOO!"

"Just tell me why, Bert. Why did you continue tuh lay with my husband and grin in my face?"

"*Because, Selma, he was beatin me and forcin me tuh do it. I'd open my do' and there he'd be, pushin, 'n' forcin his way in. As time went oan I just gave up and let him have his way.*"

"Why didn't you at least tell me 'bout him?"

"*Selma, I ain't goan lie tuh yah. I was sho' nuff scared uh him, but I enjoyed havin him 'round afta while. It's like he can put you under*" *some type uh spell uh somethin and you cain't let go.*

Believe me, I wonted tuh tell you. I really did. I hated him and what I was doin, but at the same time, I was lonely, and um scared uh Clark, he had me scared, Selma! I was mo' scared then lonely you gotta believe that!

The night I said somethin 'bout him takin Fatina home he beat me. He beat me real bad."

"So. That's what he meant when he said he'd take care uh you later? He been beatin oan you? Is that why afta that night you ain't been 'round tuh the sto' fuh almost three weeks, Bert?"

"Yeah, Selma. That's why I ain't been 'round here. I was messed up real bad."

"Oh my God, Bert. Um so, sorry. I didn't know. I really didn't know."

"Look, Selma, I know um a big old fat woman that nobody don't wont. Hurtin you was the last thang I wonted tuh do 'cause I know you really loved me lack family. But Clark had me so scared uh him I didn't know what else tuh do. At the same time, he made me feel different, and I couldn't let go afta the first time he forced hisself oan me and he wadn't goan let me no way!

I started tuh kill myself when I realized that I'd gotten use tuh Clark's mistreatment.

Now, I wish I had, Selma. Now that our friendship ruined, I might as well be dead."

"No, Bert, don't say that and don't cry. Clark the one who need tuh be dead. It wadn't enough fuh him tuh go with all them otha women so I wouldn't have no friends, he had tuh destroy our friendship, too. You know what, Bert? I ain't goan let him git 'way with it this time. Clark goan pay fuh all he done tuh me, and you."

Chapter 7

CLARK & MOTSEY

"Come here, girl."

"Not less you got some git high."

"Look in daddy's pocket, Motsey."

"Ooh, Clark, I knew you wouldn't let me down!"

"Of course I wouldn't. You know I got tuh keep my young-meat happy."

"Yo' young-meat would be even happier if huh daddy was tuh git rid uh his old sack uh potatoes."

"Why would daddy wonna go 'n' do that?"

"'Cause, then we could be tugetha proppa, instead uh bein in yo' car and meetin at all these sleazy motels 'n' junk!"

"Look, girl! We got it re-e-eal good! There ain't no since in messin up a good thang! Ain't I here whenever you wont me?"

"Yeah, daddy, but—"

"Ain't I supplyin all the crack and anythang else you wont?"

"Yeah, daddy! Don't git mad—"

"Then shut up, heffa and live with thangs the way they is or you just may end up losin that supply you need and love so much!"

"Clark. You duh one made me uh addict...!"

"I ain't made you nothin...!"

"YES YOU DID! You the one got me started oan this shit, Clark!"

"I ain't the one makin yah smoke it nigh though am I, Motsey?"

"Ah-ah Clark, that ain't right! You lit up a pipe fuh me one day, tol' me it wadn't nothin but high potency marijuana, and nigh I cain't quit!"

"I know, Motsey, and I can git you tuh do anythang I wont you tuh do tuh git it."

"Clark, um only foeteen! You done ruined me. My life ova 'cause uh you, and you talkin lack what you done tuh me ain't nothin!"

"You kin cry all you wont. But you ruined yo'self, Motsey. You and yo' mamma! You was fast, remember?"

"Naw I wadn't! And my mamma—"

"YO', MAMMA, YO', MAMMA! YO' MAMMA, WHAT, MOTSEY? DIDN'T ALLOW HUH DAUGHTA TUH RUN THE STREETS HALF NECKKED...!"

"I KEEP TELLIN YOU, THAT AIN'T NUNNA MY MAMMA FAULT! I USE TUH SNEAK AND WEAR THEM THANGS JUST LACK YOU HAD ME SNEAKIN TUH SEE YOU!"

"I ain't had you doin nothin, Motsey. You chose tuh sneak 'round with me. And you should be mo' careful how you represent yo' mamma. 'Cause no matter whatchoo do people goan blame huh. Nigh um goan explain tuh you what my mamma tried tuh explain tuh me and the first gal I evva had. Somethin that I ain't nevva paid no attention, 'cause I figured that gal shoulda been lookin out fuh huh self. I wadn't responsible fuh what that

gal did or what she let me do. Nigh you listen
good, Motsey; you listen, real good. There's
people who goan be shame uh you and some who goan
be feelin sorry fuh yah. They goan call me a dog,
but git use tuh me bein one. Me 'n' you goan be
almost blameless when peoples gits use tuh us.
But that big mouth mammy uh yours, she goan end
up takin the blame fuh all uh what you do and all
uh what I done tuh yah. 'Cause they goan thank
she done allowed it somehow. And no matter what
she do, how she act, or what she say, folks ain't
goan let huh live it down, and she ain't goan be
able tuh let go of the guilt.

Some uh them words was my own. But I Know I
ain't goan nevva fuhgit, Motsey. Um goan always
know the truth. How you use tuh strut by that
wine tree with them short skirts and them shorts
that showed yo' behind and the insides uh yo'
thighs. How I'd sweet talk yah, tell yah how
sweet, pretty, and smooth yo' thighs looked,
especially the insides of um and what I wonted
tuh do tuh yah and how yah fell fuh it. Um goan
always know the truth. You done fuhgot the truth,
silly heffa—huh, you done fuhgot that!

Look atcha...naw, you ain't fuhgot it and you
ain't fuhgot how you couldn't wait fuh me tuh do
all them thangs I promised yah eitha. How I had
yah squealin 'n' cryin, 'n' talkin outcha' head
all crazy the first time I messed with yah in

that strange way. GIRL...you was so messed up you couldn't keep yo' food down! Remember that! And I know you cain't fuhgit how all I hafta do is snap my fangas and yah do um all tuh me nigh, 'cause I ain't goan nevva letcha fuhgit!"

"Why you always talkin tuh me lack this nigh? You use tuh act lack you was so in love with me. You couldn't be without me fuh a minute. You didn't even wont none uh them otha men lookin at me and you still don't. But what happened tuh the good way you use tuh treat me, Clark? What happened...?"

"...Clark, I know you was messin with me fuh a long time that otha way, but you was the only man I'd evva let do that tuh me or touch my breasts. You was the first man I evva had sex with, Clark! I love you! Why you got tuh talk tuh me so bad, huh? Why!"

"'Cause, I can, Motsey, and you cain't do nothin 'bout it and you ain't goin no where. I done hooked you nigh, Motsey. I can do and say whatevva I wont. I done turned you into uh clown, Motsey. A silly clown who I done turned into my b—

"DON'T SAY IT CLARK! PLEASE, DON'T SAY IT!"

"Okay Motsey, I won't, but we both know you is and I control you. I control you 'cause you was too grown fuh a boy yo' own age and didn't wont tuh go tuh school. You didn't wont no summer job, and wonted all them nice clothes I boughtcha! Nigh you got um and yah got me, but look where you at. I probably don't treatcha as good as uh boy yo' age. Um resentful t'wards yah 'cause uh yah mammy, and done made you my who'e, my prostitute, my dog! You anythang and everythang I wont you tuh be, Motsey, just because you didn't wont school and no childhood, and I can supply you with them tiny little rocks you love! You must be feelin real stupid and outta place rat 'bout now!"

"Sho', you can rub it in my face nigh, but someday you'll git yours lack I got mine fuh messin 'round with you, Clark. Every demon does sooner uh later."

"Demon? Huh...! You ain't doin nothin but ticklin me, CRYIN HEFFA! You just as much uh demon as I am, Motsey! And um goan git mine...? Huh! I got this whole town under my thumb, 'specially the women folk, so how um goan git mine—Miss so smart 'til she stupid! JUST TELL ME, HOW UM GOAN GIT MINE!

Mr. Clark can git love or money anytime he wonts it. I got it made, girl, and just lack everybody else in this town you helpin me make it.

Nigh, um a lil' upset witcha fuh runnin yo' mouth but um okay. You can still make it up tuh me. Nigh I wont you tuh shut yo' mouth befo' I git real angry. Then, I'll have tuh whoop yah and you ain't goan lack that and I ain't goan lack that, 'cause when I finish whoopin yo' ass you ain't goan do nothin that I wont you tuh do fuh me the right way."

"*Clark, that's anotha thang, you caint be beatin oan me no mo', 'cause um pregnant!*"

"YOU, WHAT!"

"*I said, um pregnant!*"

"Hm. As bad as I wonted tuh hitcha when you called my wife a old sack uh potatoes I was goan let that go, Motsey. But Clark might as well take care uh that baby and what you said 'bout his wife rat nigh 'n' fuhgit 'bout you pleasin him fuh nigh...U-H-H-H!"

"A-HHHHHHH! OH NO, CLARK! OH NO!"

"Shut up, heffa!"

"But Clark, you done kicked me in my stomach! Um hurt! I caint git up! I need tuh go tuh the hospital, Clark!"

"Um goan take yah, but when we git there you'd better tell um you fell uh um goan tell um 'bout the drugs you usin. They'll call yo' mammy tuh have you locked up! Now, what you goan do when we git there?"

"U-u-um goan be quiet and let you do all the t-t-talkin—a-a-ah, um hurtin, um hurtin. Just take me tuh the hospital I'll be quiet—

"That's exactly what you goan do!"

"CLARK, DON'T HIT ME! CLARK DON'T HURT ME, PLEASE! I'LL GIT RID OF IT! I'LL GIT RID OF IT, I SWEAR—

"SHUT UP, 'CAUSE I DON'T TRUST NOTHIN' YOU SAYIN'! Me and my wife ain't got no babies runnin 'round and I be damned if um goan have um runnin 'round outside my house!

Um goan whoop you good, Motsey, real good! Um goan whoop you fuh gittin pregnant, runnin yo' mouth, fuh messin up what I planned oan you doin fuh me today, and fuh talkin 'bout my wife! When I git through whoopin you, we'll be ready tuh go!"

"NAW CLARK, NAW! DON'T KILL MY BABY! I SWEAR, I WON'T NEVVA TELL NOBODY IT'S YOURS—

"SEE, YOU WAS LYIN'! THOUGHT YOU SAID YOU WAS GOAN GIT RID UH IT, LYIN' HEFFA!"

"I WILL, CLARK AND I WONT NEVVA TALK 'BOUT YO' WIFE AGAIN EITHA, I PROMISE YOU CLARK, I PROMISE...! HELP ME, SOMEBODY! SOMEBODY HELP ME, PLEASE...

Chapter 8

DAIZELLE APOLOGIZES TO SELMA

"Um so, sorry, Selma. I shouldn'tna nevva said none uh them thangs tuh you."

"Daizelle, why you back here, ain't you done me enough evil?"

"Selma, that ain't why um here. Um really sorry 'bout what I done."

"Selma, I always been jealous uh you."

"Why, Daizelle, why? I always treated you good. I ain't nevva done nothin wrong by you."

"I know, Selma, and that's why um askin you tuh fuhgive me."

"Daizelle. I might have been able tuh fuhgive you rat here and rat nigh if you hadn't lied."

"But, Selma, I didn't lie. I saw what I saw!"

"Then why didn't you tell me Clark raped, Bert?"

"'Cause, he didn't. You been knowin me fuh almost twenty years, Selma, and you know I talks a lot. You ain't nevva know'd me tuh lie, just cheat and steal."

"So, you tellin me, Bert let him do all them thangs?"

"As bad as I wont you tuh fuhgive me I cain't lie tuh you. She let him do it, Selma."

"She tol' me he raped huh."

"Naw, Selma, he didn't rape huh. She'd been sassin 'round Clark fuh a long time. I thank that's why he treated huh lack a dog that day and made huh shame. He shamed huh real bad that day, that's why I was so surprised tuh see him goin 'round tuh huh house."

"So, she lyin, Daizelle?"

"Oh yeah, Selma, she lyin oan Clark. Clark ain't raped nobody."

"Daizelle, I thank you. Believe it uh not you done gave me enough strength tuh finally walk 'way from this mess."

"You ain't goan hurt Bert, is yah?"

"Naw, I ain't goan hurt nobody, um goan do somethin fuh everybody, includin myself.

You see, Daizelle, them women see Clark as a who'eish man. A easy man. Somethin tuh lay up with 'cause eitha they husbands ain't doin right or they ain't got nobody else. They just be usin him 'til they git somebody they wont tuh be with. He just lack that nasty yella gal...

"You mean, Clarietta."

"Yeah, Daizelle, Clarietta...the only difference is, Clarietta gits paid. Clark lays up fuh free.

He thanks he doin somethin biggity. He thank women wont him 'cause he sexy. But I know different. All them women done heard 'bout him

that's why they flirts with him in front uh me.
They know the evil thangs he be doin, that's why
um goan let him go."

"Don't let yo' husband go, Selma. Scripture
say it ain't right."

"Daizelle, scripture tell yah the only reason
fuh yah tuh let yo' husband go is that he lay
with another and he done laid with many others. I
done witnessed it."

"Selma, scripture speak uh men givin divorce,
not womens."

"Daizelle, that's because the men was the
ones askin the question 'bout divorce. If you
remember, Daizelle, the men wonted tuh divorce
them women just 'cause they was tired of um so
Jesus was clarifyin it in Matthew 5:31-32. He
never said that the men was the only ones allowed
a divorce under them circumstances. Jesus don't
discriminate. Besides, when Jesus spoke uh men.
He meant the one's with and without wombs. We
women, but that meant us too, Daizelle. Me and
you. We men with wombs. A lot uh women wont admit
that 'cause they thank God a sexist. Ain't nothin
narrow-minded 'bout God. We the ones who try tuh
put him in a box."

"Maybe you right, Selma."

"I am right, Daizelle; read the scripture!"

"I will, I will, but I just hates tuh see you
and Clark break up! Y'all been tugetha so long as
husband and wife it just won't seem right!"

"Daizelle, we been tugetha, but nevva as husband and wife. Ah-ah Daizelle. Clark ain't nevva been my husband. He was just a man I saw in the monin and went tuh bed with at night. A man that used me lack a who'e and gave me his check tuh make it all right. The man who make me too crazy tuh thank, and the only man that make me crazy enough tuh kill."

"But Selma, you was so happy. I could tell."

"Was, is right, Daizelle. Then I woke up tuh the thangs Clark was doin tuh me and had me acceptin. Somethin started happenin inside me. Once that happened I wadn't interested in that stuff Clark was doin tuh me no mo', and his cheatin' made him look like satan.

Um a Christian-woman Daizelle just lack you. I know that we don't always act lack it, but we is and we got tuh try tuh do what's right by the Lord no matter what and put him first in our lives. I ain't showin God that by holdin oan tuh Clark the way he is. I was just foolin myself, Daizelle. I don't need no Clark. It might be a little lonely 'round here without him, but thangs change and people change all the time Daizelle, but everybody gets use tuh both. So if lettin Clark go is the only way tuh keep me from hurtin somebody, then I got tuh let him go. I don't wonna spend eternity in hell fuh killin somebody who wouldn't even understand what um killin em fuh."

Chapter 9

THE SURPRISE CALL

"You really had me fooled, Bert. I really believed you was tellin the truth."

"What's wrong nigh, Selma?"

"You know what's wrong; you wrong! Daizelle came in the sto' and apologized tuh me fuh the way she been treatin me. Fo' she left, I got huh tuh tell me everythang. She tol' me you been tryin tuh git Clark tuh go tuh bed with you fuh a while...

"SHE LYIN!"

"Naw she ain't, Bert."

"I swear, Selma, Clark did what I said!"

"He mighta, but not the day Daizelle seen y'all. What really happened, Bert? Did he wont service you couldn't—wouldn't give him? Didja threaten him, didja talk 'bout me? WHAT WAS IT BERT, WHAT WAS IT!"

"YOU WONNA KNOW, SELMA! THEN I'LL TELL YOU! HE'D BEEN LAYIN UP WITH THAT YOUNG, YELLA GAL THAT DAY! AND AS USUAL HE DIDN'T MAKE IT NO SECRET! THEN HE COME TUH MY HOUSE WONTIN ME TUH DO WHAT SHE EITHA COULDN'T UH REFUSED TUH DO AND I TOL' HIM, NAW!

I thought I could whoop him 'cause he so small, but he grabbed me 'round my legs and slammed me tuh the flo'. Every time I tried tuh git up he'd slam me again. When I finally decided I'd lay there, he started stompin me. I tried tuh roll away, but he was too fast. That had made him angry so he wrestled me tuh my stomach and got oan top uh me with both knees in my back and pulled my arm up 'til he heard it snap. While I was helpless and screamin in pain, he made me do what he'd asked me and some."

"As God is my witness, Bert, I wish that I could say that I feel sorry fuh you, but I don't! 'Cause you still ain't tellin me everythang! You deceitful and disgustin just lack him! I thank if I'd been there while he was whoopin you, I woulda cheered him oan! Shoot, let me stop bein so damned modest! I woulda helped him! Maybe the both uh us coulda beatcha down tuh size!"

"You ain't got no right talkin tuh me lack that, Selma! You's a Christian—a-a-a Godly Woman!"

"Um a Christian, not some dead saint! Besides, you got a lot uh nerve tryin tuh judge me, all the while sleepin with Clark and grinnin in my face! Tuh tell you the truth you done betrayed me so bad that if you was tuh drop dead rat nigh I wouldn't feel nothin but joy. Butcha know what? Um goan pray as much as I need tuh make this leave me cause I knows in my heart, I gots tuh please my father. He's the only one that can bring me peace and true joy. I ain't goan nevva leave Jesus or put no man befo' him fuh lust and self-satisfaction no mo', 'cause my worst day with him, is better than my best day without him.

Bert, I don't need no Clark that's why um goan leave him with you and all them other desperate women out there! Um leavin', Casey Park!"

Chapter 10

THE HOSPITAL

"Naw, my daddy ain't hit me! It's just lack he said! We was standin at the top uh duh stairs strugglin. He was tryin tuh keep me from runnin 'way again."

"What do you mean by, strugglin?"

"You know; he was tryin tuh keep me there. He didn't wont me tuh run away. He was holdin me..."

"Around your waist, around your neck, where— where was he holding you, Motsey?"

"Naw, he was holdin my wrists and I pulled 'way from him and fell down the stairs. He didn't even know I was pregnant."

"I see, Ms. Talbot, but we're going to have to let him know. Does that frighten you?"

"Naw suh, it don't."

"Okay, after we tell him, we'll send him in. In the meantime you just lie there and relax."

THE WAITING ROOM

"Oh Lord, no! You tellin me my baby was pregnant and miscarried!"

"Yes sir, she was carrying your grandchild."

"It's all my fault! If I hadn't been tryin tuh keep huh from runnin off with that old, no good boy, it wouldn'tna happen."

85

"Is that what happened, Mr. Talbot?"

"Yes, suh. We was strugglin at the top uh the stairs and she pulled 'way from me and went flyin. I tried tuh catch huh, but I just wadn't fast enough."

"Don't cry. It's going to be okay sir it's over now. She's going to be all right, but she'll have to stay here a few days."

"WHAT? I cain't take my baby home?"

"No, Mr. Talbot. She's very young and we want to make sure she's going to heal correctly. Although she's stable there's still a chance of her hemorrhaging."

"When can I see huh? When can I see my baby?"

"Oh, you can go in anytime. Oh yeah. Here's her medical card. She left it at the emergency desk."

"Thank you, doctor. You been real good tuh my baby girl."

"You're welcome Mr. Talbot, but all I did was my job...

"Hey, daddy."

"Hey, sweet meat. Here go yo' medical card. Good thang you had it oan you or we might uh been in a little trouble."

"Mamma always make me carry it."

"I guess that ol', big mouth tramp good fuh somethin then. Ain't she, Motsey?"

"Clark—

"Um just teasin, um just teasin. How you feelin?"

"Um all right."

"You know daddy didn't mean what he done tuh yah, you know he sorry. You know he didn't have no otha choice but tuh do what he did tuh yah, dontcha?"

"Yeah, daddy, um—

"See, I knew you could do it. I knew you understood. I knew you could fool them doctas. Everythang came out real good and they goan git betta when you git out."

"Don't, daddy, please don't do that!"

"Hush, silly gal, all um doin is makin sho' you all right!"

"By puttin yo' mouth oan my breasts! That ain't clean, daddy! I done just lost a baby!"

"I don't believe that got nothin tuh do with it, Motsey! You wont that docta, dontcha! 'CAUSE YOU YELLA! YOU WONT THAT WHITE MAN, DONTCHA! YOU THANK HE BETTA THEN ME 'CAUSE HE WHITE, HE YOUNG, 'N' HE A DOCTA 'N' YOU LOOK HALF-WHITE! TALK TUH ME GAL OR I'LL KILL YOU RAT IN THIS HOSPITAL BED AND LEAVE YOU LYIN HERE!"

"No, Clark, I don't! I—

"YOU CALL ME DADDY WHEN UM UPSET! YOU CALL ME DADDY, YOU HERE ME!

"*Yeah, yeah, yeah, I hear you daddy! I hear you...!*"

"SHUT UP 'N' JUST BE QUIET THEN! AND STOP CRYIN! I DONE 'BOUT HAD ENOUGH UH YO' MOUTH FUH ONE DAY! YOU DONE GOAN 'N' MADE ME HURTCHA, NIGH I CAIN'T GIT SATISFIED! I'LL KILL YOU!"

"Okay daddy, you chokin me! Okay! I won't say nothin else!"

"That's good, 'cause I don't wonna hurtcha while you layin up in this here bed!"

"Okay daddy, let me go, I said, okay...

"I heard the shouting! Is everything okay?"

"Yes, nurse it is."

"Ms. Talbot?"

"Yes, ma'am. My daddy just talkin kinda loud 'cause he upset 'bout me bein pregnant and not tellin him, that's all."

"Okay, but please, try to keep your voices down. This is a hospital."

"You a smart lil' ol' somethin, aintcha...?

...I said, aintcha...!"

"Yeah, daddy, yeah!"

"Then you smart enough tuh lay oan back in this bed and keep yo' mouth closed 'til um through...

"What he doin tuh me feel real nasty...

"Um makin yah feel good, Motsey? Is it good tuh yah, Motsey?"

"Yeah, daddy, it's good."

"Then tell me yah love me and say it lack you mean it! Lack I taughtcha!"

"*I love yah daddy! I love you mo' than I love my mamma uh anybody else in my family. You everythang tuh me, daddy.*"

"You uh smart lil' thang, Motsey. Real, smart...

"He don't even care 'bout me. All he wont is my body just lack my mamma tol' me. He don't be doin nothin but feedin off my body lack the old buzzard he is, just lack my mamma said. I shoulda listened tuh huh.

Soon as they let me up outta here, um goan git 'way from him. I ain't goan nevva let no man treat me this way no mo'."

Chapter 11

CORNERED

"NIGGA! I'LL KILL YOU! AAAAAAAAAAAHG!"

"SELMA JEAN! WHAT'S DONE GOT INTO YOU?"

"YOU MEAN, WHATCHOO DONE GOT INTO, DONTCHA, CLARK! UM GOAN SPLIT YO' HEAD WITH THIS AXE, *RAT* NOW! UM GOAN KILL YOU, NIGGA!"

"WOMAN, I DON'T KNOW WHAT'S WRONG WITCHOO, BUT YOU LUCKY THAT KNIFE STUCK IN THE WALL! NIGH PUT THAT AXE DOWN, SELMA JEAN, FO' SOMEBODY GIT HURT!"

"Why'd you hafta do it, Clark? Why'd you hafta sleep with Bert...my best friend, Clark?"

"That big heffa don't mean nothin tuh me, Selma! None uh them women do, you know that!"

"I wont you out, Clark! I wont you outta here rat nigh!"

"Come oan, Selma Jean—

"GET OUT, CLARK! GET OUT!"

"Selma, let's just go tuh bed. I kin make it all up tuh ya."

"MAN, YOU KNOW I AIN'T LET YOU TOUCH ME IN ALMOST SIX MONTHS NIGH, AND AIN'T NOTHIN CHANGIN!"

"Okay, Selma Jean, okay I'll leave, but not befo' I take care uh you again...

"Oh my God! He goan try tuh take me! He goan try tuh fight me while I got this axe in my hand tuh do it...!"

"Nigh, you can eitha put the axe down so I can do what I need tuh do and be oan my way or um goan take it from yah."

"GIT AWAY FROM ME, CLARK! STAY BACK! STAY BACK! I AIN'T PLAYIN! I'LL KILL YAH...!"

"Then go 'head, Selma. Kill me. Split my head lack you promised."

"Move away from me, Clark!"

"Naw, Selma. Kill me. I done messed thangs up fuh yah, KILL ME!"

"I cain't—

"I know you cain't. Just lack I figured. NIGH, GIMME THE AXE!"

"LET GO UH ME, CLARK! LET GO UH ME!"

"Okay, Selma Jean I'll letcha go long enough fuh me tuh close up."

"LEAVE THEM BLINDS OPEN, CLARK! WE AIN'T CLOSIN!"

"Oh yeah, Selma. We closin—

"LEAVE THEM BLINDS UP, CLARK!"

"Why yo backin 'way from me, Selma Jean? Why you backin way?"

"CLARK! WHY DON'T YOU JUST LEAVE!"

"Look, Selma Jean. I done been out tuh the hospital all day 'cause I done had tuh whoop one uh y'all. Nigh, um tired and um angry—COME HERE!"

91

"NAW CLARK, NAW! PLEASE, DON'T DO THAT! NOT
IN THE STO', CLARK! NOT IN THE MIDDLE OF THE
FLO'! I TOLD YOU, UM A CHRISTIAN WOMAN! I DON'T
WONT YOU DOIN THEM WICKED THANGS TUH ME NO MO'!"

"I wont afta this, Selma Jean, less you wont
me to lack you always do when we have fights and
I make up tuh yah lack this. Nigh you lay there
and don't try tuh scratch me up and pull my hair
out lack you did last time this happened or um
goan do you lack I done Clarietta."

"PLEASE, CLARK! NO, NO, NO, NO, NO—E-E-E-E-E-
E-E-Y!"

LATER

"WHY YOU HAD TUH DO ME LACK THAT, CLARK! WHY!"

"I don't know whatchoo cryin fuh, Selma Jean.
All I done was please my wife. Nigh cut out this
nonsense. I done made up tuh yah...

"Just git out, Clark! Please, just go!"

"Selma, I don't know why you wont me tuh
leave here. You know you don't mean it. You don't
nevva mean it, 'cause you know you cain't git
enough uh me. You ain't goan nevva find anotha
man tuh give yah the money I do and make yah feel
lack that no mo'. Didn't I make yah feel good?
Dontcha wont me tuh stay and keep makin yah feel
good, baby?"

"You filthy, Clark! What you just did tuh me
is filthy and there's mo' tuh a good man than a
paycheck!"

"Is that why you always be takin my money and was holdin my head, gyratin, callin out my name, and callin oan God lack a mad who'e just nigh?"

"GIT OUT, CLARK! GIT OUT! I COULDN'T HELP THAT AND YOU KNOW IT! BUT I DON'T WONT YOU TOUCHIN ME NEVVA AGAIN!"

"Then call the police, Selma Jean! I done raped yah, Selma Jean! Call the police!"

"JUST LEAVE, CLARK!"

"Um goin, but don't come lookin fuh me when yah git the urge tuh git some uh that again, 'cause um goin tuh the lil' yella gal fuh good. She lack what I be doin. She ain't shame uh me, she ain't got no problems with what I do. She more my speed, anyway. She young and fertile. She can have babies. Me 'n' huh goan have some babies. Somethin yo' old ass couldn't make."

"That's 'cause you done pulled all the life outta me, Clark!"

"Then I shouldn't be able tuh have none eitha, nigh should I, Selma, Jean, Porter?

I done made fo' babies that you know 'bout, includin the one you was carryin' fo' we married and said was mine. I done got rid uh all of um and I had tuh do it again today!

If you barren because uh what I been doin tuh you, then I should be too, shouldn't I?"

"OH MY GOD, CLARK! JUST GIT OUT! I DON'T WONNA TALK ABOUT THAT NO MO'."

"We both know why you don't wont tuh talk about it and we both know why you don't won't tuh call the police. Selma Jean. You ain't got tuh talk tuh me or the police, but if you the Christian you say you is, you goan hafta tell the truth one day, Selma Jean."

"See yah later. Um goin tuh my, "young, yella gal."

"THEN GO 'HEAD! GO TUH HUH! JUST GIT OUT MY STO'!"

"You still my wife, Selma Jean! I got the right tuh have you anytime and any way I please, and ain't no tellin when I might wont tuh have you again! You just remember that!"

"You might wont tuh have me again! But I won't be here fuh you tuh rape again no matter what I done that's ungodly! Just git out, Clark! Please, please, please! Just git out...!"

"UM GONE! RIGHTEOUS WHO'E...! YOU BEGGED ME, SELMA JEAN! YOU, BEGGED, ME! YOU JUST REMEMBER THAT!"

"Uh—my stomach. My stomach all cramped up from what he done tuh me. He be tryin tuh drain me so no otha man kin git tuh me. UH-UH-UH-UH-UH... I cain't even stand up straight. I got tuh lean oan the counter fuh a minute. I feel lack um dyin. If I keep talkin loud I won't die. I can hear myself and I'll be okay...Where my blouse? Where my bra? Where my underwear...Oh Jesus! Oh

Jesus! Oh Jesus! Why? Why he lack he is? That nasty dog! He ain't had no right tuh rape me and put his mouth all ova me lack that. One uh these days he goan git just what he deserve."

THE WINE TREE

"Hey, Clark—Clark! What's the matter with you? Why yo' nose bleadin, man? What happened tuh—

"Oh. I didn't know it was bleadin. But I had tuh straighten Selma out, Clint, that's what happened. Nigh leave me 'lone. I ain't in the mood ...Herthenia! Can I talk tuh you fuh a minute?"

"What's up, Clark? You okay?"

"Yeah Herthenia. Um alright. Listen Herthenia. You know I ain't got no chil'ren, right?"

"Yeah, Clark. I know that."

"Herthenia. I know you prefer women and I don't see nothin wrong with that, but I been wontin you every since you been settin under this here wine tree with us ...with yo' pretty bright-skinned self."

"Clark—

"Herthenia. Wait a minute. Just listen tuh me. We both know that I mess around a lot oan Selma, but she the cause uh that. She don't know how tuh treat me in the bed. She mean, she nasty, and she barren. All she do is put me down lack I ain't good enough fuh huh. If she treated me

95

betta I wouldn't do all uh what I do in the
streets tuh git pleased. Whenevva I come under
this here wine tree you treat me special. I know
you only bein friendly, but you massage my
shoulders, go tuh the sto' fuh me, and you always
treat me just plain ol' good. You really the kind
uh woman most men would be fightin tuh git they
hands oan. The kind uh woman a man would wont his
children tuh be lack. You got a real good nature.
Herthenia. What um tryin tuh say is —I wont you
tuh have my chil'. All I wont is one time witcha.
Just one. Um willin tuh pay. You know I got
plenty money saved. I'll pay yah whether you git
pregnant or not, Herth."

"I don't know, Clark—

"Herth! You goan pass up a few thousand just
'cause you rather lay with women? What we do
won't take long. I know how tuh treat yah, Herth.
I really do. Nigh if you wont the money, meet me
at this hotel. Me and Selma done broke up. Um
goan be stayin here."

"What was you whisperin in Herthenia ear?
What y'all was talkin 'bout, Clark?"

"Business, Clint! Business!"

"What kind uh business, Clark? Can I git in
oan some uh it?"

"Naw! Herthenia tol' me don't tell nobody
else!"

"Well, if you don't, Clark that'll be a first! All you evva brag about is money and all the women you done had in Casey Park!"

"This different! I cain't say nothin 'bout this. Least not 'til it's ova...And when it is. Selma goan be the first tuh know. Um goan make sho' I let huh know that Herthenia mo' of a woman than she is even though she don't like no men. She goan know 'bout our baby, too. That's goan teach huh 'bout puttin me out. Oh, yeah. When she find out that a lesbian kin give me kids and she cain't, that's goan tear huh heart out and that's goan be just what she deserve. I cain't wait fuh Herthenia tuh birth my chil' right up under Selma's nose!"

Chapter 12

NEW FRIENDS

"Mornin, Selma...you okay?"

"Yeah. Oh yeah, Daizelle, um fine!"

"Then why you all bent ova lack that and holdin yo' stomach? Clark done that thang tuh you again?"

"What thang? What you talkin 'bout, Daizelle?"

"I know all about it, Selma. He be tellin people how he be pleasin you—

"He lyin, Daizelle. The only place Clark evva put his lips was oan mine."

"Then why you cut me so short and how you know what um talkin 'bout then?"

"Cause! I know what people be sayin—Daizelle, look! He ain't been doin nothin tuh me that ain't right!"

"Well, that ain't what he been tellin folks. Come oan Selma, you can talk tuh me."

"I SAID, IT WADN'T TRUE, DIDN'T I, DAIZELLE? NIGH, CAN WE DROP THAT SUBJECT?"

"Okay, okay, I done dropped it—what you got goin fuh today?"

"Nothin much, Daizelle. Just packin some thangs that's all."

"You really goan leave here, huh."

"Yeah, ain't nothin left here fuh me."

"Maybe you right, maybe you shoulda left fo' nigh. Shoot, Selma, I don't know how you stayed this long."

"It's all about security, Daizelle."

"I reckon it is, 'cause I was always wontin a man tuh take care me lack I seen Clark take care you, a nice place lack this one with a nice business and a nice piece uh land connected to it tuh call my own."

"Daizelle, them thangs don't mean nothin if you ain't got nobody tuh share um with!

Look at all these foolish women here in Casey Park chasin afta and fightin ova one man, mine, Clark, somebody else's husband that ain't worth the dirt he was made with! They doin it fuh comfort, but they ain't goan never be comfortable with that ignorant S.O.B. 'cause he ain't goan nevva love none of um. If they was smart they'd all try tuh find a man uh they oan somewhere. Somebody goan treat um right. Somebody that care less 'bout they figure, breast size, and what kinda sexual tricks they can git out of um."

"Selma, I gots tuh be truthful. I was jealous uh them women 'cause Clark talked tuh all of um 'cept me. I don't mean tuh upset you 'bout Bert again but—

"She don't upset me no mo'. You can say whatchoo wont."

"Well, it's just that when I seen him with huh that day in the sto', I almost flipped out 'cause I got so angry. That's the only reason why I tol' you—yah know, 'cause I was jealous and angry.

Selma what um goan say probably goan sound even mo' stupid tuh yah seein how Clark yo' husband 'n' all. But, I was wonderin why I was 'bout the only woman in Casey Park Clark hadn't tried tuh sleep with. Funny thang is, I wouldn'tna messed 'round with Clark no way 'cause fuh some reason I always looked up tuh y'all."

"Nobody could tell it Daizelle by the way you treated me."

"I knows, I knows, Ms. Daizelle ain't been too kind tuh Ms. Selma—actually, I ain't been too kind tuh nobody 'round here, but that's all goan change. Um willin tuh give my life fuh yah nigh, Selma, 'cause you the only one in this town who evva looked out fuh Ms. Daizelle and I was too stupid tuh realize that.

Afta I talked tuh the reverend, I began rememberin all the good thangs that he said 'bout you is true. Lack the time I almost died and you brung me soup, stayed with me, and nursed me back tuh health. You done brung me groceries and give me money. I might not even be here if it wadn't fuh you. Selma, you done a lot uh thangs fuh me and I returned um with evil, 'cause no matter what you did fuh me I was jealous uh what you had. I got a lot uh makin up tuh do with you 'cause I loves you now, Selma. I loves you lack a susta. The reverend helped me tuh feel this way 'bout you.

Truth is, Selma, Ms. Daizelle hated everybody 'cause Ms. Daizelle hated huhself. Now that my eyes done opened up all that's goan change. From now oan, people goan be talkin 'bout how beautiful Ms. Daizelle is instead uh how ugly she be actin. How good she be treatin people instead uh how she be sowin evil. Maybe I ain't goan be perfect Ms. Selma, but um goan be betta than yestaday and even betta tomorrow. Now come oan ova here and give yo' new susta a big hug 'cause I love you!"

"Oh, Daizelle, I love you too! Um so happy we goan be friends."

"So am I, Ms. Selma, so am I...She can say what she wont, but I can tell. He been pullin oan huh body again. He musta done it again last night tryin tuh make huh stay with him. She wadn't lookin lack that yesterday. Whatevva he done tuh huh, um glad it didn't work. He one man that needed tuh be let go 'cause he ain't no good, and ain't goan nevva be. And whatevva he doin tuh huh seem tuh be ruinin huh body. It seem tuh be drainin the life outta huh somehow. You don't know this, but um glad he gone, Miss Selma. Everythang goan be alright."

Chapter 13

MOTSEY

"What up, what up, what up! Home-girl, look at you! You gotcha nails done, yah hair done and check out them grounders, they top line! You don't even play no ball! You got it goin oan since you done left that worm carrier!"

"Tricia, girl, stop it!"

"Well it's true! He was so old he was rotten!"

"You right about that, Tricia. He was rotten from the top uh his head tuh the bottom uh his feet, and he wadn't doin nothin but drainin the life out me. He even kilt my baby."

"Naw, girl! Motsey, you lyin'!"

"Mm-hm, Tricia, he sho' did. He beat me so bad I miscarried."

"What happened, y'all got into a fight uh somethin, Motsey?"

"Naw, Tricia. He meant tuh do it."

"I don't understand that, Motsey."

"He was kinda threatnin me and I had tuh tell him I was pregnant so he wouldn't hurt my baby and it backfired. When I told him he kicked me in my stomach with them big ol' feet uh his. He ain't stopped 'til he saw my eyes roll back in my head. Then he called the ambulance."

"God, he mean!"

"You ain't gotta tell me that, Tricia."

"Did he go tuh the hospital with you, Motsey?"

"Yeah, Tricia, he went. He wonted tuh make sho' I tol' the right lie and wouldn't die. Soon as he found out he wadn't goin tuh jail fuh what he'd done tuh me and I wadn't goan die, he came in that room and started messin 'round with me again."

"How he goan have sex with you in that condition?"

"He ain't try tuh have no sex with me, he was just messin 'round with my breasts 'n' stuff. They had formed fuh the baby too."

"How they formed, Motsey? The baby wadn't full."

"'Cause, Tricia. When he killed that baby I had tuh be more than twelve weeks pregnant."

"How could he do that tuh a baby and how can he do that tuh yo' breasts knowin they was lack that?"

"I don't know, Tricia. He just a nasty old mean vicious spiteful man. And so that he wouldn't hurt me no mo', I just shut my eyes 'long with my mouth and let him do what he wonted 'til he was done. I didn't wont that evil man tuh kill me, too. He'd already threatened tuh kill me and had his hands 'round my neck, so I kept quiet. The only time I said somethin was when he started givin me orders."

Lee Charles

"What kind uh orders? You was sick. Wadn't
nothin you could do but let him take advantage uh
you. What mo' could he make you do Motsey? What
mo' could he ask you tuh do?"

"He ain't ask me nothin, Tricia. While he was
messin with me. He told me tuh hold oan tuh his
head and rub it the way I did befo' he had tuh
hurt me. He made me call him daddy and tell him I
loved him ova and ova again. He even made me say
I loved him mo' than my mamma or anybody else in
my family and I said it! That made him so excited
he got even mo' into what he was doin tuh me and
I could hear all them evil sounds he was makin.
He scared me so bad I started cryin. That made
him thank I was really enjoyin what he was doin
tuh me and kept it up fuh a long time. My breasts
felt lack rocks when he was done and I wanted
somethin, anythang, fuh pain. He called the nurse
in and she gave me somethin in a needle fuh pain.
He'd brought some git high with him and told me I
could have it if I would please him."

"Did you do it, Motsey?"

"Yeah, girl! I was strung out!"

"Aw, Motsey."

"Tricia, I wadn't the same person you see
today and I sho' wadn't the same person you use
tuh know. I tol' you, I was strung out! That shot
and that crack tuhgetha made me do exactly what
he asked me tuh do and some, rat from my hospital
bed! Once you high off that stuff, you might do
anythang! I know I did! I really thought I was

enjoyin myself 'til I came down and remembered all uh what happened!"

"Girl, you coulda overdosed!"

"I know, Tricia I know, but at least I had sense enough tuh git 'way from him and git myself straightened out. And boy do I thank God that I did!"

"How did you git away from him, Motsey?"

"Girl! Let me tell you 'bout that! I was brushin my teeth while I was in the hospital and happened tuh look up at myself in the mirror. You know how bright them bathroom lights be in the hospital. Girl. That was the first time I'd seen what I really looked lack since I'd been oan that stuff. I had these dark circles 'round my eyes. My hair wadn't shiny no mo' and it wadn't nearly as long and thick, and I hadn't cut it. My back and hip was bruised and my skin was dried out, bumpy, and disgustin lookin. I was mo' than skinny, Tricia. I was puny. I actually looked lack a crackhead. Girl! I use tuh pick at them crackheads and there I was in the mirror starin back at one! When that reflection showed me what I'd become I almost passed out oan the bathroom flo'! A light came oan in my head and I started cryin this deep, hurtful cry! Befo' he could make it back tuh git me I called my mamma. Girl! I was cryin, throwin up, and packin. When my mamma got tuh the hospital I was still cryin. Mamma hadn't seen me fuh a while so when she saw how skinny and sickly I was she started cryin too. She

105

didn't even bother gittin no wheelchair she
carried me tuh the car. It felt good tuh have my
mamma hold me in huh arms lack that. It was so
many uh us and mamma had tuh work so hard, I
didn't git a lot uh that when I was comin up.

When mamma found out I'd miscarried and that
I was strung out. She gave me a choice...jail or
treatment."

"How could she send you tuh jail fuh usin
drugs, Motsey?"

"'Cause, I'd been stealin checks from huh and
everythang else. She threatened tuh prosecute
me."

"Girl, yo' mamma wadn't goan send you tuh no
jail."

"Tricia, you don't know my mamma. She had got
my signature and pictures from the bank. Tricia,
girl, when she called me in huh room and laid all
that stuff out oan huh bed, I thought I was goan
die. My mamma told me that afta daddy left huh,
she raised seven kids without a husband or
welfare. Five of um had professional careers and
the otha two, wadn't goan do nothin no different.
She said Tyrell and me was goan straighten up
even if it killed huh, him, and me. When my mamma
tell you somethin, she don't be playin! She done
already had my baby brotha Tyrell locked up once
befo', and he huh favorite!"

"Damn, Motsey!"

"Now you understand what um tryin tuh tell yah, right, Tricia?"

"I guess I do! 'Cause, My friend Melvin—

"Tricia. You talkin 'bout the one everybody at school call Dirty Melvin, Melvin Prime?"

"Yeah, Motsey. You know him?"

"Yeah, Girl! He was only the nastiest boy in the whole school! Who don't know him!"

"He was nasty, but not with me."

"Tricia. Everybody know yo' reputation. Nobody, I mean wadn't nobody, not even nasty behind Melvin was goan try and mess with you! But he done whispered lots uh nasty thangs in my ear befo'. That shoulda been enough fuh me tuh be afraid of the thangs Clark was offerin me. But he was olda Tricia. I thought he'd treat me different."

"I don't thank age got nothin tuh do with it, Motsey. Melvin was real nasty and he was real young."

"What you mean by, "WAS, REAL NASTY"? Tricia. Ain't no way he changed all of that ignorance around!"

"Oh yes he did, Motsey! He had to! Melvin ended up with a disease! For a long time he'd wanted this girl named Blythe Turner—

"Trisha? You talkin 'bout that Trick girl?"

"Yeah, Motsey. He'd been wantin her since sixth grade, so he said! She wasn't out there then and he was tellin me that he thought she was the finest female he'd ever seen in his life, but

107

now she out there. I heard that some old man got
her out there, that's how she first got started.
Anyway, Melvin told me that when he found out
that she was walkin the streets he went up to her
like he wanted to pay for her. He took her to
that Hotel Kasheeba down on Pine Drive where they
be doin some of everything, paid for the room,
and they had sex. When she asked for her money he
started talkin' junk about her not wantin him
back in the day, but could trick for that old
pimp. He said she got nasty with him and told him
to just give her the money he owed her. He said
that's what he wanted her to do so that he'd feel
as if she'd disrespected him enough to justify
what he really wanted to do to her. He punched
Blythe—

"God, Tricia! These men 'round here love
beatin oan women! Don't they?"

"Motsey. Melvin said that he'd seen that pimp
stomp her before and what he did wasn't nothin
compared to that!"

"You know what, Tricia? That's a lie! What he
did tuh huh was worse! She thought she was okay
with what huh and that old simple- minded pimp
had! She didn't wont tuh be raped by Melvin uh
nobody else! She didn't ask him tuh rape huh or
hit huh!"

"Motsey. If she was trickin, she was askin
for it."

"Tricia, that ain't true. I was havin sex
with Clark, but I didn't wont tuh do them thangs

he made me do in the hospital and some uh them
otha' times eitha'."

"That was different, Motsey."

"Not really, Tricia, 'cause what you let one
person do tuh you don't mean you wont the same
thang from anotha'. That's why a lot uh people
don't tell when they bein abused, they thank
people goan judge um by what they did in they
past or with somebody else. It ain't right tuh
judge people lack that, Tricia! It just ain't
right!"

"You right, Motsey."

"Tricia, I ain't tryin tuh be mean uh nothin,
but if I hadn't been abused myself I might see
thangs different! People try not tuh talk about
all the sex and abuse that's goin oan and all the
otha' violence that people be commitin aginst
each otha', they don't wont tuh hear the truth. I
thank tuh justify they ignorance they pretend
that all them shows, centers, and educated talk
make all that stuff go away. They phony! And they
just foolin theyselves if they thank they foolin
me, because I know that people just keepin it mo'
quiet than they use to, that's all because uh
them abuse laws 'n' stuff. I know that I didn't
wont tuh tell oan that old dog that was messin
with me, 'cause I was too scared, but mostly
because I thought I was in love with him and
didn't wont him locked up or my mamma tuh kill
him. If I hadn't thought that, I woulda let my
mamma mess him up lack she wonted tuh in the

109

first place. Butcha know what? Just like I shoulda done Clark from the beginnin, she shoulda fought Melvin back!"

"He said she tried fightin him back, but he got the best of her, raped her and made her perform oral sex on him."

"No wonder he got a disease, Tricia. He had sex with a woman lack that without usin protection?"

"No. He told me that he used protection, but he'd put his mouth on her breasts. She was pregnant and they'd formed for the baby, but he didn't know that. The only reason why he'd ever wanted Blythe and thought that she was so fine in the first place was because she was always so big breasted, and they'd got even bigger when he'd seen her, and that made him want her real bad no matter what she was doin. He said that he thought they'd gotten that way because she'd gotten older, but he realized that somethin' was wrong with um after he'd messed with um for a while, but even that didn't bother him he wanted her so bad...

"OOH, GOD, TRICIA! HE JUST LACK THAT OLD DISGUSTIN CLARK! MEN SO NASTY!"

"Women too, Motsey."

"You mean, Blythe liked it, Tricia?"

"Melvin said she didn't. He said that she cried and begged him to not make her let him do that, and unnatural sex, because it would hurt her baby. He said he didn't mess with her

unnaturally, but he didn't care about her old
trick baby. He wasn't gonna pass up what he'd
been waitin for all them years and he messed with
Blythe until she threw up. Say he found out later
that she'd miscarried, Motsey."

"He wouldn't wont nobody messin with his old
ugly black sister lack that, Tricia. He should be
charged with rape and child abuse!"

"They both should be charged with child
abuse, Motsey! Ain't no woman got no business
sellin her body like that no way, but especially
when they pregnant!"

"So how did Melvin get that disease?"

"Blythe had it and he got it from her
breasts. He didn't realize that if she had a
disease, there was more than one way he could get
it from her. But check this out, Motsey. He told
me that he was gonna have unnatural sex with that
girl even though she was pregnant, and would have
if she hadn't thrown up like she was dyin uh
somethin."

"Then he got what he deserved, Tricia."

"I'on know, Motsey. I just hope I don't never
git none of that stuff. I ain't havin sex 'til um
married."

"Your husband kin have a disease, Tricia."

"Well, maybe, but um still waitin, at least
um goan try."

"Tricia, tuh tell the truth, I wish that I
woulda had that much sense. Maybe things woulda

111

turned out better for me than this. Maybe I wouldn'tna gotten oan them drugs and did all that stuff tuh shame my mamma."

"Maybe, Motsey, maybe, but we still love you."

"Tricia. Stop it."

"I made you smile though, Motsey."

"Motsey, you think you goan start usin again, 'cause most people do? They be goin back and forth tuh treatment all the time."

"Naw, I ain't goin back tuh that stuff. I don't even wont no drugs or nothin tuh drank no mo', 'cept juice uh pop."

"Yah know what I did, Tricia?"

"What?"

"I got myself in with this group called VTBH, Voices To Be Heard, and just be chillin' with them. They do some scripture, some counselin, some teachin, and some preachin. They use different ways tuh make you see what you missin out oan in life by abusin drugs, sex, and just plain old growin up too fast. I sho' wish I woulda stayed a chil' a little longa."

"Motsey. I really feel sorry for you about that. I mean that, Motsey. I really do."

"That's okay, Tricia. Just be glad that it wadn't you and that I was blessed enough tuh git outta that mess, git treated, and in tuh VTBH. They really help a lot."

"Can anybody join? Can I join, VTBH, Motsey?"

"Yeah, Tricia. They always lookin fuh new young people tuh join."

"When do they have meetins 'n' stuff?"

"Every night from five tuh seven. They rat oan the corner uh Park and Manor St."

"Tricia, the best thang about VTBH is that they don't try tuh force yah tuh come. They let you make that choice."

"I might not join, Motsey, but um goan come and sit in oan a meetin one night."

"Okay, Tricia, I'll be glad tuh see yah there if you decide tuh come, 'cause um there most uh the time and I ain't goan give it up. I really lack all my new friends. When you meet all them nice people you goan probably wont tuh come often too."

"Befo' I lost the baby I was goan quit smokin cigarettes. Since I been with VTBH I done quit that, too."

"Wow, Motsey. You sho' done changed...!

"I know, Tricia, and I ain't goan turn it 'round. I ain't nevva felt this good befo'!"

"Well, you look good, Motsey, and I hope you stay this way."

"Thanks Tricia. Thanks for the encouragement, I need all that I kin git."

"You deserve it, Motsey. You done come a long way."

"Tricia I'd betta get goin I got tuh go meet up with JC. Maybe I'll see you at VTBH if you decide tuh come."

"Okay, Motsey! You keep oan takin care uh yo' self! Okay!"

"I will, Tricia! I will! There ain't no better feelin than the one I got now...!"

"Motsey really did change. I know a lotta kids that could use a mamma lack hers—What am I sayin! I don't nevva wont nobody grown tuh hear me say that! But Motsey do look good."

Chapter 14

THE STRIP

"Motsey, you stay here and make sure Mason and his girl know we here. I'll go in the store and get us something to drink. You want soda or juice?"

"I'll take juice, JC."

"Who that boy, Motsey?"

"Clark! Git out my face! Whatchoo doin here! Leave me 'lone! Whatchoo doin here? You just about got me pinned tuh the wall with that truck! Git away from me! Go oan, leave me 'lone, nigh!"

"Girl, who you thank you talkin tuh lack that?"

"Clark, goan, and leave me 'lone, nigh!"

"Git in the truck, Motsey!"

"Clark, I ain't goin nowhere with you! I got a man! I don't wonna have nothin else tuh do with you!"

"Why, Motsey? My wife and me ain't tugetha no mo', Motsey! I done quit huh! I done let huh go fuh you! We kin git married nigh! You kin even git pregnant again if you wont to!"

"I don't wont tuh marry you! I don't wont tuh have no baby from you! I don't even wont you 'round me, I don't even wont you talkin tuh me, touchin me, 'cause I hate you, you old worm carrier! Just go oan and leave me 'lone!"

"OH NO, MOTSEY! YOU COMIN WITH ME! AND UM GOAN FIX THAT MOUTH UH YOURS, TOO!"

"LET ME GO, HELP ME SOMEBODY! HELP ME! AH-AH-AH-AH...You hurt my haid pullin me through that truck window lack that! Let me go, Clark, let me out the truck!"

"Come oan, Motsey, act right and I'll fuhgit about you callin me names. We can be tugetha nigh. Just me 'n' you lack you always wonted."

"Clark, look, just take me back where you got me from and leave me 'lone! That's all I wont from you! THAT'S ALL!"

"You really hate me lack you say, Motsey? All I evva tried tuh do is make you happy. I wont you back."

"Ain't you done ruined my life enough, Clark?"

"Motsey, what can that young boy do fuh you?"

"What you talkin 'bout, Clark?"

"The boy I seen go in the sto', that is supposed tuh be yo' new man, ain't it?"

"Yeah, he my man!"

"What can he do fuh you, Motsey?"

"He do everythang fuh me!"

"Even the thangs I did, Motsey?"

"Naw, he do um betta! Nigh let me go!"

"Um goan let you go, but not 'til um done witcha! Not 'til you tell me um betta than he is and not 'til you done satisfied me lack you use tuh do."

"Clark, we ain't seen each otha in ova a year, why you trippin!"

"'Cause, don't no woman uh mine hide from me that long, Motsey without lettin me know where she is or me sayin she can do it and don't no woman quit me, I quit them! Nigh here some stuff fuh you tuh git high, use it, and while um drivin I wont you tuh please me lack you use tuh do and we can fuhgit about whatchoo said and did."

"Clark, that was when I was usin, I ain't usin no mo'!"

"YOU BETTA ACT LACK YOU USIN AND TAKE THIS STUFF! NIGH DO WHAT I SAY, DAMN IT!"

"NAW! I AIN'T DOIN NOTHIN, CLARK...

"MOTSEY! MOTSEY...! That girl done goan fool crazy! She jumped out the truck! Shoot, I ain't goin back tuh look fuh huh. If she dead they goan blame me. I don't need huh no way. Um goin back tuh my hotel room. I can git me a woman tuh come up there and I know just who tuh call, too—Shoot! Fuhgit that! Um goan find me somethin betta!"

Chapter 15

BACK ON THE STRIP

"JC! JC!"

"Motsey, what's wrong? You're cryin'! Where'd you go? I thought you'd left me hangin! I told Mason and his girl that we'd meet up with um later...Why you all dirty and scratched up and stuff?"

"WHILE YOU WAS IN THE STO', THAT OLD FOOL HAD THE NERVE TUH DRIVE UP IN THE STO' PARKIN LOT AND PULL ME THROUGH HIS TRUCK WINDOW AND DRIVE OFF!"

"You're talkin' about, Clark?"

"YEAH, JC, CLARK!"

"How'd he get that close to you, Motsey?"

"WHEN I TRIED TUH RUN FROM HIM HE CIRCLED ME WITH HIS TRUCK 'TIL HE GOT ME ALMOST PINNED BETWEEN THE STO' BUILDIN AND HIS TRUCK!"

"He did this to you?"

"Naw, I jumped out his truck."

"Oh, baby, look at your arms, they're all bruised up! Come on, let me take you home so that we can put somethin on um!"

"Naw, JC, mamma goan go crazy. She might kill that old man."

"Okay, we'll go to my place. We can patch you up there."

Chapter 16

THE REUNION

"Hey, Diamond, you just as pretty as you was when we was kids at Catskin Hills College!"

"Aw, go on, Selma. You're making me blush."

"But it's true, Diamond. You looks good!"

"Selma, you're lookin as temptin as ever yourself."

"Aw, go oan!"

"Girl, I ain't lyin. You can still turn a young man's head and the old one's too. Turn around and let me look at you...Mm-hm, I'm right, everything's still in place and lookin better than ever."

"Diamond, you always made me feel good 'bout myself."

"You always deserved it, Selma. You've never been anything but a lady."

"Thank you, Diamond."

"Selma, I didn't know you attended this church."

"I've been here fuh the last ten years, Diamond."

"I've been here the past three. Why is this the first time I've seen you here, Selma?"

"Probably 'cause I usually go tuh the ten o'clock service."

"That's right, Selma. There is a ten, and a twelve o'clock service. I'd forgotten about that."

"You travel a long way tuh go tuh church in this little country town, with all us migrated, Southern Negroes, Diamond. Why is that?"

"I love Reverend Bess's sermons. Selma, I haven't heard any better."

"You sho' ain't lyin', Diamond, you sho' ain't lyin'! And he don't nevva, I mean nevva sway from the truth, or do all of that political preachin lack a lot uh these preachers do now days. Ain't nobody comin tuh church fuh that evil mess, no way. We comin tuh see how we kin make it without a man leadin us."

"That is surely the truth, Selma. The only leader we really need to be focused on is God. Most politicians are out to help themselves. I don't like it when churches get involved in that stuff either. A minister wouldn't want me to get up in his pulpit and tell him how to preach and what to preach on, and I definitely don't need a preacher telling me how to cast my votes. It offends me."

"That's the God knows truth, Diamond. The way we vote shouldn't be nobody's concern but ours, anyway."

"That's right, Selma. And I aim to keep it that way. Whenever a minister starts preaching politics. I leave that church. I'm not so ignorant that I can't distinguish fact from fiction. I know who to vote for—but let me get off this subject. My blood boils whenever this subject comes up."

"Diamond. You just lack I remember you. You still strong-headed."

"That'll never change, Selma. I've never cared for weak-minded people."

"Me either, Diamond. Me, either."

"Diamond, how yo' wife and daughter doin?"

"Selma, because we've been friends since before time I know that I can level with you. Sheila has left me again. She thinks that I'm too religious. Sadaya's been using drugs. From what I could understand from her husband, soon to be ex-husband, is that she started cheatin around with some white boy at school, then she started hangin out with nothin but the white kids and goin for white. Now, she's ashamed of her mother. She told her mother not to visit her."

"Um surprised you stand fuh that, Diamond!"

"Yah know, Selma, it's her life. I've given that girl the best of everything and so has her mother. Maybe that's the problem, but if this is her way of showing us how grateful she is, then so be it. One day she's going to wake up and realize like I did what a big mistake she's making by being underhanded and thoughtless. For now, she's in God's hands."

"What's her name—Sadaya, right?"

"Yeah, I named her after my great grandmother Sadie, remember?"

"Well, Sadaya still young, Diamond, she got a lot uh growin tuh do. What I don't understand is yo' wife leavin huh husband 'cause he in the church. That's crazy! Here I am wishin mine would go!"

"That's the way of the world, Selma, but it wasn't all Sheila. I did spend what I think was too much time on church issues and projects and not enough time with her and my son."

"Diamond, you s'pposed tuh put God first."

"Yeah, Selma, God first, not all the people in the church and everywhere else before your family. Most of us think that phrase means just that, that you should do whatever people in the church including the minister thinks or asks you to do no matter how we neglect ourselves or how it affects our families. We have a tendency to listen to what's coming out of all these voices in church instead of concentrating on the word itself and listening to God. I'm not trying to start a sermon out here, Selma, but discernment is good to have.

I'm a family man. There's a certain amount of time and attention that I need to give to my family to keep it together.

Helping the church out is good, but it's not your sole dwelling place and I've finally realized that."

"You know, Diamond, you make a lot uh since."

"Of course I do, Selma. We don't really read the bible so that it helps us. We just go along with the game."

"Oh, you talkin 'bout that old, whatever sound good is good, and if I look righteous I am righteous."

"That's exactly what I mean, Selma and that's why members leave their home church after fellowshipping there for years. They're not being spiritually fed and they know it."

"Diamond, you always had a way uh breakin thangs down so that I could understand um. You was that way even in college, although you was, a bit devilish. Why ain't you preachin?"

"Who's to say that'll never happen, Selma!"

"Diamond. It sho' ain't me."

"Selma, you've been a member here for a while. You're good with the word. Have you tried?"

"Tried, what, Diamond?"

"To preach, or just speak—you know, testify."

"Naw, Diamond, I still don't know where tuh put my to's, tuh's and ta's."

"Girl, you'll never know where to put those. You're a Southern Bell. Most of the people in Casey Park are from down your way and have the same accent. You've had yours since I've known you—

"And I ain't goan change it, Diamond."

"God's not asking you to and neither am I. We both love you the way you are, Selma. When the time comes, he'll get you in front of a congregation and everything will come out perfect."

"Yeah, maybe. That's somethin I gotta thank about."

"I understand, Selma. We all have our timing for things."

"Diamond, speakin of time. Whatever happened tuh Anthony?"

"He got married, Selma."

"You kiddin!"

"No, Selma it's been almost six years."

"Diamond, do you remember how much I loved that man?"

"Do, I, ever! Why did you and him split-up, Selma?"

" 'Cause. He idolized you too much, Diamond. He'd do anythang you tol' him."

"Anything that *I* said?"

"Yeah, Diamond, that's right. And that made me see him as a weak man. I know about the thangs y'all was doin with some uh the girls at school, too."

"They always came back for more though. Didn't they, Selma?"

"I didn't say they was smart girls, Diamond."

"Selma, you're still something else. Anthony was crazy to let you get away. You were the best thing he'd ever seen, on or off that campus."

"Even better than that wife he got now, Diamond?"

"Selma—

"Um just kiddin, Diamond. You don't hafta answer me."

"Good, because I have a long drive ahead of me. Trying to make that comparison would have me too exhausted to make it home safely... Here. Take my card and give me a call sometime. Maybe I'll have enough time and mental strength to compare you with her if you decide to give me a buzz."

"Okay, Diamond and you stay outta trouble."

"I'll try, Selma. I'll try, really hard...

"I sho' wonted tuh tell Diamond the truth. That um jealous of the idea of Anthony bein happily married, and unhappy 'cause I ain't, and why I really left him 'lone in the first place. How that one night while hidin out in they closet tryin tuh spy oan Anthony, I seen him and Anthony torturin that girl.

The screams I heard and the thangs I saw from that closet that night didn't seem real tuh me then and they still don't. Double sex, oral sex, anythang they asked huh tuh do, she did it. She even let um tie huh up. Silly thang! She let um do it just tuh be popular.

Lee Charles

Afta spyin oan Anthony that night I shoulda learned my
lesson 'bout followin and spyin' oan people. I had tuh stay
in that closet 'til they fell asleep. I always wondered if
they made huh do them thangs all ova again the next monin.
Anyway, I nevva thought I'd see anythang lack that again 'til
I met Clark. He must've been my payback fuh not tryin tuh
talk some sense in them girls. "Not me, not Selma!" Selma too
busy thankin; "They lack it, they shouldn't be there, they
ain't nothin' but who'es, I ain't goan be with no man who
treat me lack that!" Hmph, um worse, 'cause um a full-grown,
married woman bein' treated lack a who'e in my own bed. With
a husband who got mo' women than Diamond uh Anthony evva had,
and doin the same thangs they used tuh do tuh women. Some of
um worse and he doin um tuh women all by hisself.

Yeah, Selma, you done real good. A college education and
still livin in hicksville. You was goan be famous, remember?
At least you kept that promise, 'cause everybody knows you.
You the talk uh the town. You the talk uh Casey Park."

Chapter 17

THE VISITORS

"Who beatin oan my do' at this unearthly hour!
Just a minute! JUST A MINUTE, I SAID...!

...Oh my Lord, it's the police! What Clark
done did, nigh?"

"Yes, may I help y'all?"
"Ma'am, we're officers Frank and Wilcox.
Are you, Selma Porter?"
"Yes, yes, yes!"
"Is Clark Porter your husband?"
"Yes, he is, but we been separated fuh a few
months nigh. He don't live here no mo'..."
"Mrs. Porter, have a seat."
"Why, offissuh, what's goin oan? What's
wrong?"
"Please, sit, Mrs. Porter."
"No, offissuh, no. I'd ratha keep oan
standin. Just thankin 'bout what you goan say
makes me afraid that I might not be able tuh git
up no mo'."
"Mrs. Porter, we found your husband Clark
Porter...dead in his hotel room."
"OH LAWD, NO!"
"Mrs. Porter, are you going to be okay?"
"Yes, Yes suh, jus' gimme a second tuh catch
muh breath."

"Mrs. Porter. Would you like a glass of water?"

"Yes, please, the glasses in the top middle cabinet...

"Harry, would you mind?"

"Not at all Gerald, I'll get it for her."

"Here you are, Mrs. Porter."

"Thank you."

"Offissuh, tell me, how'd it happen?"

"He was shot."

"Was he by hisself, was he aurguin with somebody or what, offissuh? Why'd they kill him?"

"Mrs. Porter, we haven't gotten the answers to those questions yet. We're still investigating the incident. As soon as we get more information we'll let you know exactly what took place."

"Are you going to be okay if you're left alone here all night or can we call someone for you?"

"Offissuh, I would be pleased if you'd call Daizelle fuh me."

"You mean, thee, Ms., Daizelle Washington?"

"Oh, y'all know huh too."

"I'm afraid so. Are you sure you want us to call, her?"

"Offissuh, I know how everybody feel 'bout Daizelle, but she been really helpin me out lately. She done changed."

"Okay Mrs. Porter, if you insist, we'll give her a call."

"Good, here's huh number."

"That's okay Mrs. Porter. The entire station has it memorized."

"Mrs. Porter, she's on her way. Officer Wilcox and I are going to leave. Here are our cards. If you happen to think of anything that might help us solve your husband's murder, call us immediately, okay?"

"Yes, offissuh Frank, I'll do that."

"Good night, ma'am."

"Good night, offisuhs."

"Oh my God, I caint believe it, Clark, Dead...!"

Chapter 18

AT THE HOTEL

"It's like I tol' the other offissuhs in uniform. I nevva saw nobody go in and I nevva seen nobody go out! This hotel so cheap most everybody here is a permanent resident. I'd known if somebody different entered the hotel."

"Are you the only one who works the desk during these hours?"

"No, offissuh, it's me and Jim Miles, the only otha white guy who works the desk during those hours. We switch up oan a monthly basis."

"What are your regular hours?"

"From ten p.m. tuh six a.m."

"Were you here last night?"

"I came oan 'bout midnight. Jim covered for me for the first two hours 'cause I had somethin tuh take care of."

"Thank you, Mr...?"

"The name's Leedage, Samuel Leedage."

"Mr. Leedage, we're going to question some of your other guests to see what they might have seen or heard."

"Okay, offissuh, help yo'self. I ain't goan git in the way. Sorry I couldn't be of more help."

"That's okay, Mr. Leedage. Here's my card. If you happen to recall seeing anything unusual, call me, will yah?"

"Yes, suh, I'll do just that."

"Wilcox, we'll take the floor where he was killed together. We'll split-up for the first and third...

SOMETIME LATER

"It's a shame, I tell yah, a filthy shame."

"What is, Mr. Percell?"

"What I saw."

"What did you see, Mr. Percell?"

"It's just too awful to repeat, officer."

"Sir, if you don't want to tell us what you saw...

"Oh no, officer, I want to tell you what I saw!"

"Then please, feel free to do so, Mr. Percy."

"It's, Percell, officer, Percell!"

"Forgive me, Mr. Percell. Go ahead and tell us what you saw."

"My lover and I had just dozed off from some heavy lovemaking—

"Did she see anything? We'd like to question her, too. Is she in?"

"SHE...who said anything about a she? My lover is Darnell Thompson who's a beautiful cocoa tan, thank you! With biceps and triceps that

would put yours to shame! Besides, he slept
through the whole thing...and don't look at me in
amazement, with that puzzled look on your
face...The answer is yes! I'm gay! My lover's
black! I'm white! And, YES! We make love just
like anyone else does...!"
   "Not quiet."
   "Did you say something, officer?"
   "No, Mr. Percell, I did not, I was just
wondering if you'd like to continue, nothing
else...

   "Perce! I heard the shouting, who are these
gentlemen?"
   "Go back to bed, DT...That's my lover,
Darnell. Everyone calls him DT, officer...Go back
to bed, DT, they're just askin about the man
across the hall—
   "You mean the old, pervert!"
   "Yes, yes, and let me handle this—and put
some clothes on, you're showing them all of my
property—okay!"

   "Now, where did I leave off? Oh yeah, I woke
up to what sounded like a little girl crying. I
looked out my peephole and there he was...
   "He, who?"
   "The deceased of course."
   "Go ahead, Mr. Percell."
   "He was loaded as usual. But there was
something different about him the other night.

His eyes were bugged out and wild looking. He
must have been doing drugs, too. He looked crazy.

He had this little girl who appeared to be no
more than twelve years old. He was holding her by
the arm with one hand and his key in the other.
He was struggling with the lock, but he wouldn't
let go of that child. He didn't want her to get
away! When he opened his door, I could see
directly into his room. The bed was in plain
view. As soon as he was inside, he just slung her
on the bed. Before she could do anything he
simply removed her upper clothing, and attacked
her without closing the door or restraining her.
I got somewhat sexually excited myself until I
saw the way the little thing was trying to fight
him off and was begging and pleading with him not
to have sex with her. She really didn't want
that. He wasn't listening he was too busy pawing
her. He was especially interested in her breasts.
I couldn't understand why, the poor little thing
barely had any, but he was pulling on them so
hard with his mouth the force made her fragile
body raise up from the bed. Oh my goodness what a
horrible site! What a horrible thing to do to a
mere child! A sparsely developed child at
that...!"

"Mr. Percell—

"Okay, okay! She tried to push his face away
from her, but he was too aggressive. He was like
an untamed beast. Her fighting seemed to make him

want her more. He had absolutely, no compassion for that baby!"

"And neither did you, yah pervert, or you would have called the cops...Okay, sir, what else happened."

"I didn't mean to go on like that and change the subject, but that was so, awful! He should pay for making that poor child suffer. She was screaming, kicking, struggling, hitting him, crying, and complaining about how sore her breasts were, while begging him not to rape her.

He must've fooled her in from off the streets, 'cause I'd never seen her around here before."

"What was the young girl wearing, Mr. Percell, did he call her by name?"

"I never heard him call her anything but baby, but she was wearing this lightweight white sweater, powder blue skirt, and white tennis shoes. She was a pretty little thing. Like an angel...

"Mr. Percell. Do you want to finish telling us what happened?"

"Oh-oh, yeah, officer. Oh yeah. Let me finish telling you what I saw. He straddled that young thing while she was lying on the bed, held her arms down, and began kissing her breast nipples while talking sweet to her. I could see tears rolling down her face, and her moving her head in agreement. He was talking low, but I could hear him telling her that he only wanted to put his mouth on her private area, saying that he wanted to know what it would be like with someone who's never been touched. He flattered her for a long time before she calmed down and totally consented. But officer, that was definitely the child's first encounter with that type of sex. The strained look on her face and the awful sound that came from her tiny body made that clear. Before she could collect herself, he literally jacked her up against the wall and violently raped her. All I could see was his naked rear gyrating, her feet dangling and kicking, with only one tennis shoe and her underwear around her ankles. She was screaming as if he was ripping her guts out...And oh my God! I thought he had the way her shoe flew off...

"For a man who thought a child was being treated unjustly, this guy saw an awful lot and did nothing...

...Then, in walks this other woman wearing a trench coat. She starts screaming at him, waving her arms all around, and threatening him. He let the girl drop to the floor as if she was nothing. She quickly pulled up her underwear, grabbed her other clothes off his bed, and ran out of the room crying. I heard him say to the woman, "You see what you let get away," and began savagely beating her. I saw the fire in his eyes. He was angry enough to kill her. He beat this woman until she bled. Her face was swollen and her eyes were partially shut. She looked so bad it made me sick. He didn't seem to care, though...

"It made him sick all right. The kind of sick he seemed to enjoy! This guy is full of it...!

...He put that woman in a chokehold, brutally sodomized and forced her to do to him what he'd done to that child, earlier on.

The way he had that woman screaming, gasping, and choking, I thought he was going to kill her. She got through that ordeal though and I thought it was over, I think she did too, but he beat her some more—somethin awful, I mean, horribly!

She somehow got her hand in the pocket of her trench coat, and pulled out a gun. That's when he stepped back and she pulled the trigger, shooting him four times. "Twice in his chest, once in his stomach, and once in his head. That's when he fell to the floor and she just sat in the middle of it holding the gun in her trembling hands.

If she hadn't shot him, he was definitely going to kill her...and that child! He was definitely going to finish ruining her if she hadn't gotten away. He might have even killed her! I could tell that by the way he handled her. He was going to make sure that none of her would remain innocent."

"Are you sure that's what you saw and heard, Mr. Percell?"

"Yes, absolutely, I am! These walls and doors are paper-thin. And like I told you before, he left his door wide open, which put his bed in the direct view of my peephole!"

"It's amazing, Mr. Percell!"

"It sure is, officer! I can't believe the way people carry on!"

"No, Mr. Percell. I mean it's amazing how you could watch all of that go on and not call the police! You might have prevented a death and a rape! You said that you thought he'd fooled the girl in off the street and did nothing, absolutely nothing to help her! I don't know who's worse. You or the corpse!"

"Maybe you see me as a monster, officer, but you just can't get involved around here!"

"Even if children are being mistreated. Huh, Mr. Percell?"

"Well, yes—w-w-well, no, well, you know, it's just hard, that's all!"

"Then why are you so eager to tell us about it now?"

"Because, you're here, he's dead, and guilt got the best of me! Look, officers. He always has some woman or other over there doing things to him most of them are real, young. There are always weird sounds coming from his room. He even has this lesbian who goes over there. Herthenia I think is her name! I don't know how he hooked her, but he has her doing weird things, too! She even has his child! As a matter of fact, she and that other woman came to his room earlier—separately, but they were both there and they both saw what he was doing to that child and never said a word! All of his women were afraid

of him, a lot of us were afraid of him, even that
lesbian, Herthenia was afraid of him!"

"How do you know she's a lesbian, Mr.
Percell?"

"We ran in some of the same circles—at least
she was a lesbian, officer! I've seen her over
there quite regularly, so I don't know what's
going on with her now. Some gays are switch
hitters."

"Are you always watching and listening?"

"No! Not always, I mean...!"

"What do you mean?"

"My God, officer, give me a break! I am the
one who called the police you know!"

"BIG, DEAL!"

"Okay, okay! I'll admit! It was thoughtless
of me! But when I started watching I was half
asleep. My thoughts were "She's a young hooker."
Darnell and I often entertain ourselves by
watching him through our peephole. That scene was
different, but not unusual for him. When I became
coherent enough to realize what was really going
on, I couldn't believe what I was seeing and
hearing. It was all like a movie, none of it
seemed real. No one around here ever complains
about the weird things that go on including me,
so I watched like always. It wasn't until he
began to beat the woman the second time, that I'd
finally gotten myself together enough to do
something. Before I could pull myself away from
the door, she'd shot him and I knew it was too

late. The way he'd beaten her, I knew she was terrified and wouldn't stop with one bullet.

You have to understand officer this isn't a five-star hotel, it hardly bares one star. Things of that nature happen all the time and no one ever gets killed. Like I said, no one even complains.

Johns, hookers of all ages, sexes, and colors, gay lifestyles, and pimps beating women, it's a way of life around here! This is not a monastery!

If I could've adjusted my thinking sooner, you're right, not only would I have saved a life, but that young girl would never have gotten raped by that piece of dirt, some might so lovingly call, a corpse!"

Chapter 19

REALITY

"He won't be comin home no mo', Daizelle, drunk
uh sobuh, he won't be comin home. You tol' me not
tuh put him out. You warned me and I wouldn't
listen."

"Selma, what happened tuh Clark wadn't none
uh yo' fault. I know you ain't s'pposed tuh say
nothin bad 'bout dead folk, but Clark was a
wicked, evil, selfish man. What people wouldn't
give him, he took. He was bound fuh the ground."

"Daizelle, he was *still* my husband and I
still loved him. I was upset and was just puttin
him out fuh a while, just a while. I thought that
maybe he'd git betta if we was apart, just fuh a
while, Daizelle, just fuh a while."

"I know, Selma, I know. But sometimes the
truth kin help yah tuh move oan. Ain't no need in
you feelin guilty, 'cause Clark was a full-grown
man, he was goan do, what he was goan do, with or
without yo' consent.

Much as I hate seein yah lack this, Selma, I
got tuh be truthful. Dyin probably the best thang
that man ever done fuh you. I know he left you
plenty money."

"Daizelle, we wadn't rich, but we always had
plenty money. That money ain't important tuh me.

Money ain't nevva been important tuh me and it
mean even less when you lose somebody you love."

"When them checks start rollin in you goan
change yo' tune. You deserve them checks, Selma.
You took a lot from that man.

Bad as I was treatin you, I always knew you
was good, too good. That could be the reason why
Clark walked all ova you too."

"He did not!"

"Come oan nigh, Selma. Clark did anythang he
wonted tuh and you took it."

"I didn't wonna lose him, Daizelle."

"You nevva really had him, Selma. You know
it. You said it. He was a man you went tuh bed
with at night and woke up to in the monin. He
spent most his time everywhere else.

I know it's too late nigh, but you gotta let
peoples know where you stand in a relationship.
If you don't they walks all ova you. That's
probably why I tried treatin you so bad, Selma.
You gotta put peoples in they place."

"You ain't lyin, Daizelle. I nevva stood up
tuh Clark. He could do anythang he wonted and I
nevva said a word.

All the time he was messin with women and
young girls—oh yeah, Daizelle, don't look at me
in shock. I knew 'bout that. I chose tuh look the
otha way. I coulda at least done somethin 'bout

them young ones. I coulda probably helped him tuh be mo' of a man. Nigh he dead and there ain't no chance uh me doin none uh that."

"Did the police tell you how he died, Selma?"

"Daizelle. All they tol' me, is he was shot fo' times."

"They didn't tell you nothin else, Selma?"

"Naw, but I sho' wont tuh know all uh what happened, 'cause it's bothin me not tuh."

"Don't worry Selma, I'll find out fuh yah."

"Would you really go tuh that trouble fuh me, Daizelle?"

"It ain't no trouble compared tuh what I use tuh put you through. Anyway, I done tol' you, um goan do everythang that I can tuh make up fuh the way I mistreated you in the past. Ms. Daizelle goan do right by you and a lot uh otha folks fo' she leave this here world."

Chapter 20

AT THE POLICE STATION

"Yes, detective. I covered for him a couple hours that night, but I don't remember hearing or seeing anything stranger than usual...wait a minute, I do recall an older man and a young girl coming through right before midnight."

"Had you seen them before, sir?"

"Only the older man, he'd just recently moved in a few months ago."

"Do remember what the girl was wearing?"

"Wait a minute. Let me think officer.
Hm-mmm...oh yeah! I think she was wearing a light colored blouse and skirt, with white tennis shoes."

"Do you remember what color the blouse and skirt was?"

"No, officer. I'm afraid I don't. You see. I'm a little color blind, but I think that it was actually a sweater and it was white. Her tennis shoes were exceptionally clean and noticeable, maybe new. Even for a person with my vision they'd be hard to miss."

"Did the young girl seem frightened to you?"

"Yes, now that you mention it officer, she did seem frightened. She kept telling me to make the man let her go. He told me to stay out of it;

she was his daughter. He said that he had to take charge of her because her mother let her run around at all times of night unsupervised. It was late, she was young—they seemed legit!"

"What about later, did you see an older woman come in wearing a trench coat...?"

"Yes, and a wig. She seemed to be full of good spirits, officer. She teased with me, then threw her coat open exposing herself to me. She was wearing what looked like a black panty and garter outfit with a white, see-through apron. I thought she was a hooker. She seemed high, so I humored her. She pressed her breasts to my face and when I did what I thought she wanted she left her handprint on the side of my face. Before I could recover from the stinging pain enough to let go of my face and lift my head, she was gone.

"Are you able to identify these two females?"

"Oh, sure, officer! Sure! The young girl was what black people call brown-skinned, very tiny—no more than four feet, with medium length hair and small features. The woman was very busty and dark skinned, not heavy and not skinny, just healthy. She was very attractive, but the young girl was very pretty...I tell yah, that young one's going tuh be a real looker when she gets older...!"

"Did you hear the man call the girl's name?"

"No, no I didn't, but when he got tired of her pulling away from him, he lifted her under his arm like an empty suitcase and carried her on upstairs, kicking and screaming."

"Thank you sir for coming down. If you hear, see or remember anything else give us a call."

"Yes, officer, I'll do that...Oh, wait a minute, officer! Wait a minute!"

"Yes, Mr. Miles. Is there something else?"

"Officer! I just remembered something! Now, how in the world could I forget this! After the woman slapped me, a few minutes later I went to do my rounds. I have the first and ground floor. As I was checking the exits, storage, and supply rooms I saw light under a door and heard moaning coming from one of the basement rooms rarely used. The door wasn't exactly open, but it wasn't connected to the latch, either. It's my job to check each room so I pulled it open a little bit. That big breasted woman was in there with this other woman. They were—you know! I watched for a while then completed my rounds. Which is probably why I never heard the shots."

"Why didn't you interrupt them, Mr. Miles?"

"I was angry with the busty woman for slapping me. For humiliation I'd intended to return by the time they were done and make them pay for the use of that empty storage room."

"Mr. Miles...!"

"Well! I was!"

"The other woman. Have you seen her before, Mr. Miles?"

"Oh, sure. Many, many times, officer. When Mr. Porter—the deceased moved in. She became a regular here."

"Can you describe her, Mr. Miles?"

"She was tall and thin, like a model, but more shapely. Her hair is a reddish brown. Oh yeah, and it's also very long and wavy. But of course I never knew that until I caught her in that storage room with that woman. The times I've seen her she's worn it pulled back in a bun. She looks white or something. She's very light. Which seemed to be Mr. Porter's preference."

"Thank you Mr. Miles you've been more than helpful."

Chapter 21

DAIZELLE'S REPORT

"Selma, all I could git from the man who lived 'cross the hall from Clark was that they was both black. One looked lack she was only twelve with a very small build and the otha was an older woman. He knew she was bigger than the girl was, but couldn't really git a good look at huh 'cause she was wearin a wig and trench coat.

He said when Clark started beatin the woman the wig fell off, but he jumped oan huh almost as soon as she come through the do' so he still couldn't git a good look at huh. He said when Clark finished beatin huh, she was so swollen and messed up that he couldn't tell what she looked lack anyway."

"Daizelle, he had two women in his room?"
"Sit down, Selma, it's mo' tuh it then that."
"JUST TELL ME, DAIZELLE!"
"Come oan nigh, baby. Sit down, this goan be hard oan you."

"Here, take the pills the docta give yah and drank yo' tea. Um goan tell you everythang the man tol' me ...Clark was uh, um, hum, a...

"WHAT, DAIZELLE, WHAT! TELL ME! If people goan be lookin at me stranger than usual I wont tuh know why!"

"Okay, okay Selma, gimme a chance tuh git the words out...He pulled some young girl off the street. She was comin from a friend's house. At least that's what the man 'cross the hall said he'd heard the girl sayin tuh Clark."

"WHY WOULD SHE TELL CLARK SOMETHIN LACK THAT IF HE WAS GOAN PURPOSELY RAPE HUH!"

"'Cause, Clark was tellin huh she shouldn't be oan the streets late at night 'cause she might run in tuh somethin lack him. She tol' him she was only comin from a friend's house. She kept tellin Clark tuh let huh go home and Clark didn't pay huh no 'tention.

He say Clark went crazy oan that girl. He raped that chil' in his room with the do' wide open."

"I don't believe it! Clark ain't nevva had tuh rape no woman!"

"The man said he saw him, Selma. He said he could see everythang from his peephole."

"How he goan see everythang that go oan in anotha person's room, Daizelle!"

"'Cause, Selma, his do' right 'cross from Clark's. And the man said, many nights Clark be drunk and high and leave his do' open while he take care uh business.

Selma, the man said Clark was so rough with that chil' she was screamin 'n' kickin. He say Clark was even messin with huh breasts."

"Daizelle, Clark wouldn't do nothin lack that tuh no chil'!"

"Selma, the man said they found one uh huh shoes in his room. He also said the walls in that place already thin, and Clark was so outta control that night that he probably didn't know if that do' was open uh closed. He say Clark was wild lookin. Say he done seen Clark supplyin most his women with that crack and he thank Clark had got messed up oan that stuff hisself. He said Clark asked that girl if she wonted some tuh try and calm huh down and she refused it. Then he asked the girl if she was a virgin and was that why she was cryin. When the girl tol' him yeah he begged that chil' tuh let him put his mouth oan huh 'cause she hadn't been touched befo'. Say Clark pretended he wonted tuh know what that was lack and tol' huh he was goan let huh go if she just let him do that. He only wonted tuh calm that chil' down so he could have his way with huh. When he calmed huh down, he said Clark treated that chil' lack a grown woman. The chil' was groanin and gaspin from the strain he put oan huh body. She was clawin Clark up tuh git him tuh stop. He said Clark didn't care he kept oan doin it 'til he got tired. I thank he'd turned crazy, Selma. I thank that stuff had Clark, goan! The man say he didn't tell the police everythang he told me, 'cause he didn't remember some of it 'til they left."

"YOU LYIN, DAIZELLE AND HE LYIN! Y'ALL LYIN! CLARK DIDN'T NEED NO DRUGS! I KEPT PLENTY FUH HIM TUH DRANK RAT HERE IN THE STO'! AND HE DIDN'T NEED NO BABY TUH PLEASE HIM! HE HAD ME AND ALL THEM OTHA WOMEN! WHAT HE GOAN RAPE A BABY FUH! SHE PROBABLY THAT SAME GAL YOU 'TOL ME 'BOUT BEFO.' THE ONE CLARK WAS BRAGGIN 'BOUT UNDER THE WINE TREE —YEAH, THAT'S IT, AIN'T IT! AND THAT MAN YOU TALKED TO LYIN! WHY HE GOAN TELL YOU SOMETHING HE WON'T TELL THE POLICE!

THEM FASS ASS GALS ALWAYS GITS WHAT THEY DESERVE—FLOUNCIN 'ROUND MY HUSBAND—SHE WADN'T NO GOOD! CLARK BEIN AN OLD MAN, HE DON'T KNOW NOTHIN 'BOUT NO DRUGS! SHE PROBABLY FOOLED HIM IN TUH TAKIN THAT STUFF! EVERYBODY KNOWS THAT ALL THEM YOUNG WHO'ES WONT FROM THEM OLD MEN IS MONEY AND HOW THEY LACKS GITTIN HIGH! SHE WAS TRASH AND THAT'S WHAT CLARK WAS TREATIN HUH LACK! HE AIN'T RAPE HUH, HE AIN'T RAPED, NOBODY! AND YOU! YOU AIN'T DOIN NOTHIN BUT LYIN!"

"Selma, you begged me tuh find out what happened, then you call me a liar...? HE HURT THAT CHIL', SELMA! HE HURT HUH, DON'T YOU UNDERSTAND!"

"SHUT UP, DAIZELLE; SHUT UP!"

"NAW, SELMA, NOT THIS TIME! NOT 'TIL UM DONE! THE MAN SAY HE SLAMMED THAT CHIL' UP 'GINST THE WALL AND HAD THE ROUGHEST SEX HE EVER SEEN. ALL

HE COULD SEE WAS CLARK'S NAKED ASS AND THAT
CHIL'S FEET DANGLIN AND KICKIN.

SELMA, LISTEN TUH ME! The man say he watched
the police remove all kinds uh dirty videos,
books, and magazines from Clark's room. Clark
even had weed and otha drugs, probably that crack
cocaine stuff, in his room that the police took.
He say that he done seen Clark bring home many
different women and how it seem lack Clark be
practicin some uh the thangs he see oan them
videos and read from them books oan them women.
Say one time when he was spyin oan Clark he had a
towel 'round some women neck chokin huh while he
was havin sex with huh. She'd let him do it, but
Clark just about killed that woman. He say that
woman was tryin tuh tell Clark tuh loosen up his
hold, but he kept oan like he hadn't heard huh.
Just so happened, Clark got pleased is why the
woman still alive.

He say that woman took hold huh neck and
started coughin and spitin up blood. Clark
grabbed that woman hair flipped huh oan huh
stomach and finished destroyin huh. He made huh
git out afta that. He say the po' woman passed
out in the hallway. He had tuh call the ambulance
Clark wouldn't do it.

I believe he was goan do that chil' the same
way. He was goan continue tuh molest huh 'til he

Lee Charles

got tired of huh. If she small as that man say
she is somethin lack that probably woulda killed
huh. He probably woulda killed huh Selma if that
woman hadn't come in the room and caught him. She
came in the room yellin, he let that gal drop tuh
the flo' and that's how she got 'way. The woman
musta scared him. From what the man tol' me, that
was the only way she was goan git out that room
alive.

He wadn't finished with that gal that's why
he beat that woman almost tuh death.

Selma, he was cruel. He put that woman in a
chokehold and sodomized huh. He made huh do tuh
him what he'd begged that chil' to let him do tuh
huh. Then he beat huh some mo'.
While he was kickin huh, she went in huh
pocket, took out a gun, and shot him. The man
said if she hadn't, Clark was goan kill huh.

Selma, I know you loved Clark, but you don't
need tuh be frettin ova no Clark. He treated you
and otha women lack they was nothin. He lived
indecent and he died the same way. You goan just
have tuh accept that.

You a pretty woman, Selma, with a lot goin
fuh yah. You didn't need me, Clark uh Bert tuh
make you. You always had mo' oan the ball then
us.

You goan git through this, Selma and I'll
help yah as much as I kin, but I don't wont you
tuh keep oan lookin back, 'cause that ain't what
life all about.

You still young and pretty and you ain't lost
yo' figure. It ain't too late fuh you tuh be
happy, happier then you evva been with Clark.
When God got somethin fuh yah, sometimes the old
got tuh be removed fo' he brang in the new...I
hate tuh have tuh tell huh 'bout Herthenia, but when she
settle down um goan hafta tell huh that, too. It's betta
comin from me than a stranger or hearin it oan the streets. I
gotta tell huh, I just got tuh wait fuh the rat time."

Chapter 22

SLEEPLESSNESS

"Hello."

"Diamond, it's me...Selma. Um so sorry tuh wake you up, but I needed tuh talk tuh somebody."

"Selma, is something wrong?"

"Clark, dead."

"I'm sorry, Selma, I'm still half-asleep. What did you say?"

"Clark, dead, he gone, Diamond. I ain't goan nevva see him no mo'."

"Oh my God, Selma, I'm so, sorry. What happened?"

"Somebody killed him."

"Who, Selma, who would kill your husband?"

"Probably any woman in this town, he was messin with most of um. Even this pretty lesbian by the name uh Herthenia. He even paid huh tuh sleep with him and have his chil' tuh spite me 'cause I didn't wont tuh have nothin else tuh do with him and put him out when I found out my friend Bert was messin with him too."

"Oh, Selma, baby...

"Diamond. I don't know why I still feel somethin fuh Clark, he'd moved out months ago. The day I put him out he raped me fo' he left here, called me a who'e, and thought it was all right."

"What did the police do, Selma?"

"Nothin, nothin—I didn't call—I couldn't call! I'd threatened him first with a meat cleaver. He took it from me, grabbed me 'round my neck, and took his knife out his pocket. I thought he was 'bout tuh kill me, but he drug me tuh the middle of the flo', throwed me down, cut my clothes off me, and raped me in the middle of the sto'. I looked and felt so bad when it was ova I just couldn't tell nobody. Not even the police. I was embarrassed, Diamond, embarrassed. I didn't wont nobody tuh see me lack that, or tuh know that my own husband would treat me that bad. And you know the police. They wonna know mo' than what you wonna tell um and more than they needed tuh know. I decided tuh suffer through it."

"Oh, Selma. I'm so, sorry. Do you need me to come out there?"

"Naw, Diamond. You remember what happened between us in college while Anthony was away."

"Yeah, I almost didn't marry Sheila."

"You hadn't even started talkin tuh Sheila yet."

"And I never would have if you would've married me like I'd asked you to."

"I didn't wont you and Anthony tuh fall out lack that."

"You'd wanted me for a long time, Selma and I wanted you. I was in love with you. I'd get a feeling of lightheadedness whenever I saw you. No

other woman had ever made me feel that way until
I met Sheila."

"Tell me, did you know that Anthony was out
of town when you came by that night?"

"Naw, Anthony was always absent-minded, he
fuhgot tuh tell me he was goin away ova'night. I
thank we both just wanted what happened tuh
happen. Tuh be honest with you Diamond, I wonted
tuh see you afta that.

I wadn't goan tell you this, but one night I
tried tuh spy oan Anthony from y'all bedroom
closet and I saw y'all in bed with this girl.
What y'all did tuh huh made me stay 'way from
you. You just didn't seem lack you could treat no
woman lack that no matter what."

"There's only one who's perfect, Selma and
you know that."

"Yeah, I do nigh. Everythang seem tuh be
fallin intuh place."

"Diamond, um a rich lady nigh. You got tuh
git up and go tuh work in the monin. I betta let
you go."

"Selma, the work that I go to is mine.
Believe me, I'm not needed there. So you go ahead
and talk as much as you need to. Clark's death is
more important. It must be hard on you. You seem
to be holding up very well."

"That's just oan the outside, Diamond. That's
oan the outside, only."

"Diamond, I don't know what happened. It wadn't lack I wadn't a good wife. I tried tuh please him in anyway and every way possible."

"Maybe you tried too hard, Selma."

"Maybe I did, Diamond, but I loved him, still do, and it don't seem lack I kin help it."

"I know I said that I was going to let you talk, Selma, but I have to say this. I use to cheat on Sheila, it wasn't intentional, but I did it. And once I started it was hard for me to stop. Women went out of their way to get me and they went out of their way to please me. They didn't care if I was married, single, engaged, crazy, handicapped, diseased, or gay, and they very seldom asked, and most of the one's that did still wanted me to sleep with them. All they saw was what they thought was a clean, disease-free, attractive man, who looked like he had money and a job. Some of them didn't even care about my financial status, just my sexual ability. Selma. I'd never make it a point to sleep with those women right away because I knew that they were so anxious that they'd do whatever it took to get me in their beds right away. And Selma, that didn't exclude the ones I'd met the day or night before, and they'd keep on doing whatever they could until I'd decide to commit myself to a bedroom relationship...

"Diamond. Clark was good lookin, but not lack you."

"That doesn't matter, Selma. Many lonely misguided women who instead of looking for God, look for some male image to depend on, even a married or no-good one. When I was cheating on my wife I was blind and immature just like them. The only difference was that those women made me feel like a god, I let them and used and abused them. I stripped them of their dignity! What they wouldn't give I took! I'd beat, rape, and sodomize them if they made me angry enough, then force them to perform various sexual acts for me, and their knowledge didn't matter, because after I was finished with them they'd be well schooled, because if they'd refuse, I'd make it worse. I'd hire people to join me and we'd all use them and there was no where for them to run or hide. I've even sent them to hospitals and mental institutions and they'd come back for more.

You see, Selma, if people have low self-esteem, they allow others to mistreat them. Those of us who use them aren't any better. I thought I was being a masculine leader when I was misusing women, but just like them, I was also a victim of ignorance and low self-esteem. I'd fallen prey to the circumstances I'd created. Like a drug dealer I got addicted to what I'd produced. There's nothing masculine about that. You can't build yourself up off of someone else's humiliation or weaknesses. When I took my life to God, that's when I began to realize that. I stopped seeing people as insignificant objects and saw them as people—real people, with flesh, blood, and feelings, just like me. I don't let a day go by without thanking God for changing me."

"In a way, I can understand some of Clark's behavior, Selma. He was a victim of circumstance just like I was."

"I don't understand what yo mean, Diamond."

"Selma, just like me, Clark probably couldn't walk down the street without some woman trying to go to bed with him...

"OH, GOD!"

"Oh yeah, Selma. It happens to men, too. So don't gasp in surprise. Once the word gets out that you're a good lover or you'll be sexual with women no matter who they are, you're doomed. All of the love starved women come out of the woodwork. They chase you down like men chase down the town whore or prostitute, or he can be just plain old vulnerable prey. It might start out as an ego booster, but being constantly sought out for sex becomes aggravating and it's a struggle losing that reputation."

"You tellin me what happened tuh Clark was them women fault?"

"No, Selma. What I'm saying is that Clark probably started off by having an affair somewhere and the rumors started to fly. The affairs didn't necessarily have to start while he was married to you, but probably at some point he began having an affair with another woman, then another found out and another until the stories about his sex drive and manhood, got blown out of proportion. Then his lovemaking became the talk of the town. Some mythical, some fact. That gave him a big head and he acquired a habit he couldn't break."

"You mean a sex habit, Diamond?"

"No, Selma. Clark's real addiction was ego. He was use to being the king, a god, somebody the women looked up to and thought was a great lover and ladies man. He might have thought he had a sex habit, but it was probably more psychological than anything else. Something in his mind told him he needed to keep up this physical image, Selma. That something was his ego, his master. And he kept it fed so that he could brag to the guys about the women he had to somewhat woo, and the vulnerable ones that it didn't take much effort to pursue. But he probably never let on about the vulnerable ones being vulnerable, that would tear down some of his image. He had a need to make it sound as if he had something special, something that made all the ladies attracted to him. He thought that made him look like a big man to them. Some of them I'm sure were jealous, didn't like it or didn't want to hear it, and others probably even loathed his behavior but never said anything about it. If they had that might have helped Clark.

For some reason Selma, men will go along with what's being said and hardly ever speak out in disapproval. The truth is, more of us should. Disease is a big issue today."

"Diamond, did you evva brag when you cheated oan yo' wife lack Clark did?"

"No, Selma, but that was probably the only difference in what we were doing. That and the fact that I was blessed enough to find the Lord and was willing to change before the world took me out of here."

"He goin tuh hell, ain't he, Diamond?"

"Selma, all I know is that God gives all of us chances, warnings, and a will of our own so that we can make our own choices.

Continue talking to God, Selma. That's the only way you'll be able to ease your mind. He's the only one that will get you through this rough period. He might use me and others for you to lean on along the way, but he's the only one who can really answer your questions and ease your pain."

Chapter 23

THE CONFESSION

"May I help you?"

"Yes, I need tuh see uh offissuh."

"I'm an officer."

"Naw, naw, I need tuh see the one who handled the shootin the otha night at the Hotel Kasheeba."

"Oh, you mean officers Frank and Wilcox!"

"I guess I do."

"Just a minute, I'll get them for you."

"Thank you...

"Hi. I'm officer, Frank. You have information on the shooting at the Hotel Kasheeba?"

"Yes."

"Come on into my office..."

"...Have a seat...

"Thank you."

"...May I have your name?"

"If you don't mind, I wonna tell you what happened first."

"By all means, go ahead."

"I'd been seein him fuh a long time...

"Him, who, ma'am...?"

"Clark Porter."

"Okay, go ahead...

"He wouldn't see me no mo'.

I knew he was separated from his wife and was stayin at the Hotel Kasheeba. I thought he was goan git tired uh stayin there and come be with me. That didn't nevva happen.

I wonted him so bad I couldn't even eat no mo'. I went from a size eighteen tuh a size twelve from worryin. I couldn't take it no mo' so I got drunk tuh build up my nerve. Then I dressed up in this lil' black negligee and wig, put oan my coat; took my gun 'cause it was late, and went tuh the hotel."

"Is the gun registered, miss?"

"Oh, yes suh. It's legal. I'd gotten threats from some uh his women is why I bought it. You can check yo' records...

"Continue."

"When I got tuh his room, his do' was wide open. At first, I stood there lookin. He had this gal who looked lack uh baby all up 'ginst the wall and was havin sex with huh lack he was uh wild animal uh somethin and makin huh holla'. Seemed lack the louder she screamed the worse he got. I was goan run, 'cause the way it looked scared me, but the way that gal was squeelin in pain and the way he was moanin in plesha and kept wrappin that gal's arms 'round his neck every time they fell down, made me angry and jealous. I wonted him tuh wont me that bad.

All of uh sudden, I couldn't stand it no mo'. I was so jealous I started yellin. He let that gal fall tuh the flo' and he jumped oan me. He was beatin me and forcin me tuh do thangs I didn't wont tuh do.

I don't quite remember what he was sayin tuh me. I do know that he was mad 'cause that gal got out the room.

He beat me so bad I could barely see. I remembered I had the gun. I thought he was goan kill me so I went tuh strugglin tuh git tuh my pocket. Looked like he went tuh kick me again in my face. By that time I had the gun out. The blood in my face and my swollen eyes made everythang look hazy but I could see somethin movin. I didn't know if he was reachin fuh me, uh comin towards me tuh beat me some mo' or what. I was scared and I started shootin 'til I saw what was comin near me hit the flo'. I staggered from his room, took the fire exit, and fell down most the stairs, then stumbled tuh my car. I'd parked almost in front uh the hotel so it wadn't too hard fuh me tuh find it. My face and eyes was so swollen I had tuh pat my car lack a blind person tuh find the do' handle. Maybe 'cause he done sent me there so many times, I don't know, but somehow I drove myself tuh the hospital with my eyes half shut and bloody from that beatin.

My negligee was bloody and ripped all up and so was my coat.

All I could thank about oan my way tuh the hospital was how he'd shamed me.
He didn't even notice the weight I lost uh nothin. He didn't even wont me and I do remember him tellin me that and how he was goan make me do what that gal didn't git chance tuh do.

Offissuh, that wadn't the first time he'd done me lack that but that was the first time he'd beat me that bad and tol' me he didn't wont me no mo' at all—that I wadn't good enough!

I knew he didn't claim tuh love nobody but his wife, but I thought that was goan change when they separated. It didn't. He still didn't wont me. He didn't wont no parts uh me. He put me totally out his life! And I always lied when he'd send me tuh that hospital! They thought I was a prostitute who got beat up by different men all the time! *I couldn't believe he'd do me lack that afta' all I'd done tuh keep him from goin tuh jail...!*"
"It's okay, ma'am, it's okay. Here's some tissue. Everything's going to be okay."
"*...He lacked tuh molest young girls, offissuh and gave um money and drugs tuh keep um. When they wouldn't do what he wonted, I'd have*

tuh make up fuh it. That's all the good I was tuh him and if I refused, he'd hurt me.

He'd come tuh my house and make me cook and everythang lack I was his wife, but he treated me lack a dog. Sometimes, if he saw me bendin ova he'd kick me in my behind and make me fall ova just 'cause he was nasty. He was always nasty tuh me."

"Ma'am, what happened to the woman in the storage room?"

"What, woman! What storage room?"

"We were told by the night clerk that you and another woman was in one of the storage rooms at the hotel Kasheeba, being intimate. Was she involved in this homicide? What can you tell me about her?"

"Offissuh, please—

"Ma'am. Do you have children?"

"Yes, suh."

"Then tell the truth. You don't want to end up doing someone else's time for a crime that wasn't totally your doing. And you might not want your children to know of this woman. If this hits the news it's going to be on every local station and in every local newspaper. The relationship between you and this mysterious woman might surface...

"Offissuh, she didn't have nothin tuh do with murderin Clark! I tol' you the truth 'bout that!

It was all my doin! It all happened afta me and huh had been tuhgetha!

Offissuh. I passed huh as she was comin downstairs. She had huh head down and huh hands in huh pockets. She looked up and saw me. I knew she was one uh Clark's women and she knew me. She tol' me not tuh go up there but I didn't pay huh no mind. She wonted Clark just lack I did...Okay, Offissuh I'll tell you 'bout that too. I went tuh his room twice I was so determined tuh have him make love tuh me. When I got there he had his head between that baby's legs. She was screamin between clenched teeth and poundin oan his back with them little fists uh huhs. He acted lack he didn't even feel it and he probably didn't. I don't know what he'd gotten hold of, but he was worse than I'd evva seen him befo'. I was angry, but I was leavin. I kept walkin towards the otha end uh the hall where the exit was lack I hadn't seen nothin. When I decided tuh look back she was there. Herthenia was behind me and I don't know why. I don't know what she come back fuh. Maybe tuh lay with me, I don't know. I took the back exit down so that I wouldn't run into that desk clerk again and she followed me. When we got tuh the basement, Herthenia wonted tuh talk about what we was goan do 'bout Clark. I was cryin so hard I couldn't say nothin. She hugged me and kept tellin me it was alright. She led me tuh this storage room. We was both lonely and it happened. She was the one who did it all. I didn't do none uh that stuff back.

Offissuh, me, and Herthenia had been secretly seein each otha since I lost weight. She talked me in tuh that. I wadn't goan do it. *I swear tuh God I wadn't offissuh! But, I was so lonely I was desperate, and tried claimin tuh myself that I was goan only do it once. She'd given me huh number and tol' me tuh call huh if I decided tuh be with huh. When I realized that Clark wadn't goan come 'round no mo' them calls to Herthenia got mo' regular than I'd planned oan. Oh, God, um so shame!"*

"Come on now, ma'am. It's going to be okay."

"But, I just recently found out about huh and Clark, maybe, two, three weeks ago. She done had his baby."

"How'd you find out?"

"Them people under the gossipin wine tree."

"Oh, yeah. I know the one."

"Well, I hadn't seen Clark in a while and hadn't been out uh the house. I'd been sittin up in there waitin oan him tuh come by lack he told me I'd betta' do, but I got tired uh that and had tuh git some air uh answers uh somethin' tuh ease my mind. I went there lookin fuh Clark and that's when they tol' me who he was with and where he was. One of um wonted tuh sleep with me so he took me tuh where they was. I didn't let oan, but I knew where Herthenia lived. She'd gave me a key later in our relationship. When we got tuh

Herthenia's house Clark's truck was parked in front of it. I tol' my ride tuh pull 'round the back and not tuh git out the car. I went 'round tuh the front do' and used my key. They was tuhgetha alright. *He was doin thangs tuh Herthenia, a lesbian, that he'd nevva even planned oan doin tuh me. I couldn't believe it offissuh. Me and Herthenia was supposed tuh have a special relationship and there she was, layin up with my man, too. I didn't say nothin 'bout me and Herthenia tuh Clark. But she knew she couldn't come 'round tuh my house no mo'. She sit up under that wine tree with all them men everyday. She knew I was messin 'round with Clark.*

Clark usually beat me fuh followin him. He didn't wont nothin else tuh do with me since he had Herthenia. He nevva even noticed the weight I'd lost. He just tol' me tuh git outta Herthenia house. He didn't thank I was movin fast enough. He got up and physically removed me. He got outta Herthenia bed necked, put my arm behind my back with one hand, grabbed the back of my blouse with his other, put his foot in my behind, and kicked me out. Herthenia didn't git up uh say, nothin! I knew rat then that was the end uh me and Clark. I shoulda just stayed 'way from him. I wish I had. If I hadn't been drankin that night, I probably would have, but when me and Herthenia was done I went back tuh his room and that's when it all happened. *I seen Clark with that chil', started yellin, and he beat me 'cause she got 'way from him."*

"Ms., would you like to tell me your name, now?"

"*It's Bertha Mae Martin, Offissuh.*"

"Ms. Martin, I'm going to have to read you your rights."

"*I understand, offissuh...*

"You'll get to make some phone calls, Ms. Martin. I suggest that you make one of them to your attorney."

Chapter 24

THE PHONE CALL

"Hello."

"Hello, Selma, it's Bert."

"WHAT THE HELL YOU CALLIN MY HOUSE FUH!"

"Selma, please, calm down and listen tuh me...Um in jail."

"Why ain't I surprised, Bert?"

"Selma, I know yah mad at me, but I just wonna tell yah some thangs yah need tuh know."

"LACK, WHAT!"

"Lack, how much Clark loved yah. He was goin crazy 'cause you left him. He didn't know what tuh do withoutcha."

"How you know how my husband felt 'bout me? You was too busy tryin tuh git with him yo'sself. But that don't matter nigh, 'cause he dead. Some woman he was beatin oan did it. So neither one uh us don't have tuh worry 'bout him lovin, nobody!"

"Selma, I know he dead, um the woman he was beatin. Um the woman he was beatin in the hotel."

"YOU! YOU KILLED MY CLARK!"

"Yes, Selma, I did it. That's why um callin you from jail. I done turned myself in."

"WELL, WELL, WELL, GOOD FUH YOU! YOU KIN GIT OUTTA JAIL! BUT WHAT ABOUT MY CLARK, HUH? YOU DONE SENT HIM TUH HELL BEFO' HE COULD REPENT, BUT

YOU GOAN GIT OUTTA JAIL...! IF YOU AIN'T THE
LOYALIST FRIEND I COULDA EVVA HAD! FISH 'N' GRITS
IN THE MONIN' AND BETRAYAL BEFO' IT'S DARK! FIRST
YAH LAY UP WITH HIM THEN YAH KILL HIM! AIN'T YOU
SOMETHIN ELSE! YAH KNOW WHAT, BERT, JAIL AIN'T
ENOUGH! I HOPE THEY GIVE YOU THE DEATH SENTENCE!"

"So do I, Selma."

"THEN AT LEAST WE BOTH AGREE OAN SOMETHIN!"

"Selma, I know I done wrong by you. All I
wont tuh letcha know is that Clark didn't have no
feelins fuh me. All he evva did was use and abuse
me. He done stomped me mo' times than I can
recall, but the night I killed him was worse than
anythang he'd evva done tuh me."

"I DON'T WONNA HEAR NOTHIN ELSE YOU GOT TUH
SAY 'BOUT MY DE-A-A-A-A-A-D, HUSBAND!"

"I know yah don't and um goan let yah go afta
I say this. If I hadn't decided tuh go tuh
Clark's room when I did, he might have killed
that young gal. He might be the one here, instead
uh me."

"SO!"

"So, yah might have two deaths oan yo' mind
rat nigh instead uh one. Clark killin that gal
fuh nothin and him gittin a harsh sentence fuh
doin it."

"BERT! IF THAT'S S'PPOSE TUH MAKE ME FEEL
BETTA, IT DON'T!"

"Um sho' it don't rat nigh, but if you'd seen
that chil' wrenchin, strugglin, screamin, and

gaspin fuh breath lack I did, you'd probably see
thangs different.

Selma, I deserved what I got 'cause I was the
one who messed with Clark first. That gal was
just a chil', a baby. She hadn't done nothin tuh
him befo'."

"HOW DO YOU, KNOW THAT, BERT! AND YOU WADN'T
UP THERE FUH THE GOOD UH THAT CHIL' NO WAY!"

"I know I wasn't, Selma, I know I wasn't, but
I knew all the young gals Clark was messin with
and she wadn't one of um, Selma. Um sho' Daizelle
can tell you the same thang...

"Ms. Martin, your time is almost up."

...Selma, you know Clark didn't lack
rejection and that gal probably tol' him no and
he snatched huh."

"Befo' I go I gotta tell yah somethin 'bout
Clark I shoulda tol' you long time ago."

"BERT! AIN'T NOTHIN YOU CAN TELL ME 'BOUT
THAT MAN I DON'T ALREADY KNOW OR SOMEBODY ELSE
AIN'T TOL' ME...

"Selma. He raped Baby Fatina."

"WHAT! WHY YOU LYIN, NO GOOD, FILTHY, FAT,
LOW DOWN WHO'E—

"Selma. You kin yell and call me all the
names you wont, but that ain't goan change
nothin. Fatina told me huhself afta church a few
Sundays ago what he'd done. She say he took huh

the night he was suppose tuh be droppin huh off
at home, and he messed with huh again that Sunday
at church in the ladies bathroom. She even tol'
me huh daddy been kissin huh in the wrong place
and I tol' huh that was wrong, too.

Selma, the reason why you ain't seen Fatina
no mo' is because she ended up in the hospital
about a week afta Clark touched huh. She was
pretty messed up afta what Clark done to huh.
Anita thought Fatina was messin 'round with boys
and Baby Tina wouldn't tell huh no different.
Clark had threatened tuh kill huh if she did.
Odell, Fatina daddy, he left home. I believe he
thought what he was doin tuh Fatina somehow
caused it and she was goan tell what he was doin
to huh and he'd get in trouble. Even go tuh jail.

I didn't mean tuh hurt Clark, Selma, but he
was hurtin me that night. He done hurt a lot uh
people includin you and Baby Fatina. You know
that, Selma. Nigh, I wont you tuh thank about
what I tol' you and thank about them otha thangs
Clark done tuh you. Yo' heart a git lighter. You
won't feel so guilty 'bout puttin him out 'cause
you done the right thang."

"WHO IS YOU, TUH GIVE ME ADVICE, BERT!"

"SELMA! Long as I know'd you, you was always
blamin the womens instead uh Clark! He was wrong,
too!

Selma, just lack I was wrong tuh mess with him, he was wrong tuh mess with me! He coulda walked 'way! He coulda said no, no matter how he felt about what I'd done tuh him!"

"BERTHA, MAE, MARTIN, I KNOW'D HOW WHO'EISH HE WAS! BUT YOU, YOU WAS SUPPOSED TUH BE MY FRIEND! MY, BEST, FRIEND! SO DON'T YOU TELL ME NOTHIN 'BOUT WHAT MY HUSBAND COULDA DONE! YOU HEAR ME! BERTHA? UM TALKIN TUH YOU! BERTHA! BERTHA! BERTHA...!

Chapter 25

DAIZELLE GETS FED UP

"Why you yellin lack that, Selma?"

"'Cause, that fool ass Bert called me from jail tellin me she the one killed, Clark...!"

"...Well, ain't you goan say somethin, Daizelle! You actin lack it ain't no big deal!"

"Selma, listen tuh me. I kinda figured it was Bert who killed Clark. She was in love with him and he treated huh lack a dog. She wonted tuh be with him, but he'd stopped seein huh."

"How come everybody knows mo' 'bout my business then I do, huh, why is that?"

"'Cause, you turned yo' head the otha way, Selma. Folks out in the streets ain't goan do that!"

"Um goan tell you the truth, Selma. I was oan the otha line listenin. Not oan purpose, I was gittin ready tuh make a phone call. I was goan hang up 'til I heard Bert's voice. She betrayed you, but what she was sayin made good sense."

"Daizelle, please."

"Well, it did."

"I'll give Clark points fuh bein a good provida, Selma. But it takes mo' then provisions tuh make a good man! He got tuh love and respect his woman. He supposed tuh love huh so much that he at least try tuh hide what he doin. Clark ain't nevva tried tuh hide nothin from you 'cept him rapin Baby Tina and I know you kinda know'd 'bout that, too."

"Why, Daizelle! Why you talkin 'bout my husband lack that and he dead?"

"Um sorry, Selma. I know yah ain't supposed tuh talk 'bout the dead less yah got somethin good tuh say, but Clark wadn't no good and you helped him stay that way and you know that.

What Bert said 'bout him hurtin that chil' he didn't even know in his hotel room, you know was true, 'cause you heard it from me fo' she tol' you. Nigh, we all ain't lyin oan Clark?

Selma, if you evva wont tuh git ova feelin guilty 'bout puttin Clark out, you goan have tuh accept the truth. He was a man who didn't have no respect fuh you, hisself, and nobody else, and you know that. He didn't care if he was the one who started up with them women uh not! He always wonted tuh be the one who ended it! And Selma! You know full well that anybody, anybody, includin you, caught hell from that man until he decided it was ova!"

"I know, Daizelle, but I just couldn't let him go. I had done got so use tuh him I just couldn't let go. And I was too afraid uh bein alone. Nigh, I ain't got no choice, Daizelle. What um goan do? *What um goan do*...

"That's right, Selma, cry. Let it oan out. It's good, it's good tuh see yah cryin, 'cause when you finish, you goan thank some mo' 'bout what everybody been tryin tuh tell yah and what you already knew."

Chapter 26

SELMA ACCEPTS THE FACTS

"They right, they all, right. I let Clark do whatever he wonted. No matter what kind uh sex he wonted, how he bragged 'bout his women 'round town, him havin otha women, it didn't matter I let him do it so he'd stay with me. Nigh, I regret it.

If I woulda left that no good man long ago, he'd probably be alive today. Then again, he probably was goan find anotha' woman just as foolish as me. He was messin 'round with anythang wearin a skirt. Um sho' there was anotha' fool lack me in that bunch, but that wouldn'tna been my concern.

Daizelle and Bert right, though. I need tuh git myself tugetha and try tuh go ahead with my life instead uh grievin ova a man who was s'pposed tuh be my husband but only spent the night with me. Besides, I know Bert wadn't lyin 'bout Clark hurtin that chil' he was a heartless man. And he was pure puke, fuh ruinin Baby Fatina. How could he do it? She was lack his own chil'. We practically raised that baby. The only thang I caint deny, is how good him beatin oan Bert makes me feel."

HERTHENIA

"Herthenia Nittles?"
   "Yes, officer, yes! That's me!"
   "May we come in? We need to talk to you."
   "Yes, of course. But what's this all about...?"

"Ms. Nittles—wait a minute. I know you...

"I don't think so. I'm not originally from Casey Park. I'm from Northbury...

"I knew it! I knew it! You're Little Hearty Herthy! How could I not know? I mean, how could I ever forget...!"

"I've changed since Northbury. Are you here for anything specific? I mean, other than reminiscing?"

"Oh. Yes, yes. We're investigating the homicide of Mr. Clark Porter...

"I didn't kill him!"

"We're not accusing you, Ms. Nittles. We just want to know if you could give us any information on what happened the night he was killed."

"I wasn't even there. I—

"Ms. Nittles. We have three witnesses that place you at the hotel before and after Mr. Porter died. Do you want to change that statement?"

"Oh, all right! I was there! But, I didn't kill him. I didn't even get a chance to talk to him. When I got there he was with this kid. He was performing oral sex on her. I was angry, but I never said anything. I didn't even let him see me. He'd told me before if I ever saw him with someone else I should just leave and not say anything and I did. He had a bad temper and a reputation for beating his disobedient women. I've seen what he's like when he's beating them and I didn't want to experience it.

On my way out I saw this woman named Bertha that I'd had an affair with and that also messed around with him. I hadn't seen her at the hotel before so by the time I got to the front door I'd collected myself enough to think, "Is she going to tell Clark about us?" I thought she wanted revenge. She'd caught me and him in bed together. When I called her house to apologize and explain myself she'd cursed me out.

You see; Clark knew that I liked women, but once I got involved with him he wouldn't let me see them right out. I had to sneak around. When he asked me about her, he didn't just ask. He had me pinned to the bed and waved his fist in my face. I had to lie to him. I knew that he didn't think much of her so I told him that I'd paid her to help me clean, and that I'd given her a key to come in to do it in case I was away and she must have thought that I was out. I went back up there to make sure she wouldn't tell him the truth. He would've killed me! He still punched me in the middle of my back that day and left a large bruise. He said that it was something to make me remember who gave the orders. Anyway. She never talked to him either. She took the back exit out of the hotel to the stairs and I followed her! That's all that happened, officer! I swear to you! That's all that happened!"

"If that's all that happened then how'd you two end up being intimate that night?"

"He—We were never intimate—

"Hearty—I mean Herthy. You might as well tell the truth. Mrs. Martin has already told us—

"Officer, we both needed comfort! It just happened! Just goes to show. You can't do nothin without somebody seeing you do it...!"

"Did you say something Ms. Nittles?"

"No. I was just wondering if you were finished questioning me?"

"Yes, we are. But, if you remember anything else give us a call. Here's my card."

"Was that any way for an officer to talk to a witness, Officer Wilcox? Ms. Martin has already admitted to committing the crime."

"No, but I knew her! She's from my hometown!"

"You really do know her, Wilcox?"

"Yeah, I know her! She was Hearty Herthy and she knows it. We could pay her a buck to get her to go down on us! She'd put her heart into it, man! She wasn't but twelve years old!"

"How old were you, Wilcox?"

"Sixteen."

"And you let a kid do somethin like that to you and you knew she was a kid?"

"Yep! And I'd let her do it again if she calls. She was good!"

"How old is your daughter now, Wilcox?"

"Fifteen, why?"

"What would you do if you found out boys were using her that way?"

"THAT'S NOT EVEN A QUESTION, FRANK! I'D KILL UM! I'D—

"Then shouldn't you be dead, Wilcox?"

"For what, Frank? That girl? She's trash!"

"What would your daughter be, Wilcox, if she was being molested by boys older than she is?"

"Aa-a-a-h! You're crazy, Frank!"

"Maybe. But never, in thirty-nine years have I been crazy enough to mess with someone else's child no matter what her reputation was, and I hope I never will be."

Chapter 27

THE REVEREND

"It's nice uh you tuh call and check oan me from time tuh time, reverend. I appreciate yo' concern."

"Selma, I know that your husband's passing has been hard on you, but that's not the only reason why I call.

You know, it's been over a year now and I've been watching you for a long time trying to build up my nerve to ask you out."

"Reverend, are you askin me out oan a date?"

"Yes, Selma, yes, I am."

"Reverend, I'm so flattered. But, why me?"

"Selma you are, and always have, carried yourself like a queen in my presence.

I think that I've been interested in you longer than I can remember."

"Really, reverend?"

"It's the truth, Selma."

"I know that Clark never treated you very nice and neither did some of the other people around here. That happens when someone such as yourself doesn't get involved with all of the local gossip and carrying-on's. Personally, I've always admired you for that."

"Thank you reverend, you just don't know how that make me feel. But, I was a big part of that gossip. Some even thank that I coulda controlled Clark more than I did."

"It's not your fault that Clark's dead, Selma, no matter what people may think. Husbands and wives are to guide each other, but they can't control each other. Selma. None of us can do what God won't do. He'll direct our paths, but he won't force us to take it. So come down off the cross, Selma. Stop punishing yourself. You deserve to feel good you're a good woman. A woman who with the right partner can make many wonderful things happen."

"Thank you reverend fuh the kind words, but some uh what they sayin is true 'cause I didn't even try tuh guide, Clark, and he sho' nuff didn't respect me."

"Selma, when we allow people to mistreat us it's usually because we don't want to face the negative consequences that might come if we confront them. God is the master and our world leader. He has the utmost respect for all of us. If the world leader and master holds us in such great esteem, no man should treat us any less important regardless of who he or she is. Even the Bible tells us not to cast our pearls amongst the swine, Selma. We should know when to be humble, when to speak, and when to walk away from coarseness. Discernment allows us to know these things. But when we continuously allow ourselves

to be misused by man out of fear alone, we're
putting man first instead of God. I know that
Clark didn't treat you as if you were one of
God's children, but there's nothin that you can
do about that now so you're going to have to make
a decision. You can die with Clark or live your
life. I'm hoping that you'll choose to live,
Selma. I'd really like to get to know you
better."

"Reverend, it will be my pleasure to go out
with you."

"What about tomorrow night?"

"That's perfect, reverend. What time should I
be ready?"

"Eight o'clock is good, Selma. I want to
spend as much time with you as possible."

"Reverend, um flattered."

"Selma, call me, Paul."

"Reverend, I couldn't!"

"Please, Selma, I insist."

"Reverend, I just caint call you by yo' first
name rat nigh. Maybe afta we get tuh know each
otha oan a mo' personal level I'll be able tuh,
but rat nigh, I caint."

"Okay Selma, we'll do it your way.

Now, I want you ready on time tomorrow night
and I want you to be ready to have some fun. I
don't want you thinking that just because I'm a
reverend I don't like to have fun."

"Oh, no, reverend, I don't thank that at all. Tuh be honest with you, you probably mo' up tuh date then me. Clark nevva took me no where and I nevva bothered askin him."

"Well, Miss Selma, you get prepared to have some good times. I'm going to make sure that you have so much fun, it'll make up for everything you've missed out on, okay!"

"Okay reverend, okay!"

"Then I'll see you tomorrow night at eight."

Chapter 28

SELMA TALKS ABOUT HER DATE

"He took yah tuh the ballroom?"

"Yeah, Daizelle. Afta we had the lobster dinner at Shade Nine—

"He took yah there! That's an expensive restaurant...!"

"I know, Daizelle! I know!"

"Go 'head, Selma! Tell me what else happened!"

"We went tuh the movie. I thought we was goin home when it was ova, instead he turned tuh me and said in that proppa way uh his "You like dancing," and you know I said yes. I nevva danced so much in my life. He even kissed me oan the cheek and held my hand. He made me feel lack a school girl again. I thank um fallin in love with the reverend, Daizelle. I thank um goan stay in Casey Park a bit longa!"

"Ain't nothin wrong with that, Selma. Um glad you havin a good time. You deserve it yah know."

"I reckon I do."

"Naw, Selma, you really deserves it. You done been through hell. There ain't many people in this town who can say they done been through what you have and still able tuh do as much fuh otha folks as you do. Um goan tell you somethin else."

"What's that, Daizelle?"

"Um glad you stayin and um glad you and me friends, 'cause you real serious 'bout bein a person's friend."

"Daizelle, you don't hafta say that."

"Yes I do 'cause I mean it. You one uh the best people in this town. There ain't many people lack you."

"Thank you Daizelle, you a good friend, too. You really been lookin out fuh me and I really appreciate it."

Chapter 29

SELMA AND THE REVEREND

"Selma, I know we've only been seeing each other a short while, but I love you, Selma. I always have."

"Reverend—

"Call me Paul, Selma, call me, Paul."

"Paul, I—

"Selma, I want you to marry me."

"Paul, I don't know what tuh say!"

"Do you enjoy my company, Selma?"

"Yes, I do."

"Do I make you happy?"

"Yes Paul, very happy."

"Do you have deep feelings for me, Selma?"

"Of course Paul, I thank about you all the time."

"Then say yes, Selma so that we can make each other happy for the rest of our lives...please. Accept this and say, yes."

"Oh, Paul, this ring is beautiful!"

Chapter 30

SELMA CALLS DIAMOND

"So, you told the rev you'd marry him, huh?"
    "Yes, I did."

    "Yah know, Diamond, I always had a secret
crush oan him rat from the beginnin. Now that's a
man who's as handsome as you is."
    "Girl, how you goan play me like that! You
just up and tell me the reverend look as good as
me...please! If he ain't careful, I'll steal you
from him!"
    "Diamond, stop it, you too much."
    "Okay, I won't tease you anymore, but tell me
one thing."
    "What?"
    "Does he kiss as good as I do?"
    "DIAMOND! You makin me blush!"
    "Good, that's payback for tellin me the rev
looks as good as I do."
    "Diamond, I don't know what um goan do with
you."
    "I do, you're going to invite me to the
wedding!"
    "You right, I am. Will you come?"
    "You know I'll be there, but I have to warn
you. If you see the rev trip, look at me. I'll be

sittin there with my foot stuck out in the
aisle."

"Diamond, you betta not cut up."

"You know I'm teasin you, Selma. I've been
praying that God would bring something good into
your life, and look at what happened. Men don't
come any better than Reverend Bess. You couldn't
have said yes to a better man than the reverend.
He's real people. He takes his ministry seriously
and you never hear any gossip about him. It must
have been hard for him all these years, him being
a single man, if you know what I mean."

"Yeah, I know what you mean, Diamond. He tol'
me he had tuh do a lot uh prayin tuh keep from
strayin."

"Diamond, even if I did hear somethin 'bout
the reverend—I mean, Paul, I wouldn't take it tuh
heart."

"What do you mean, Selma?"

"I mean, he's been so good tuh all uh us, and
so decent, that it wouldn't matter. Besides, he
human just lack the rest of us.

With all uh the wickedness in the world and
in that church, it's almost impossible not tuh do
somethin wrong every nigh 'n' then."

"Amen to that, Selma, amen to that! You being
such a strong woman, I know that you'll be able
to stand by the rev no matter what happens—you
know what, there's no need for negative thinking!
We're going to put all of our trust in the Lord

and believe for only the best! Before I hang up this phone, you and I are going to pray and ask God to bless your marriage. Dear Lord, I am in agreement with my sister today asking that you watch over her, and her soon to be husband, Brother, Reverend, Paul Bess, before, during, and after they are married. Anoint their marriage with the goodness and prosperity that only you can supply Lord.

Grant my sister and brother the blessing of fertility Lord. She has been waiting for a long time.

Continue to ease her mind and give her direction, for she has suffered long and hard. Show my sister the true suffering that is needed and paths to take for prosperity and to be worthy to take a seat in the kingdom.

Thank you Lord, in Jesus' name, amen."

Chapter 31

BERTHA

"Sister Martin?"

"Reverend Bess!"

"I thought that was you, sister! Give me a
great big hug! You've lost a tremendous amount of
weight! I can almost fit my arms around you
twice!"

"I ain't that small, reverend!"

"Really Sister Martin, you look good! Have
you been dieting!"

"Naw, not really."

"Well, whatever you're doing certainly agrees
with you."

"Thank you, reverend."

"Just telling you the truth, Sister Martin,
the plain truth! I haven't seen you at service
lately and the weight loss makes you look so
different, I almost didn't recognize you!

Are you coming back, sister? Are you coming
back to church? I miss hearing your amen's and
thank you lord's. They were so powerful!"

"Reverend. Sometimes the most powerful amen
can be the most wicked. I now you done heard by
nigh just lack everybody else in town how my
chil'ren was taken from me fuh a while 'cause I

was messin 'round with Selma Jean's husband, Clark, and killed him."

"Yes, I have, sister, but none of us can stop you from entering God's house.

Do you think that God doesn't love you anymore because of what's happened in your past...?

...Come on now sister hold your head up like you know Jesus. Rest in his arms."

"How can I, reverend? I done slept with muh best friend husband, let him sodomize me, and only me and God knows what else. Then I turn 'round and tol' huh all kind uh lies 'bout huh husband rapin me. I feel so dirty. Too dirty tuh step in the Lord's house."

"Sister, remember Mark 2:17. Those who are well have no need of a physician, but those who are sick. I did not come to call the righteous, but sinners to repentance.

Who is really righteous, sister? Me, Selma, Clark, the others who were also involved with Clark, but by grace were blessed not to be in the way of the devil during the time of Clark's demise? No, Sister Martin, none of us, we all fall short. We all took part in the death of Clark Porter. We either kept quiet or went along with what he was doing.

Come to church this Sunday, sister. If we can't support you then why do we stand? You need us to help you at this time."

"I don't thank that I can, reverend."

"Nothing's impossible, Sister Martin."

"But, Selma Jean hates me so, reverend. As good as she is, she wonted me dead when she found out 'bout me and Clark."

"I wasn't going to mention this to you sister, but Selma and I are going to be married in a couple of weeks—

"Oh Lord, thank you Jesus...!"

"Sister, are you okay?"

"Yes, reverend, yes. It's just that I'd been prayin fuh somethin good tuh happen tuh Selma, and tuh hear you say that overwhelmed me with the joy of The Holy Spirit. God is, so good!"

"That's right, sister and my congregation and my future wife will be good to you, too.

When I go home, I'm going to call and talk to her. What we talked about today will be my sermon for next Sunday. So don't let me down, sister, be there."

"Yes, reverend, I promise, I will."

Chapter 32

THE REVEREND CALLS SELMA

"Will you come over for breakfast, Selma?"

"Of course I'll come fuh breakfast as long as somebody else doin the cookin! You goan be doin the cookin, right?"

"Yes, Selma, I'm going to cook."

"Then I'll be there."

"Selma, I went to the market this morning. I ran into an old friend of yours."

"A friend uh mine?"

"Yes, Selma. A friend of yours; Bertha Martin."

"Paul, I don't wont tuh talk 'bout no Bertha Mae Martin."

"Selma. You're going to have to talk about what happened and forgive Bertha, or you're headed for illness, and unforgiveness of your sins."

"Paul, I don't—

"Selma, the way everyone's been treating that woman you'd think they were all perfect saints.

What Bertha did was wrong, but so was Clark and the others, but the only one who's suffering from the finger pointing is Sister Martin.

Maybe it makes you feel good that the entire town is on your side, but she's lost an enormous amount of weight. Even for a woman of her previous size, that may not be good. Do you want to be responsible for her health?"

"Paul, I just don't thank I kin evva feel right about that woman again."

"Would it help any if I told you that she's been praying for you?"

"Prayin fuh me, why would she pray fuh me and not huhself?"

"Apparently, she feels a lot of guilt. When I told her that you and I were getting married she almost passed out. She began thanking the Lord right there in the market. That's when she told me she'd been praying for you."

"She need tuh pray fuh huhself!"

"No, Selma! We need to pray for her! She's feeling unworthy. She may be contemplating suicide.

Please, Selma, call Sister Martin. Talk to her; forgive her. Remember; life and death are in our words. You don't want her suicide on your conscience."

Chapter 33

AFTER THE REVEREND HANGS UP

"BERTHA! BERTHA MAE, PLEASE, PICK UP THE PHONE! BERTHA MAE, YOU THERE? PICK UP THE PHONE, PLEASE!"

"Hello, hello."

"Bertha, please fuhgive me fuh what I said tuh yah! Um sho' you done asked God tuh fuhgive you!"

"I have, Selma, ova, and ova again."

"Bertha, I fuhgive yah too. Come tuh church oan Sunday. The reverend and me goan be sho' that everybody know how wrong we all been.

Here we is treatin you lack you the only one who was wrong. You know what, you the only one who done somethin right. It's just lack the reverend said, you prayin and we pointin fangas lack we so righteous.

Bert, I don't wonna be responsible fuh keepin you from servin the Lawd the way you wont to. I just don't have the right."

"Selma, it ain't really yo' fault. I been thankin 'bout what happened and prayin ova and ova. I was wrong. Nothin shouldn'tna nevva happened between me and Clark in the first place. When I found out I had feelins fuh Clark I shoulda at least got from 'round you."

"Bertha, it's lack you said, he coulda said no."

"Selma, he did in a way. He kept avoidin me 'til he couldn't avoid me no mo'.

Um goan be truthful, Selma, that's the only way um goan make it through. Them otha women, Clark went afta most of um. He didn't come afta me. I seduced Clark just lack Daizelle said. He come in drunk while you was gone one day when you had me watchin the sto'. Daizelle wadn't in the sto' that day, nobody was. As soon as I heard him git quiet upstairs, I closed down. I went up there hopin he was sleep and he was. He was in that big rocka, wearin only his T-shirt and boxers. I kneeled in front uh him, gently reached into his underwear and started pleasin him. He called yo' name and I didn't say nothin. He squinted his eyes tuhgetha, looked down at me and said, "Bertha, what you doin?" I tol' him tuh relax, it was goan be all right. He was so drunk he couldn't git up out the chair and I knew it. He tried not tuh give in and I knew he was holdin back, but there ain't too much a person kin do when they in that position. He was pushin up oan the arms uh the chair tryin tuh stand up, but I made him holla' out. Me and that liquor had him so weak, Selma. He fell back down in the chair. I got up and was walkin out the do'. He called out my name and I looked back at him. He had got hisself tugetha enough tuh raise up and say,

"Bert, um goan git you fuh this, you hear, um goan git you." I ignored him 'cause I thought he was just talkin from a drunken mind and I'd done it befo' tuh otha men while they was drunk. Clark wadn't the only one. Clark was the only one tuh beat, sodomize, rape, and embarrass me though.

I thought he was just goan be willin tuh have sex with me lack the otha men did if I kept oan pleasin him that way, but he didn't. He nevva got ova what I'd done tuh him.

See, Selma, the other men would pay me tuh have sex with um that way and tuh have sex with me. They would even meet me and tell me what outfits tuh wear, and how they lacked big women, especially in sexy night clothes. Most of um rat in our congregation, Selma, and nigh, everyone of um, they pointin fangas at me.

All the thangs I tol' you he done tuh me afta he'd been with otha women is true, but it was my fault fuh messin with him in the first place. I seduced, Clark, I molested him, I raped him, and he was gittin back at me and I deserved every bit of it.

The night I shot him he kept tellin me how he didn't wont me, how I wadn't nothin, and he'd heard 'bout me 'round town. Selma, he kept sayin, "Do I have tuh keep oan showin you what I do tuh dog bitches." I couldn't believe that he thought he was betta then me afta all the women he done had, afta all he'd made me do—but seein him with that young girl in his room made me burn inside. I felt more insecure than evva, and him sayin them thangs tuh me and beatin me while he was sayin um drove me crazy."

"Bertha, just stop cryin nigh just stop cryin. Clark was nasty and spiteful. You was lonely and feelin inferior 'cause you was heavy. You need tuh know that you don't have tuh do all them thangs tuh men tuh make um lack you. You ain't got nothin tuh prove tuh nobody. It's a shame that I didn't learn that myself 'til afta Clark died, but it's true. He made me feel inferior too. Nigh I know I don't have tuh feel that way."

"I know that nigh too, Selma, 'cause what I done tuh Clark, done brought me closer tuh God. Believe me, if time could go backwards there'd be a lot uh changes in my life."

"Bert, we all say that. What we got tuh do is look ahead and learn from our mistakes. If we don't nevva make no mistakes, we wouldn't nevva learn nothin. Nigh would we?"

"Selma, I know what I did learn, not tuh nevva mess with otha women's mens, 'specially my best friend's, no Matta what. That was real stupid uh me."

"Yah know, Bert, Diamond tol' me that men git a reputation just lack women when they loose and that's what happened with Clark. Clark ways got him killed. You only pulled the trigga."

"Um still responsible, Selma."

"Bert, I thank all uh us who was involved with Clark can take credit fuh what happened tuh him. Most everybody in this town supposed tuh be Christians, but they all encouraged him. The folks that would listen tuh him brag, and the ones who didn't refuse tuh have a relationship with him and his surly ways. They knew he was doin wrong, but they tolerated him 'cause they lacked tuh hear gossip. Even I coulda said no, that woulda at least slowed him down. I would nevva say no 'cause I was scared uh him leavin me. I was lack a frightened chil' when it came tuh Clark Porter leavin me. Nigh, all I can thank about is he coulda give me a disease, and he goan, anyway. Diseases ain't nothin tuh be playin with nigh days."

"I know, Selma, but I didn't care, either, as long as I had a man, any man tuh make me feel lack a woman."

"Bert, the only man that can make you feel complete is God. I had tuh learn that the hard way."

"So did I, Selma. All the time I been lookin at the wrong thang tuh make me feel whole. Men flesh-n-blood just lack us. They caint do no mo' than we kin."

"I guess God got tired uh me playin with him and cursed me tuh be alone. That way I could learn about him and myself without anythang gittin in my way."

"He musta cursed both of us, Bert. I thought Clark was goan be 'round fuh evva."

"Selma, is we goan be friends again?"

"Let's take it one day at a time, Bert."

"Why, Selma, do yah still hate me?"

"Naw, I don't hate you no mo', but we each need tuh stay oan our paths with God 'til he tells us exactly what tuh do."

"Okay, Selma, we'll do that. We'll take it one day at a time and leave the rest up tuh the Lord. Um sho' he'll get us tuhgetha when the time is right."

Chapter 34

THE FIRST TO KNOW

"Diamond, yah know me and the rev been married fuh a while, nigh."

"Yeah, I know that. You tryin tuh rub it in, Selma?"

"Naw, Diamond, nigh stop clownin and listen. The reverend don't even know yet, you the first tuh know! Um pregnant!"

"Selma, you're kidding!"

"Naw, Diamond, I ain't."

"Why haven't you told Paul?"

"He still out uh town and I just found out today."

"Selma, he's going to be disappointed that you didn't keep the good news until he got home."

"I know, but I just had tuh tell somebody! I could barely believe it myself! Um so excited I can barely stay still! Um finally goan have some kids uh my own!"

"I knew only good would be coming to you, Selma."

"You mean, besides bein married tuh the rev, bein pregnant with twins is the best thang that coulda evva happened tuh me!"

"TWINS? You're pregnant with twins?"

"Yes, suh."

"When is your due date?"

"Nigh, you really ain't goan believe this! It's in fo' months and I ain't nevva had monin sickness! The only reason why I know um pregnant is because I went tuh the docta tuh see why my period hadn't come oan in these last two months! I thought I was goin through early menopause!"

"Girl, I can understand that, 'cause all women don't get those symptoms and I've only seen you a few times at service, that's if you come late, but you look the same to me! How in the world have you been carrying twins around all this time without knowing you're pregnant!"

"My hips, Diamond, my hips! That's where um carryin um, in my hips! You know how broad they are!"

"Oh, yeah, I remember them. I remember holding onto them and how smooth they are—

"Come on nigh, Diamond, don't talk to a pregnant, preacher's wife lack that."

"I really couldn't help myself that time, Selma. That's why I'm so glad we have a God to serve. He'll forgive me if every now and then I tell the truth and not bridle my tongue for the wrong reasons. You know what else?"

"What."

"I'm going to be honest with you, Selma. I still have feelings for you. When I saw you at church I wanted you. When you kissed the rev, I got angry."

"Diamond, I thank you bein a little lustful 'cause you miss, Sheila."

"No, Selma, it's more than that."

"Diamond, if you talkin 'bout the night we had sex it was full uh lust. Anthony neglecting me, and hearin about the thangs you and Anthony did tuh girls is what made me do some uh what I did with you that night. I knew that Anthony was betrayin me and I was angry when I proved it by watchin y'all with that girl, but not too angry tuh enjoy the surprised look oan huh face. She was shocked when she found out she wadn't goan have sex with y'all one at a time. When she started screamin from the pain and embarrassment I was glad. I've always held resentment fuh people who I thought had hurt me. A lot uh people don't know that 'bout me though.

I shouldn'tna been watchin and hopin that what y'all did tuh that girl that night would go oan 'til the next day then sneaked outta that closet and not help huh. I believe that's what doomed me with Clark."

"Selma, you're trying to talk around it, but you're still wondering about that, aren't you?"

"Wonderin? About what, Diamond?"

"That night, Selma. You're wondering what else Anthony and I did to that girl."

"Naw, Diamond. I was just runnin my mouth. I ain't wonderin about—

"Yes you are, Selma. I know you...

"Diamond—

"I'm going to tell you exactly what happened, Selma so that you can stop wondering and bringing it up."

"Naw, Diamond, don't! You don't have tuh do that!"

"Yes I do, Selma. Every time we talk you bring up Anthony's name. You're searching for something, Selma. The only way you're going to stop questioning me in your mind is that I tell you what happened...

"Diamond—

"She tried to slip away, Selma. That girl had no idea how cruel Me and Anthony were until she was forced to sleep with both of us—

"Diamond...!"

"Be quiet, Selma and listen. Anthony and I were still sleeping and she'd gotten loose somehow and got up to get dressed. We caught her and forced her to drink vodka, which we'd laced with something like Spanish fly. It didn't work. We couldn't get enough in her. So we tied her to the bed and kept raping her. I'd had enough, but Anthony continued to mess with her breasts and other areas of her body with his mouth and hands until she was screaming in pain and begging him to stop.

I told him to let her go, but he acted as if he didn't hear me. He seemed to have hate in his heart for her for some reason.

He straddled the girl's chest and forced her
to do what he wanted. She pleased him and I
thought he was going to let her up, but he stayed
on her like that until he was ready again and
made her do it again. The girl could barely
breathe. When I saw that he wasn't going to let
up on her, I pulled him off her, untied her, and
let her go.

He was totally vicious, Selma. I'd never seen
him like that before. He was wild-eyed and out of
control. He was so volatile I had to hold him
back. He started yelling at me and telling me he
wasn't done with her and how he was sick of
whores coming to our room. He told her if he saw
her again on campus he was going to finish the
job. He wanted to kill that girl and she knew it.
She was so hysterical they ended up taking her to
the college sanitarium."

"What made him act lack that, Diamond?"

"I really don't know, Selma. Maybe he had a
flashback of some sort. But he's never really
discussed any past molestation of any sort with
me. Maybe he'd taken some drug that I didn't know
about. It could have been the mixtures of
alcohol. It could have been a number of things,
Selma. We'd been partying all night."

"Did she tell oan Anthony?"

"I don't think so because no one ever said
anything to him. She was probably too frightened
to talk about it.

I think of that night quite often, too, Selma. Sometimes it makes me cry and I wonder how I did something like that to such a pretty little thing—to any woman. All she wanted was for one of us to like her. To this day, I don't know if that girl ever got right again. What I do know is that it made me wake up. At the rate me and Anthony were going someone was bound to get hurt more seriously. I got my own room, explained to the other guys what had happened, and we stopped the orgies. We were lucky that none of us ended up in jail and that none of those other girls ever got hurt more seriously.

The same way you feel about Clark being your doom, Sadaya's mine. Everything that I did to those girls, someone's either forced my baby to do or she's done them willingly. So you're right, Selma, you have to be very careful about what you do in life. It can fall back on you and your family members."

"At least you kinda helped that girl, Diamond. If I woulda come out the closet that night, y'all wouldn'tna sent huh tuh that mental ward."

"That's possible, but you only saw a mild case of what we were capable of."

"Y'all was worse!"

"A lot worse."

"I caint even imagine that, Diamond."

"I'm not going to lie to you, Selma. Most of the time there would be more than Anthony and me. We did some horrible things to those girls. We'd tie girl's hands together, in the front or back of them and take turns sodomizing or anything else we'd want to do to them in front of a crowd. Sometimes we'd have two females who were friends in the same room tied up like that and facing each other so that they could see and hear each other suffer. We embarrassed them, to amuse us."

"What made y'all do thangs lack that, Diamond?"

"We saw those girls as freaks and whores. We didn't see them as human. We thought we were better than them. We felt as if we could do what we wanted to them and anyone else and it was all right. In our minds we were the great jocks, the masters of the campus, the most popular, the best-looking, and the most important guys on campus. We felt that no one could touch us no matter what we did.

When the abusive parties ended we'd all sit around getting high, and bragging about who'd been the cruelest. We'd talk about the girls as if they weren't real. We believed that any woman who would willingly lay up with a bunch of men just to be popular knew what to expect from them."

211

"But them poor girls had tuh be screamin they heads off lack crazy. Lack that girl you and Anthony had with y'all that night."

"They would. Sometimes we'd gag them, at other times, if we were drunk enough, we didn't care."

"Where did such young men lack y'all, pick up the act uh sodomizin somebody?"

"I don't know about the others, and I never asked them. I'd been introduced to various kinds of it by some of my aunt's girlfriends when I was very young. Several of them molested me when I was young, and liked that kind of sex, even preferred it."

"Oh my God, Diamond, I nevva knew that!"

"It's true, Selma."

"I believe you, Diamond and um sorry."

"Selma, don't feel sorry for me, feel sorry for those old women. When I realized what they'd done to me nothin could stop me from doing what I saw fit for retribution. Some of um couldn't finish what they'd started and I threatened to tell my aunt, their boyfriends, husbands, or whoever would listen to me if they didn't do whatever I wanted. Unfortunately, my abusive ways spilled over into my college life. I'd abuse those girls out of lust and revenge. Sometimes while I was abusing them, I'd pretend they were one of my aunt's friends. I'd remember how one of them would get me drunk, or catch me off guard

and seduce me. That would make me more forceful
and brutal."

"Diamond, how can a woman force a man tuh
have sex with huh?"

"Selma, when an adult offers you something to
drink when you're young you think they understand
you. You trust them.

The first one got me falling out drunk when I
was sixteen. She called my aunt and told her I
wasn't feeling well and that I was going to lie
down at her place for a while. I thought she
meant well, but she ended up performing oral sex
on me while I was in a semiconscious state and
told me it would be our secret.

She told me how gorgeous I was, how I should
be pampered that way all the time, and to never
allow those young girls to talk me into having
any other type of sex with me unless they were
good enough. She never gave me a chance to
respond. She told me if I liked what she'd done
to me to come over or call and she'd be there for
me. For assurance, she did it again before I
left. I began to go to her house regularly. This
went on for quite a while.

She knew that I was hooked so she made me an
offer that I couldn't refuse. I'd have sex with
her or the sessions would stop. She was the first
to teach me about different types of sex. The
next two got me drunk after I tried to cry on

their shoulders about what happened to me with the first one and they ended up seducing me the same way. The only difference was they never got me to have sex with them until I got ready, and that usually wasn't until all I could think about was what they'd done to me after trusting them and how much I wanted revenge. I'd gotten hip to their tactics and wouldn't return after that.

The last two caught me off guard. One caught me as I was coming out of her bathroom, and the other while I was naked and sleeping by what I called my swimming creek.

The one by the pond kept up with me and became my live-in maid some years later. I didn't recognize her until after we'd hired her. Actually, Sheila wanted to hire her, I didn't. I thought she was much too young and inexperienced. Boy was I wrong. She was experienced alright, but in the wrong area. She'd flirt with me and try to entice me."

"How could she do that with Sheila rat there in the same house, Diamond?"

"She'd leave her bedroom door open so that I could see her nude. She'd purposely rub up against me anytime Sheila wouldn't be around. Once she even pretended to faint so that I'd carry her to her room. As soon as I lay her on the bed she threw both arms around my neck and pulled me to her and kissed me. When I refused her, she exposed her breasts to me and asked me to make her feel good. It was a struggle not to comply. She had the body of a goddess. She was beautiful.

One morning, I woke up to what I thought was my Sheila having sex with me. She'd climbed on top of me and her hair had fallen into my face. Being half-asleep, it took a minute to sense it wasn't Sheila and to realize Sheila had just cut her hair...well, that, along with the feel of her body, and the sound of her voice when she began to moan and call out my name was some other clues.

I was holding on to her hips and enjoying her, but I immediately tried to push her away when I became coherent enough to realize that it wasn't Sheila, but just like at the creek, I was no match for that innocent looking serpent. I'd never had a woman who was as sexually aggressive as she was with me. Later I made her pay for her aggressiveness. I felt as if she'd emasculated me.

Sheila left me not long after that but not because of her. That didn't matter to me though. I made her pay for it anyway. I also hadn't gotten over the anger I felt for her somewhat molesting me at the creek. I initiated a relationship with her and I wanted it to be a cruel, vengeful one. I did it slowly, but I began abusing her physically, mentally, and sexually. During this time she thought that I didn't recognize her from the creek. One night she upset

Sadaya. So for what I thought would be one of my final vengeful gestures I reminded her of it and forced her to repeat what had happened there. During the entire time I'd been abusing her, up until that night I'd never even mentioned oral sex to her although I'd been exceptionally intimate with her. The special attention was to keep her attached to me. I wasn't as willing to let her go as I was the others. I was willing to let her slide for a long time because of her body, the way she looked, and made me feel, but that night triggered the beast in me. She could see the coldness in my eyes and began begging me not to make her do it. She was saying "Please, Diamond, please! I'll do what you want, but not while you're angry, please! I know that you're going to make this painful somehow!" She was right, but her plea fell on deaf ears. I always made my victims pay the maximum price and that's all she was to me at that point and she knew just how cruel I could be when I was upset.

When Sadaya went to bed I turned into a monster. When I entered her room she was sitting on her bed crying, with her arms wrapped around her waist, and rocking. The first thing I did was backhand her as hard as I could. She went flying off the bed onto the floor. I straddled and beat her. I drug her back to the bed and tied her face down on it and beat her some more with my belt like she was a slave, because that's the way I felt about her—about every woman who acted the way she did with me. Her back and behind were red and full of welts. While she was still tied down, I forced indecent sex on her and held her mouth so tight she couldn't scream. Her lips bled. Then I told her, "Seduce me, Daijah, seduce me like you did the day at the creek!" I said it wickedly too, and forced her to do it. I even made her stay in her room so that Sadaya wouldn't see how I'd beaten her.

Sadaya was very close to Daijah. To keep Sadaya away from Daijah's room, I pretended Daijah was real sick with something contagious that I wasn't afraid to get, but didn't want Sadaya to get and served Daijah her meals in her room. I would even wrap Daijah in blankets to transport her back and forth to the bathroom so that Sadaya wouldn't see the bruises.

I had a doctor come in to look at her. I told him one of her boyfriends had beat her and that she didn't want anyone to know. We're good friends and he never mentioned it after examining her. As soon as I found out she'd be okay the sexual misconduct started again. And it didn't stop until my rage ended and depending on how insulted I felt that could take months sometimes, and hurting my baby was almost the biggest insult someone could impose on me, and I was determined to make Daijah pay for that.

In the shower I'd let the water get as hot as I could stand it. She could never take it. When it got hot enough, I'd call her in. If she'd hesitate I'd drag her in and slam her, face first into the tiles and brutally rape her. I remember her crying like a little baby—like she'd been defeated and there was nothing left to live for. That wasn't enough for me. When that was over I'd drag her out and force her to please me and continue talking about the creek and the morning she'd seduced me—no the morning she raped me was the way I'd say it. I can't believe my heart was so cold and wicked, Selma. It makes me sick just thinking about the things I did to her and made her do to me that night and the days that followed."

"Diamond, who wouldn't feel vengeful, evil and dirty afta what they did tuh you? Even Christians feel lack gittin back at somebody every nigh 'n' then whether they do it uh not.

People nasty these days, Diamond, they don't care who they hurt just as long as they git what they wont.

I know how you feel, Diamond. I done been betrayed many times. When I was younga this woman who was supposed tuh be my friend cooked up what I believe was a scheme with this man. He fixed my car and charged me mo' than double what I owed. I was keepin my susta's kids at the time and was

strugglin tuh keep um fed. My, "so-called friend"
knew this. What She didn't know was that I knew
she was havin an affair with this man. I've been
quiet about it fuh almost twenty years."

"Why would she do that to you, Selma?"

"Jealousy! Huh and huh sustas was always
jealous uh me and was always talkin 'bout me.
Shoot, they was always talkin 'bout everybody
lack they had the market cornered oan looks 'n'
perfection uh somethin. But them was some uh the
homeliest gals I'd evva seen befo' in my life and
they was always talkin 'bout somebody, I just
couldn't understand that."

"That's sad, Selma, real sad, and low."

"You thank that's sad and low? Listen tuh
this. She knew that I was in love with this boy
and was goan marry him...that was fo' I went tuh
college. She got tuhgetha with this woman who
knew one uh the girls who had a baby from him and
was givin out information 'bout me and him. She
did everythang she could tuh help break me and
that man up. She was wicked. She was angry 'cause
I'd tol' huh how close me and him was and she
ain't nevva experienced nothin lack that with a
man uh nobody else.

I shoulda got suspicious 'bout huh when he
stopped talkin negative 'bout huh and all of a
sudden took up fuh huh one day.

I didn't try tuh git back at huh, I just
prayed, watched, and waited oan God. Sho' nuff,
huh life was almost destroyed.

What she couldn't conceive was that huh life
stayed full uh turmoil 'cause uh huh ways.

Tuh this day, when I talk about this mutual
friend uh ours she goes back and tells that too.
I ain't supposed tuh know that.

She even be tellin my in-laws thangs I be
sayin. Maybe she don't know this, but that's why
I tells huh thangs 'bout um. They just lack
Clark, they ain't the sweetest people tuh call
friends, either."

"Why, Selma? What gain can she get from
that?"

"Diamond, she the kinda person who wonts tuh
be lacked the best by everybody and know
everythang 'bout everythang, and everythang 'bout
everybody. She always had tuh know mo' 'bout
everybody than I did and would be tryin tuh keep
up with whatevva I did. She'd even try tuh buy
everythang I bought, or if I'd pick out a name
fuh one uh my nieces uh nephews, she'd make sho'
tuh steal it and give it tuh somebody else tuh
use. She even bought a piece uh furniture lack
the one I said I was goan buy, then got mad at me
'cause I changed my mind and bought somethin
different."

"Selma, she sounds like she needs a
psychiatrist."

"I thank she do. I see rat through huh, but she tries tuh hide huh real character from people. Fuh these reasons this child's life is always in turmoil. I kept tryin tuh tell huh that jealously, wickedness, and evil doins would kill people. All she would evva say was; "I know, I don't know why people act the way they do."

I thank huh susta's need a psychiatrist too. One of um didn't wont tuh pay no rent. She got tuh messin 'round with huh landlord. He was pretty well tuh do. She got him tuh smokin that crack stuff. Just lack Clark had got this young girl he had strung out, she'd tol' him it was finely ground weed mixed with a little cocaine in a pipe. He smoked it once, lacked it, and couldn't quit. He kept goin 'round tuh that gal's house 'til he got strung out. His habit got worse and worse. He started losin thangs left and right, includin weight. First he lost his job, then his family and house. He had these antique cars, and one by one, he sold um all. He was so desperate he practically gave them cars 'way. That man had no idea that stuff was goan make him lack that. He didn't know it was lack bein addicted tuh a no good somebody...that once you touch it, if it make you feel good enough you ain't able tuh leave it 'lone."

"Selma, lots of landlords smoke that stuff. A lot of professional people do too."

Lee Charles

"I've heard that, Diamond and I found out
it's true. I saw my ex-doctor, and me and Clark's
ex-lawyer comin out of one of them crack
houses...two different crack houses. I guess they
ain't met up with each other yet."

"You never know, Selma. They try to keep
those things a secret."

"Well. It wadn't no secret from me afta that
day. I stopped doin business with both of um."

"Maybe your so-called friend was on that
stuff, too, Selma. That could be the reason why
she acts the way she does. Maybe you should cut
ties with here, too."

"Diamond, that's funny, but that stuff she
done tuh me don't even matta no mo'. I prefer tuh
be a comfort tuh people not a thorn in they
side."

"Selma, I believe you. You've always been
there for me even if we did make the mistake of
having sex that one night."

"Diamond, if we goan be honest, let's be
honest. Even though I wonted tuh git back at
Anthony that wadn't no mistake, we both know
that. I knew you wonted me and I wonted you too.
My biggest reason fuh dressin up so special when
I'd come tuh see Anthony was fuh you.

Anyway, I always thought Anthony was gay 'til
that night I caught y'all with that girl. He'd
nevva had sex with me."

"You're, kidding!"

"No, Diamond, we nevva did."

"I know you tol' me he got married, but tell me Diamond, is he gay?"

"Selma, why—

"Was he? I know that you know, Diamond."

"Well, he'd had some thoughts that he might be, but that was all he'd ever said to me about it back then."

"You tellin me the truth?"

"What difference does it make, Selma? He's married now and so are you!"

"It makes a lot uh difference. I felt sick afta seein him and you with a woman. He'd nevva as much as asked me fuh a kiss. I thought you and him was, you know..."

"Makin out, Selma? Is that what you're trying to say?"

"I guess it is."

"No, sweet, sweet Selma, we never made out!"

"What about all them rumors I heard about him and men?"

"I don't know, Selma; I never heard any rumors... honestly."

"Oh, I didn't know that."

"OH! So the truth comes out, huh, Selma!"

"Whatchoo mean, Diamond?"

"I mean, the real reason why you were hiding in the closet. You weren't just curious about Anthony cheating on you. You were curious about Anthony cheating on you, with me."

"Naw, Diamond—not really—that's silly."

"Yes you were, Selma and I'm not being silly. I know what, "not really" means."

"What did you think you were going to see, Selma? A couple of jocks gettin it on?"

"Diamond, um sorry! I didn't mean tuh offend you! Really, I didn't!"

"Then why would you question me about Anthony's and my relationship? Why do you still care? Why do you keep on questioning me about his sexuality in different ways?"

"Diamond, I said um sorry."

"I know, Selma, but you somehow push me into giving you dirty details that are better left in the past."

"So you do know somethin!"

"You see what I mean, Selma! You ask people questions and if what they have to say is too difficult for you to digest you become angry or judgmental."

"No I don't!"

"Oh, you don't! Then what do you call suspecting Anthony and me of being sexual partners, Selma?"

"Diamond, that was a perfectly reasonable assumption. I tol' you, he'd nevva tried anythang with me!"

"Selma, this is not the first time you've done that. You've always judged situations by the way they looked."

"I didn't realize I did that. I really didn't Diamond."

"Selma, just as well as me, you're a Christian. We have to begin to look at others and ourselves differently and work on our negative characteristics. We're now, God's disciples."

"Diamond, how did you get all of that out of what I asked you? All I wanted was a truthful answer."

"Selma, I have no problem with that, and God probably doesn't either. What I do have a problem with is when I give you the truth you act as if the person who told you is the one who committed the sin or injustice against you. If you can't accept the total truth, you're going to have to stop asking questions that you don't want a truthful answer to. People are going to tell you some of what you do and don't want to hear. No one can tailor make an answer for you.

Please, Selma, for your own well being; leave the subject of Anthony's sexuality alone. If or when God gets ready for you to find out those things about Anthony, he'll show them to you.

Enjoy your new husband and babies, Selma. Promise me you'll do that, Selma."

"But—

"No, "buts'" Selma, promise me you'll put the past away where it belongs. You won't survive if you don't."

Chapter 35

THE ARRIVAL

"Selma, Louise, Bess! I been knowin you since you was a chil' and I know you can do betta then that! Nigh, PUSH!"

"I cain't do it Doctor Leander, I cain't do it!"

"Yes you can!"

"Sweetheart, come on now, you have to try! Have you forgotten how badly we want these babies?"

"No, Paul, no!"

"Then we're going to make it happen together... Take a breath, Selma."

"UH-UH-UH-UH-UH-UH-P-A-A-A-A-A-UL...!"

"That's good, Selma, real good! Now relax and do the breathing patterns that you were taught in the natural child birthing classes...

"That's right, Selma Louise. Listen tuh yo', Yankee reverend husband!"

"Very funny, Dr. Leander...

"Paul, Paul, Paaaaaaaaul...!"

"I'm right here, Selma you're doing real good. Take my hand and squeeze it as hard as you want!"

Lee Charles

"Reverend, are you aware uh how strong these women git when they're in this condition?"

"Yes, doctor. I've walked many women through this procedure. I have very strong hands. I got them from doing strenuous farm work. I can't compare childbirth to what I've seen on the farm, but I've also helped the vet deliver many folds from the time I was six or seven—

"Dr. Leander—PAUL!"

"I'm sorry, Selma...SELMA, SELMA, I CAN SEE ONE OF THE BABIES, HONEY! IT'S COMING!"

"One mo' push, Selma, come oan, one mo'!"

"OKAY DR. LEANDER! OKAY...UH-H-H-H-H-H-H-H-H-H-H-H!"

"Good girl, Selma! Nigh bare with me, um goan cut the umbilical cord and let y'all hold it."

"Here's one uh yo' new babies, reverend."

"She's beautiful, Dr. Leander!"

"Is it a girl, Paul? Is it a girl?"

"Yes, and she's beautiful! Look, honey, look!"

"Hold oan nigh, here come the otha. Push Selma Jean, push!"

"UH-H-H-H-H-H-H-H-H-H-H-H-H-UH-H-H-H-H-H-H-H-H-H-H!"

"Come oan lil' one, come oan. Yo' parent's anxious tuh gitcha...It's another girl! Selma, Paul! I think they identical!"

"Oh my God! My babies are beautiful! Just look at um, Selma! Just look!"

"Mr. Bess."

"Yes, nurse?"

"They'll look more beautiful after they're cleaned up. I promise to bring them back as soon as I'm done."

"How are you feeling, Selma? Are you okay? Are you in pain?"

"Um in pain, but the doctor can give me somethin fuh it. All I wont is my babies rat nigh."

"Selma—

"Don't worry, Paul. I'll be okay."

"Selma, honey, this is one of the proudest and happiest days of my life. I can't begin to express the love that I have for you and our daughters."

"You don't have to, Paul. Some thangs don't hafta be said. Yo' smile tells me all I need tuh know."

Chapter 36

LATER AT THE HOSPITAL

"Hey Daizelle 'n' Bert. Y'all didn't hafta come way out here tuh see me."

"Selma, you know we wouldn'tna missed this fuh the world."

"Oh my goodness. Look at these babies, Bert. They angels, pure, angels. They beautiful."

"They sho' is, Daizelle. They just as pretty as they mamma. They must've had tuh knock you out extra with twins—Whatchoo name um Selma?"

"Well, Bert, Paul actually named um, Nina Cetedra and Nia Catraya, Bess. But we went natural with these babies."

"Lovely names, Selma, but I thought afta a certain age they gave C-Sections."

"They tried tuh talk me intuh that, but I insisted oan the natural, Bert, they just watched me extra close, that's all. It was tryin, runnin back 'n' forth tuh the docta, it was well worth it, but I ain't doin it again. And thank you fuh complimentin my babies names. But they should be lovely. It took us the full nine months tuh come up with um."

"Oh, girl, that ain't nothin, it usually does."

"Really, Bert?"

"Oh, yeah. Some people don't even be done namin they chil' 'til afta they done left the hospital."

"I didn't know that."

"Bert ain't lyin, Selma. Them baby names kin be somethin else tuh pick out."

"Then I guess um a betta mother than I thought, Daizell."

"Selma, you a perfect mother."

"Thanks, Daizell—Have a seat, y'all. I need tuh catch up oan what's been happenin 'round town."

"Girl, ain't nothin much been happenin. Since you moved out here with the rev, I don't hardly have nobody tuh talk to no mo', 'cept fuh Bert."

"You mean the crowd don't hang 'round the sto' and tree no mo'?"

"Well, they still shop there Selma, and hang 'round that old, good fuh nothin tree, but they don't stay long neitha places no mo'. They don't have nothin much tuh say or do with me. All them people use tuh come 'round tuh see you and Clark. Clark kept thangs jumpin and you was always sweet and encouragin."

"I ain't no perfect saint, Daizelle. Just lack everybody else, I got some changin tuh do too."

"Saint or not, you still sweet, Selma and you got a good heart, too.

People 'round town, includin me, feel yo' loss, I can tell by the looks on they faces.

Shoot, most everybody 'round there knows you was one uh the brightest lights that burnt in Casey Park. It just ain't the same withoutcha."

Chapter 37

THE ENCOUNTER

"Hey! I know you!"

"Don't tell me we went tuh school tuhgetha. You look young enough tuh be my daughter."

"Naw, naw. Didn't you know Clark Porter?"

"Yeah, baby...um the one who killed him."

"Miss, um so, sorry. Really, I didn't know 'bout that. I mean, I knew a woman had killed him, but I didn't know it was you."

"Then where do you know me from?"

"I know you from Clark. He tol' me you his wife."

"I still don't understand, honey."

"You know what, um sorry miss...

"They call me, Bert."

"Um sorry Miss Bert, if I had known—

"It's alright, honey...

"Call me, Motsey. My name, Motsey."

"Okay, Motsey. First of all I wonna letcha know that um gittin ova all the stuff that happened so don't let it worry you. Nigh, you was sayin?"

"Miss Bert—

"Just call me, Bert."

"Bert, I was just goan offer my condolences that's all. I just didn't know how tuh go 'bout it."

"Naw, naw, naw, nigh child, that ain't what you was talkin 'bout! You done gone this far, tell me the rest!"

"It's ova, Bert, let's leave it where it's at."

"It's ova fuh you, it's ova fuh his wife, it's ova fuh Clark, and it's ova fuh the people here in Casey Park. Motsey. Um still dealin with it. Nigh go head, tell me. Tell me 'bout him sayin um his wife...

...Don't be shame, don't drop yah head, Motsey, tell me."

"Okay, Miss Bert—I mean, Bert. My mamma wadn't home and he'd got me high oan crack and showed me some new sexual stuff. It was the first time I'd been with him sexually, at least real sex. He usually did all them otha thangs tuh me in his truck in back uh the all night sto', way back where all them trees 'n' stuff be growin when he was tryin tuh hook me. But he ain't nevva had sex with me there until he did git me hooked oan him and got me tuh smoke that crack. And the way he talked me into that was just horrible. Tuh this day, I don't even know why I done it there—maybe 'cause I thought I owed him fuh all the money and stuff he was given me and was guilty 'bout the way he was touchin me and I wadn't doin none uh that stuff back. Maybe I thought he wouldn't brang me nothin else tuh git high oan, uh touch me that way no mo', Bert! Maybe I was

234

too high that night! I'on know, Bert, but I let
somebody who wadn't worth the dirt oan my shoes
have me when I was still clean, Bert! And I'll
nevva git that back! Nevva git that back! It's
too late fuh me tuh change my mind!

*He wadn't even romantic uh nothin—he did all
that extra stuff tuh me befo' he ruined me so I'd
wont him, but he just wadn't romantic or gentle
when he took me. When he got hold uh me he just
about ripped me apart and I was a virgin, too...*
"Motsey? You cryin?"
"*Every time I thank about it I cry, Bert.*"
"Come oan, baby. You talk while we walk
'round this sto' lookin at all these fine
clothes, okay? That way, won't nobody notice yo'
tears but me."
"*Okay, Bert. We kin do that.*"
"Then go oan and finish talkin, baby. He
ain't here tuh hurtcha nigh."
"*I know.*"
"Then go oan and git it all off yo' chest,
baby. That's the only way you goan git ova' what
he done tuh you."
"*Okay, Bert, well, anyway, he was thankin
he'd start me out there just in case I made too
much noise, and he done right, 'cause lack I tol'
you, he ripped me apart in that car that night.
He didn't stop 'til he was good 'n' tired and I
was too hoarse from screaming, and wore out from
the struggle. I was too naïve tuh know it then,*

*and too ashamed and scared tuh believe it when I
did understand, but, Bert, he had a sex problem.
Only God saved me that night from his demon,
'cause as messed up as I was he tol' me tuh turn
ova' oan my stomach and I couldn't. When he saw
what condition I was in he tol' me nevva mind and
went in the back uh his truck and got some stuff
tuh clean me up. All the while he talked tuh me
real nice. He was makin sho' I wouldn't tell
nobody what had just happened. Then, he sat in
that truck talkin sweet tuh me and rubbin my
stomach while I was cryin and all cramped up. He
was tellin me that I was probably carryin his
baby. He was just talkin trash and stallin'. He
didn't wont no kids. He was just waitin 'til my
mamma left fuh work so that she wouldn't see what
he'd done tuh me. Bert. I had tuh literally crawl
up them steps tuh my bed that night. When I got
in the bathroom and got a good look at my
clothes, I thanked God that my mamma was goan tuh
work. I don't know what she woulda done if she'd
seen me lack that. Anyway, I took some aspirin
lack I do when I git my periods, and as bad as I
was still hurtin I washed them clothes out and
hid um in my room before I went tuh bed so they'd
be dry before I put um in with the laundry. My
mamma go ova every thang close and I know she
woulda asked me 'bout them clothes. She know when
my monthly come oan.*

I was limpin the next mornin when my mamma
got in and she asked me what was wrong. I tol'
huh that I'd fell and hurt myself at the sto' and
that's why I didn't git back home befo' she left
fuh work. She tol' me that she'd almost come
lookin fuh me. I tried tuh make it sound good by
sayin, "I wish you would have, mamma, I wish you
woulda" and I started cryin. She tol' me tuh stay
home that day with huh, but I tol' huh I'd be
okay and left the house lack I was goin tuh
school, but I really went lookin all around fuh
Clark."

"Didn't nobody see y'all uh hear you screamin
behind that sto', Motsey?"

"Naw, Bert, I fuhgot tuh tell you. He didn't
stay parked at the sto' that night. Afta he found
out it wadn't goan be that easy to you know,
penetrate me and how bad I was goan carry oan
while he tried, he took me someplace else. It was
far out, 'cause even all them trees and stuff in
the back uh that sto' couldn't cover up them
sounds."

"Here, Motsey. Here some tissue. Blow yah
nose."

"Thanks, Bert."

"Didn't you git scared when he changed up,
Motsey?"

"Naw, Bert. I figured I was with my man.
Wadn't no need fuh me tuh git scared. Bert, I
figured he'd leave his wife and marry me lack

he'd said, and we'd be doin that at my mamma's
house in huh basement while she was goan, anyway—
at least until he left his wife. See. He'd tol'
me how good he could handle women, any woman,
includin my mamma. He said that once she approved
uh him seein me he'd make huh thank that he
wadn't tryin tuh sleep with me 'cause he had too
much respect tuh do that. Then, he'd sneak ova'
and we could use the basement instead uh his
truck when we wonted tuh be tugethta. We both
believed that he could con huh and that he'd be
comin by my house afta' that, but that nevva
happened. We ended up usin his truck or some old
sleazy motel once he found out how my mamma is.
You see, he didn't dare come 'round when my mamma
was home. He was scared uh huh. She'd cussed him
out real good and threatened tuh kill him befo'
he even got through huh do'. She tol' him that he
must thank she crazy. That maybe I didn't, but
she knew 'bout him and his reputation 'round
town. She said that she'd have him put 'way fuh
messin with huh baby, but by the time the cops
would git tuh him they wouldn't have nothin tuh
cart off tuh jail, 'cause she'd be done cut him
up. She tol' him she'd start off with that part
she say most men thank with and end with his
scalp. She meant it too, 'cause she mean lack
that and I'd told Clark that befo' he even
attempted tuh go talk to huh, but he tol' me he
could handle huh, said he could handle any woman.
I'd begged him not tuh come 'round tuh my mamma's

house, Bert, but he did it anyway tryin tuh be
Mr. Big shot and thankin that no woman could
resist him. Bert. My mamma had Clark sweatin
bullets by the time she got through cussin him
out. She didn't know it was too late, that Clark
had done talked me in tuh lettin him be with me
in huh basement a few nights befo' that while she
was at work, and had already messed me up in his
truck afta that. And his main reason fuh comin
'round there that night was tuh git me again by
pretendin he was standin up tuh my mamma fuh our
love. That was his way of pretendin tuh apologize
tuh me about me bein mad with him fuh some ol'
silly mess that I don't even remember. What I do
know is that it was all phony and he was tryin
tuh impress me and my mamma at the same time, but
my mamma nevva let him in and I nevva got a
chance tuh say nothin tuh him that night. Afta'
she finished cussin him out she just slammed the
do' in his face. Then she cussed me out fuh him
comin 'round there. I was surprised when she
didn't punish me, and told me that she knew I
didn't know no betta and let it go.

She just didn't know, Bert. I wonted tuh see
him bad. I wonted to see him, real bad that
night. 'Cause lack I said, afta that night he'd
messed me up I hadn't seen him fuh a while. Bert.
I was sufferin from lovesickness and I was ready
fuh him tuh take me again.

Befo' all that happened he'd usually be
waitin fuh me at the all night sto' every
Wednesday and Friday at seven. That way I could
tell my mamma I was goin tuh the sto' and be back
befo' she'd miss me, but he stopped bein there
afta' all that happened. He'd even bought me a
pager so that he could git a hold uh me, but he
wadn't pagin me. I had tuh lie tuh my mamma 'bout
that pager, too—Oh, wait a minute. I remember
what I was mad about—why he was pretendin tuh be
so polite tuh my mamma and stuff. It seemed as
soon as he'd finished ruinin me that night he
brought me home and left my house, even afta' I'd
begged him tuh take me with him so that I
wouldn't hafta face my mamma alone. He tol' me
tuh stop poutin, whinin, and givin him uh hard
time. That I was actin lack a silly baby, then he
walked out oan me. The next day when I felt
betta' and went lookin fuh Clark and couldn't
find him I went tuh meet up with some uh my
friends instead, 'cause I was mad about Clark not
callin uh comin' 'round afta' he'd got what he
wonted. I took the shortcut through Feld's Alley
and saw his car parked there. You was sittin in
his truck and he was beatin you and you was
cryin. Then I saw him grab a hand full uh yo'
hair. It was light and shorter then, but he had a
good hold oan it and he forced yo' head down. He
was the first man who'd evva done somethin lack
that tuh me, so it didn't take me long tuh figure
out what he was makin you do.

I could feel the blood rush tuh my face and my ears started burnin. Instead uh hangin out with my friends, I ran back home cryin.

When I finally saw Clark again I tol' him what I'd seen that day afta' he'd ruined me. That's when he tol' me you was his wife. I tol' him I was jealous and didn't lack what I'd seen. He tol' me if I didn't wont his wife doin stuff lack that tuh him I'd hafta learn. Shoot. I didn't know how tuh do none uh that stuff so I just went oan back home all depressed 'n' junk. The next thang I knew he come 'round tuh talk with my mamma, and that's when she cussed him out. He ended up pagin me the next day so that I could meet him at the all night sto'. He got me real high that time and he showed me what tuh do. At the end of our relationship I found out he was just gittin back at my mamma through me fuh the way she treated him. Bert, once I started, he wouldn't let me stop. From then oan he used and abused me. The beatins, name callin, and me bein forced tuh do whatever he wonted seemed lack it didn't have no end."

"Baby, Clark was lack that all right.

Chil', once you started somethin with him you'd betta be able tuh go as far as he wonted you tuh, or you'd pay his price."

"I know that, Bert, but most uh the time I didn't care, 'cause he kept me high."

"Motsey, he done me the same way, only he ain't nevva got me high, not fuh free anyway, and he ain't nevva repaid none uh the favas I done fuh him. The time you saw him beatin me and forcin me tuh be good tuh him was somethin he did tuh me oan a regular basis. Specially when eitha' you wouldn't uh couldn't."

"So. He musta been with you all that time I hadn't seen him afta my mamma had cussed him out."

"Maybe he was, Motsey, 'cause he'd been hangin 'round my house all that week makin me do thangs and I wonted tuh git rid uh him real bad. It was gittin harder and harder fuh me tuh figure out what tuh do with my kids, and he was treatin me bad every day he was there, too. He did them same thangs tuh me the night I killed him, only difference about that time was that I thought fuh sho' he was goan kill me, first."

"Bert, what really happened that night?"

"Well, Motsey, first of all I gotta tell you this. He was my best friend's husband—

"So what? A lot of the females I know do that. If a man wont you he just wont you. So what!"

"Motsey. You and yo' friends betta wake up and learn somethin'. Men that mess with family and friends is just lack Clark was, no good. And no matter what you hear, you don't need tuh mess with nobody else man, especially yo' friend's uh family's. First of all, every time you have sex

with somebody you havin sex with everybody they
done had sex with. And believe it uh not, each
time you back do' somebody close tuh you it's
goan come back on you in a way you cain't handle.
And a man that will cheat with you oan somebody
else will cheat oan you with somebody else,
'cause ain't no ethics in cheatin, baby, ain't no
ethics in cheatin.

I'd been flirtin with Clark 'cause I was
heavy and thought I couldn't git no other man. I
knew he had a reputation as a lady's man, uh
who'eish, uh howevva you wonna put it, and
figured he'd be easy tuh lay with and nobody
would evva know, not even Selma, his wife and my
best friend. But baby! That mess caught up with
me when I least expected it! And it came fast and
hard, too...!"
    "Bert, I thought only men went afta women
that acted lack that."
    "Naw, honey, women do it too. Men just don't
see it lack that 'cause they men. A lot of um
thank it's okay fuh them tuh act who'eish...Okay,
nigh, where was I? Oh, yeah. I felt lack I
couldn't git nobody else 'cause I was ova weight.
So I'd flirt and flirt with Clark, because I just
knew that he was a sho' thang. All the rumors
about him led me tuh believe that. So. While my
best friend was out uh town and had me watchin
huh sto' I made my move. I waited fuh Clark tuh
git drunk, go up tuh they apartment, and fall

asleep in that old rocka uh his. When he woke up
I was kneelin in front uh him. He was so drunk
wadn't nothin he could do but react. When I was
done he mumbled, "Um goan git you." I thought he
was jokin uh talkin out a drunken head. The next
day he came by my house, and God knows I was
happy tuh see him. I thought that he was goan do
what I wonted, but he tol' me not until he'd got
what he'd come fuh. Afta I'd goan outta my way
fuh him he just up and left. The next day or so
while his wife was still out of town he started
up with me rat there in that sto' and I was
ready. What I wadn't ready fuh was the treatment
he give me. You see, Motsey, all the otha men I'd
done that to only wonted sex. Clark was
different. He wonted my soul if he could take it.
He started off by puttin his mouth oan my breasts
and makin me moan. Then he tol' me tuh git oan my
knees. Chil'! I remember the feelins that come
ova me that day as soon as he said that! I was
excited and breathin hard. I thought he was goan
make love tuh me lack that, but once he got me
down there he straddled my back. He musta cuffed
his hands tuhgetha 'cause I felt a sharp blow
against my neck and shoulders. I fell hard tuh
the flo'. When I tried tuh git up he done it
again and I stayed there feelin dizzy. Felt lack
my head was spinnin 'round and 'round. I could
feel him pullin my underclothes down—I knew what
he was goan do tuh me but all I could do was try
tuh turn over and beg him not tuh take me

unnatural. He pulled both my arms back and acted
lack he didn't even hear me. When I tried tuh
stop him he'd punch me in my face. He took
advantage uh me while I was lack that and I was
tremblin and scared tuh move.

Motsey, it was so painful I cried out fuh the
lord, 'cause Clark sho' didn't have no mercy oan
me.

When he got done messin me up and makin me do
all the thangs he wonted, he tow most my clothes
off and sent me half-naked into the streets."
"Is that the day you killed him?"
"Naw, but I shoulda, um gittin tuh that. I
thought I could whoop Clark afta that 'cause he
was so small and he'd caught me off guard that
day in the sto', so I tried him the first time he
come 'round tuh my house with that mess. He
grabbed me by my legs and slammed me oan the flo'
so many times I saw stars.

The whole time I was messin 'round with him,
he was forcin hisself in my house, makin me wash
his clothes, cook fuh him 'n' anythang else he
wonted, and I have kids, too, Motsey!"
"Yeah, Bert, I know, you tol' me that
already."
"Oh, yeah, I did, didn't I?"

"Yeah, Bert. You tol' me that. See. Clark still gittin tuh you, too. He musta really did treat you as bad as he treated me."

"Naw, Motsey. He treated me worse. But the thang about it, my kids nevva seen him hit me. They just thought he was a man that wonted me and I didn't wont him, but I helped him out from time tuh time. They thought that I'd be sendin them up tuh they room and different places so that me and him could talk. He'd take me in the basement tuh abuse me if they was home, uh wait 'til I'd find someplace tuh send um fo' he'd abuse me so that they wouldn't know, and I had tuh beg him tuh do that! He even threatened tuh mess with my daughter 'cause he said I'd ran my mouth too much about his business one time, and I had tuh beg him not tuh do that, too. To this day I still thank he found a way tuh do somethin to huh. She started runnin every time she saw him afta' he'd made that threat."

"Bert, did you ask yo' daughter if he'd done somethin to huh?"

"Naw. She seemed tuh git betta once she found out he was dead. But I thank he touched huh 'cause when he was with me one time he said, "Yo' daughter softer then you." That made me scream and he threatened tuh wake huh up if I didn't shut up, so I shut up screamin real quick. When he finally left me 'lone I ran up them steps real quick and examined my baby. But she didn't have no marks uh nothin oan huh—nothin tuh indicate

that Clark had been with huh. God knows that man
loved messin 'round with young gals. But I was
determined tuh always be one uh his women no
matta what, and I cain't believe how I just about
sacrificed my children tuh do it.

I knew 'bout you, Motsey, but I hadn't seen
yah. See; he'd always talk about his, young,
yella gal, wadn't doin right, and he needed tuh
be treated right. Believe me, when you wadn't
actin right I didn't only hear 'bout it I'd feel
the pain.

Believe it uh not, Motsey, as nasty as he was
tuh me I thought I loved him even afta he'd
slowed down messin with me, but thangs got worse.
Afta Selma put him out he left me 'lone
completely and I couldn't handle it. I lost ova
eighty-five pounds from worriation 'n' love
sickness. All I did was drank, thank 'bout him
and who he might be sleepin with, 'cause I wadn't
hearin 'bout the yella gal no mo'. Fuh some
reason him sayin that gave me sort of a sense of
security."

"Why, Bert, why would him tellin you 'bout
another woman make you feel secure?"

"In my mind I thought that was my way of
keepin up with him when he wadn't 'round."

"But, Bert, he'd been layin up with me and
then he'd come tuh you. I was usin all them
drugs! I coulda been messin 'round with more then

Clark tuh git high! The only reason why I wadn't
was 'cause Clark was keepin me fed, but—

"I know, Motsey, I know, but I was weaker
then, much weaker and he'd beat me whenever I'd
call myself reminded him uh what he was doin with
you uh what I heard you was into.

Anyway, I knew where he was stayin afta he'd
left Selma. I made sho' I didn't lose him all
tuhgetha and I went there. It was late so I took
my gun fuh protection. When I got there what I
saw made me crazy. He had a little gal all jacked
up ginst the wall 'n' she was screamin—well, I'd
seen him messin with that chil' earlier, but
didn't have nerve enough tuh say nothin and kept
goin past his room—

"He had his do' open, Bert?"

"Yeah, Motsey and he acted lack he didn't
care—lack it wadn't no big deal! All the while he
was with that gal he was moanin and stuff lack
he'd nevva had sex befo'. I started yellin. He
let go uh that gal, she fell tuh the flo', then
jumped up and ran. He said tuh me in a real nasty
tone, "You see whatchoo done let git 'way," and
reached fuh me. He beat me and forced me tuh do
what you'd seen when you was comin through the
alley, and I could smell that otha female oan
him, too. Then he raped me unnaturally as many
times as he could, makin me feel the dampness of
what he'd done tuh that chil' oan my bare skin.
All that had me crazy enough, but then he beat me

some mo', and I thought he was goan kill me,
Motsey. He was oan somethin that night. Somethin
that had him extra crazy. He beat me so bad my
eyes was almost swollen shut. All I could see was
this blurry figure comin near me, that I thought
was him, and if he got hold uh me again, he was
goan kill me.

You know, Motsey, at times, we be sittin
'round feelin bad and miserable about different
thangs that make us feel lack we wont tuh die.
But um goan tell you somethin. When you lookin at
death straight oan lack I was, reality be starin
back cold 'n' hard and you change yo' mind real
fast. 'Cause as miserable as I thought I was, and
as much pain as I was in, I still didn't wont tuh
die. The thought of him killin me just about
scared the life outta me. And when he reached fuh
me again I could feel death comin. My whole life
flashed before my eyes.

I remembered the gun, went intuh my coat
pocket, and pulled it out. I shot until I saw him
fall tuh the flo', or what I thought was him fall
tuh the flo'.

It was a good thang that I'd parked my car
close tuh the hotel, 'cause I wouldn'tna nevva
made it tuh the hospital by myself if I hadn't.

Um sorry I killed him and um sorry I messed 'round with my best friend's man. Nigh I got tuh live the rest uh my life with both them thangs oan my conscience, and always wonderin if he really did touch my daughter Lashella."

"Bert? Yo' daughter named Lashella?"

"Yeah. Why, Motsey?"

"Bert. I gotta tell you somethin...

"Oh, no. He did mess with my baby, didn't he, Motsey?"

"Bert. He picked huh up from school one mornin while he was drivin his wife car. I was in the car with him. I'd been skippin uh lotta school myself, rat before I got totally strung out oan that stuff and left home. He tol' me tuh wait in the car he had tuh go pick up his niece. I don't know what he tol' them at that school, but she came out holdin oan tuh Clark's hand. He was smilin from ear tuh ear, and she was skippin and sangin lack she was really his niece, and I didn't thank nothin of it.

Bert. I thought him pickin me up in the mornin time and him makin all them plans the night befo' fuh me tuh meet him at a certain time and place and him bein extra nice was strange, but I just thought he was changin 'n' stuff. He'd tol' me that he was goan make up fuh mistreatin me and I assumed the way he was actin was part of it. When he picked me up that mornin and tol' me we was goin tuh the amusement park I was excited

and I just figured him takin his niece with us
was a nice thang fuh him tuh do. I was excited
about goin and at huh age I woulda wonted tuh go
too if my uncle woulda came tuh school and got
me, so I thought it was cool. He put huh in the
back seat and tol' huh tuh put huh seat belt oan.
When we got tuh the park he gave me some money
and tol' me tuh go ahead and git the tickets that
him and Lashella would be in afta' he parked the
car. They was takin too long so I walked around
that parkin lot fuh almost an hour befo' I found
Clark's car. At first I thought they'd gotten out
and was oan they way inside until I noticed
Clark's hat. He'd got in the back seat and had
his back sorta tuh the window and seemed tuh be
strugglin uh somethin'. It was lack I was walkin
up tuh that car in slow motion. When I got close
enough I heard Lashella sayin stop it you hurtin
me, you makin me burn. Lashella was still sittin
oan the seat, and I could see Clark's hand under
huh dress and she was tryin tuh push it away. I
froze rat there. Then I heard him tell huh tuh
quiet down he wouldn't do that no mo' and that
he'd let huh out the car so that she could go in
the amusement park if she just laid oan the seat
until he was done. Lashella wouldn't listen tuh
him and he pushed huh back oan the seat with one
hand tuh hold huh down pulled huh panties down
with the otha, then put his head down. Befo'
Lashella made any sounds I knew what was
happenin, but that's when I figured out why he'd

even bothered tuh brang me along. I was just
extra bait. I made it easier fuh huh tuh trust
him enough tuh git in his car—

"Why didn't you stop him, Motsey? Why you let
him hurt my baby?"

"I was too scared, Bert. All I could remember
was what he'd done tuh me and this otha' girl
befo' and I didn't wont him tuh go no further
with Lashella. Bert, I figured if he knew that
I'd seen what had happened he'd make us both go
through some worse stuff than that and I didn't
wont Lashella tuh be anotha' me, anotha' one uh
Clark's nothin's. Bert, um sorry, but I figured
if I just waited 'til he did that, me and
Lashella would be okay. So when I heard her make
that sound that I was so familiar with I started
callin Clark's name and then said, oh there y'all
is I thought ya'll had gone inside and I'd missed
y'all. I saw Lashella pullin up her underwear
real fast, but I asked him why he was in the back
seat, because I knew if I ignored that he'd git
suspicious and would figure out that I'd seen
what he'd done, and me or Lashella wouldn'tna
been safe afta that. He told me that he was
chastisin huh about that seat belt and showin huh
why it was a good idea tuh wear it, because she
didn't put it oan when he tol' huh to back at the
school. Although I knew she had put it oan, I
didn't say nothin 'cause he was capable of doin
too many mean thangs. When he let Lashella out
the back seat she was still snifflin. I wonted

tuh hug huh, but I was too busy tryin tuh figure
Clark's next move. While I was thankin he grabbed
my arm and made huh walk ahead uh us. Then he
asked me what I'd seen. Bert, I knew that me and
huh had tuh make it back home with him so I
played crazy. I asked him what he was talkin
'bout, then I said, "Clark? Was you messin with
that baby uh somethin?" He kinda laughed and
said, "Naw, girl, naw. You know that ain't what
um about." So I asked him why he asked me that
question and he tol' me that he'd spanked huh and
thought that I'd turn him in fuh that. I tol' him
that I hadn't seen him spank huh, and he was okay
with that answer. Lashella finally stopped
snifflin and cryin, but was quiet the whole time
we was at the park. I made sho' I kept huh real
close tuh me while we was there. Clark sat oan
this bench in one spot until he decided it was
time fuh us tuh go. He wonted tuh drop me off
first and Lashella last. I talked him outta it. I
tol' him that it would be betta if he dropped huh
off at school. That if she played with the otha
kids fuh a while she'd probably fuhgit about the
whippin he gave huh and everythang would be okay,
that if she tol' he might git in trouble fuh
child abuse. He dropped us both off there. Said
he had tuh git the car back tuh his wife. I sat
outside with Lashella and waited fuh yo' otha'
kids tuh come out so that she'd have somebody she
really knew tuh walk home with huh, and tol' huh

not tuh evva again go home with nobody but the parent she live with, or huh brothas."

"She'd been havin nightmares, Motsey. She'd been havin nightmares and wettin the bed until she heard he was dead, and it's all my fault."

"Ms. Bert, I know I shouldn't say this, but um glad he ain't 'round here no mo'. He was lack a devil uh somethin. I heard he raped his eleven-year-old goddaughter, too. He didn't care 'bout nobody. He even killed my baby, that's probably why he dead."

"He killed yo' baby?"

"Yeah, he beat me and I lost it."

"What he beat you fo'?"

"It don't matter, Bert. He ain't got no right tuh be hittin oan me no matter what! But he beat me so I would lose the baby. I thought he was goan be happy 'cause uh what he said tuh me, and the way he treated me in his truck the first time we laid tuhgetha, and what he'd said that time he mistreated me and that girl, but he wadn't happy. He kicked me in my stomach and kept oan stompin me in my side and everywhere 'til he saw me bleed and my eyes roll back in my head. He was evil, Bert, *real* evil.

He took me tuh the hospital and pretended tuh be my daddy and made me tell a lie 'bout fallin down the stairs. They believed it and took care uh me. As soon as he saw I was goan be all right he come in that room and started messin 'round

with me. He fed me drugs and made me do
everythang but have sex with him rat in that
hospital room.

   Bert. I shoulda got away from that crazy man
the first time he hit me that day just because we
wadn't speakin and then forced hisself oan me
even afta I'd tol' him I didn't wont tuh see him
no mo'. I'll nevva fuhgit that day, Bert, that's
why I didn't wont tuh stop him too soon with
Lashella, 'cause this what happened tuh me and
that otha' girl I was talkin 'bout, my white
friend, Gail. We'd been ridin in huh car and was
stopped at a light. This gray car with light
tinted windows was in front uh us. I could see
one uh the men starin at us through the rearview
mirror and the otha' one was starin at us through
the passenger one. The man oan the passenger side
got out. It was Clark he was ridin with Otis Coy.
He headed fuh us. He snatched the car do' open
and Gail freaked. She started screamin, "Don't
hurt me, C! Don't hurt me!" I was lack, "*What*?
What she talkin 'bout?" Then, Clark said, "I
ain't afta you rat nigh old crazy, white trash,
um here fuh Motsey...git in the back seat,
Motsey! Git in the back seat!" I was arguin with
Clark when the light changed, cars was blowin at
us 'n' everythang, Clark didn't care. Finally I
gave up arguin and was gittin out. I wadn't movin
fast enough and he pulled me oan out the front
seat and throwed me back there. Gail was cryin,

cryin, cryin and sayin, "Please, just help us Jesus. Please, just help us." I was wonderin why she was so scared uh Clark. It all came tuh light afta he got me in that back seat.

I didn't wonna tell this, but Gail baby was back there screamin and cryin too.

Clark made Gail drive while he raped me 'n' stuff with huh baby in the back seat. When he got finished, I was sore and bruised from the beatin and what he'd done tuh me.

He started in oan Gail. Said he'd finally caught up to huh and was goan take care uh huh lack he'd promised he would if he evva saw huh again. She talked him in tuh lettin huh drive out some place. Bert. It just so happen tuh be the same place he was takin me every time he wonted tuh lay with me. She tol' me tuh take huh baby out the car and go sit by this big tree 'til it was ova.

At first Gail tried tuh fight him. I could hear him talkin tuh Gail. He was chokin huh and tellin huh tuh let him do what he'd set out tuh do or he'd kill huh and huh baby. She still didn't give up that easy. She was fightin him. Gail was screamin, the car was movin, and they was wrestlin 'round. One of um kicked the do' open and it stayed that way 'til Clark was satisfied. Bert, I thought I couldn't feel no dirtier, but when I saw what he was doin tuh Gail, I finished breakin down. I held oan tuh huh baby, threw up, and cried lack I was one, too.

Bert, that baby Gail had was his and he did some real nasty stuff tuh Gail that day because it was—because she'd had it! He did thangs tuh Gail I wish I could fuhgit. How can a person be so wicked and evil, Bert? He raped me with that baby in the car and was gonna rape it's mother in front uh him if Gail hadn't tol' me tuh go sit by that tree with him."

"GIRL, ARE YOU SERIOUS! THAT WAS REALLY HIS CHIL' HE DID ALL THAT IN FRONT UH YOU AND HIS *OWN*, CHIL'!"

"Yes ma'am. Gail went away tuh have that baby then came back. That's how come Clark didn't git tuh it. When she'd first tol' him 'bout bein pregnant, she say Clark whooped huh and left huh 'lone, 'cause he thought the baby wadn't goan make it. He said if it didn't die, the next time he saw huh, he was goan stomp huh, and kill it. Well, it didn't and he kept his promise, too— well, he didn't bother huh baby, and he really didn't stomp huh, but she probably wished he had after all he made huh go through. But she was still smarter then me. She left town tuh have that baby then came back."

"Motsey, I don't know if I'd call havin a baby by Clark a smart thang."

Lee Charles

"Well, Bert—

"Motsey! It was two uh y'all! Why didn't
y'all fight him uh tell oan him, uh somethin?"

"We tried tuh tell oan him, but by the time
we got smart, and brave enough tuh do that, I'd
just turned sixteen and Gail was eighteen. We was
both old enough fuh him tuh mess with. He tol' um
we was both messin with him and was jealous so we
teamed up against him. He said we'd lied about
our ages. That Gail was mad 'cause he left huh
afta she got pregnant and that I was jealous
'cause he had a baby by Gail and she was my
friend and a white girl. And if you know Clark
lack I do you know there wadn't no way me and
Gail was goan git the best uh him in no fist
fight. It take a woman lack my mamma tuh handle a
man lack Clark. He one uh them tall, thin men who
real solid and strong. He so firm you can see
them big veins uh his through his muscles. What
else can I say, Bert! He was just too strong fuh
us, Bert, and we knew that! We was both too
scared tuh try him! I guess we both figured we
couldn't win! We let him do what he wonted and he
let us go lack he promised. Only thang was he
made Gail drop him home while I was still in the
car. He didn't say a word the whole time. When he
got home, he took Gail by the arm and drug huh
out the car and took huh tuh the back uh his
house with him and stayed a long time. All I
heard was garbage cans movin and then some
moanin, lack Clark had his hand ova Gail mouth uh

258

somethin. I was so scared I thought I was goan
lose my mind. His wife must've heard it too. They
upstairs light came oan and I saw huh look out
the window. She didn't see me though. It was too
dark.

I couldn't help Gail and I tried hard not tuh
thank about what he was doin to huh. But I knew
it was somethin dirty. She'd had that baby he
didn't wont and she'd tried tuh fight him back
and I knew his mind stayed oan that the whole
time we rode. I don't know what happened back
there and I didn't ask Gail. But fuh him tuh take
huh outta my site, and the way Gail was cryin
when she got back in the car, it must've been
somethin real dirty, something real bad. I had
tuh drive huh home and spend the night with huh.
She wouldn't calm down. Gail almost lost huh
mind, too.

He'd hurt me, my friend, and disrespected his
own baby. I wonted tuh kill him, Bert, but lack I
said, I knew he was too strong even fuh the both
uh us. If we had jumped oan him and didn't beat
him good enough he was goan hurt us real bad,
Bert. Maybe even kill us and his baby. He was
downright filthy, but he caught me one day and
apologized real sweet. He tol' me he couldn't
stand me not talkin tuh him and what he'd done
tuh Gail he'd done it fuh our love. He lied and
said that if anybody was supposed tuh have his

baby I was. I was young and simple-minded, and
believed all them lies he was tellin me. And when
Clark done all them thangs tuh me again tuh prove
his love fuh me, gave me all that money, and got
me high! Shoot, Bert! I fuhgot he'd evva hit me
and Gail, disrespected his own chil' or been with
us tuhgetha, and I went back with him. The mo' I
got strung out oan them drugs the less I cared
about. He'd mistreat me mo', and make up less. I
was foolish enough tuh git pregnant thankin he
really wonted me tuh have his chil', would marry
me, stop messin 'round and stop hittin me
altogether and I thought I was in love with him
too. Bert. He was just too strong fuh me in every
way. My thoughts was that goin back tuh Clark was
betta then tryin tuh fight with somebody lack him
and havin tuh fend fuh myself tuh feed my habit."

"He was real strong lack you say, Motsey. He
probably woulda hurt y'all real bad if y'all had
tried tuh double team him and didn't git the best
uh him. He was crazy. But what I cain't
understand is why he didn't wont y'all tuh have
them babies. The way he lacked tuh brag, seems
tuh me he'd uh been proud tuh have a young gal
carryin his chil', Motsey. I don't mean no harm,
but especially a high yella one and a white gal."

"Naw, Bert, he didn't wont no kids outside
his house no matta what color they'd be. He'd
made that clear tuh me, fo' killin mine."

"I believe yah, Motsey, he was just that mean
and evil. But you know he paid that lesbian he

use tuh sit under the wine tree with tuh sleep
with him and have his baby...

"BERT! YOU MEAN, HERTHENIA?"

"Yep! He did it mostly tuh spite, Selma.
Herthenia knew it and kept oan seein him. She
couldn't leave Clark alone neither. She was one
uh the women goin tuh his hotel room oan a
regular basis. I found that out at the police
station and I'd seen huh there the night I killed
him. He was mistreatin Herthenia too. Motsey.
That man was purely, mean and evil."

"He was mean and he was evil, but I just
caint picture it, Bert..."

"Picture what, Motsey?"

"How you let a small man lack that, beat you
so bad, Bert?"

"The same way he beat you and Gail, Motsey!"

"But, Bert, you bigga then us."

"And there was two uh y'all. Wadn't it,
Motsey?"

"Yeah, but—

"But that don't necessarily mean nothin when
it come tuh the strength of a man, Motsey.
Besides, I wadn't eatin and takin care uh myself
lack I shoulda been, but if I had that still
wadn't goan be enough fuh me tuh whoop no man
lack Clark, or stop him from whoopin me.

I ain't goan deny it, Motsey. He done beat me
and broke my arm when I was heavier. He done beat
me, broke parts uh my body, and abused me

sexually fuh just sayin no when I was heavier. So
I know exactly what you and Gail went through
'cause I done suffered his abuse many, many
times. I can probably tell you exactly what he
done tuh Gail behind his house, and his wife
probably did see it. She looked the otha way when
it came tuh Clark's mess—his little problem. Lack
I tol' you, I even tried fightin him back when I
was put in the same position as Gail, but he was
too strong fuh me. The worst thang about it, he
wadn't doin none uh that stuff tuh his wife, at
least she never mentioned it tuh me and it made
me mad 'cause she nevva did.

Motsey, I remember the time he asked me tuh
cook him some greens, chitlins, cornbread, and
macaroni 'n' cheese. I tol' him I didn't know
how. He tol' me that was just lack tellin him no.
He made me git oan my knees lack a dog and
whooped me with a board. I ended up in the
hospital. My behind and insides was bruised up. I
was too afraid tuh tell the doctas what really
happened. If I had, um sho' I'd be occupyin that
grave instead uh him if he woulda spent even one
day in jail. But the worst whoopin I got was the
time I mentioned him rapin his eleven year old
goddaughter."

"So, it's true? He raped his own, god-child,
Miss Bert?"

"He took you and that chil' in his hotel room, Motsey! You say he was messin with my baby and you stopped him! What that tell you?"

"Well, he didn't do Lashella too bad and he didn't know that girl lack that and he ain't really raped me—at least not in the beginnin, we was messin 'round, but what made him wont a little girl he just about raised as his own?"

"Motsey. A man lack Clark kin git turned oan by most anythang, but he said he'd done it mostly tuh git back at me and his wife fuh tryin tuh talk 'bout him behind his back, and um sure he got afta' Lashella fuh the same reason, tuh git at me."

"Well, Bert. I do know one thang. He lacked tuh beat oan people and force hisself oan um."

"Motsey, it might sound crazy, but I lacked fuh him tuh beat me."

"WHAT! BERT! YOU CRAZY! YOU LYIN!"

"Naw, Motsey, you heard right, and yeah you right, I was stupid. I thought he loved me when he beat me and took what he wonted and I felt lack the worse the beatin the mo' he loved me no matta how much he said he didn't, or how bad he treated me."

"Um sorry fuh you, Bert, but I felt the opposite. When he hit me, I started hatin him. It's a shame, Bert, he dead and I still hate him."

"That's 'cause he killed yo' chil'."

"Naw, Bert, it's mo' then that. He didn't only kill my chil'; he killed the chil' in me."

"True, Motsey, but you goan hafta accept the fact that you allowed him tuh do it just lack I did."

"Nigh you sound lack him."

"Motsey, um only tellin you somethin you need tuh hear. We put ourselves in bad situations with a person and then we wonts tuh put all the blame oan the otha person. I knew Clark had threatened harm tuh my baby, but I wouldn't let go then, or even afta' I knew he didn't wont me no mo'. I coulda goan someplace that woulda helped me tuh git rid uh Clark but I didn't. You tol' me yo'self yo' mamma didn't approve uh Clark."

"She didn't."

"Why didn't she, Motsey?"

"'Cause, he was too old fuh me."

"You see, Motsey, that was a sign rat there...

"But, he didn't start off bein nasty. He was bein nice tuh me at first. He was always buyin me expensive clothes 'n' stuff and I didn't hafta work no summa job!"

"Laziness ain't no excuse, Motsey! Anythang given tuh yah fuh the wrong reasons, you won't keep! Anythang stolen is always repaid with a bigga price! Anythang yah hafta fight too hard fuh tuh git, uh keep, will always give yah trouble. When somethin fuh yah, it usually come tuh yah. When you s'ppose tuh fight fuh somethin,

God will show you what steps tuh take and he'll
do the rest! Workin hard towards a dream
different, but we have tuh choose our battles
wisely, we caint let um choose us."

"I realize that now, Miss Bert. But why did
you mess 'round with him?"

"'Cause, I just realized that too, but I was
a lot heavier and ignorant at the time and
thought I couldn't git nobody else. God done
show'd me different."

"You see, Bert, we both thought we had good
reasons!"

"CHIL'! MINE WADN'T NO BETTA!"

"How old you, Motsey, seventeen or eighteen?"

"Naw, Ms. Bert. Um sixteen. I'll be seventeen
next month."

"How old was yah when Clark ruined yah?"

"I'd just turned foeteen. Why is you askin me
all these stupid questions? What they got tuh do
with that low-lifeded man?"

"Everythang, Motsey, everythang, 'cause um
tryin tuh make a point! Nigh listen tuh me and
listen tuh me good. Thank you fuh savin my baby's
life, 'cause um sho' Clark woulda took it away
from huh somehow if you wouldn'tna stepped in.
'Cause I was shonuff too foolish tuh leave that
man alone although I love all my chil'ren the
same as yo' mamma love you. I know yah know that.
Dontcha, Motsey? You know yo' mamma love you,
dontcha?"

"Yeah, I know that, Bert."

"Then yah know she ain't goan tell you nothin wrong, nigh dontcha?"

"Yeah."

"So. When she run Clark from 'round y'all house and tol' yah he was too old fuh yah and no good, why didn't yah listen?"

"'Cause, I—

"'Cause, you thought you was grown."

"When yo' mamma run him from round yo' house you coulda stopped everythang rat there, but you didn't, Motsey. Once you made that decision everythang that happened afta that was really yo' fault."

"How can that be?"

"You have the ability tuh refuse a situation or accept it oan yo' own free will, but when yo' mamma ran him 'way that was yo' back up rat there.

Motsey, I know it's too late nigh, but them old men don't be doin nothin but feedin off uh young girl body just lack the old buzzards they is."

"My mamma said the same thang, Bert, but he used you too."

"Um old, baby—I still was wrong fuh what I did, but um old. When I met Clark I was old and I'd done lived some uh my life. Clark done used up all uh his, and some uh yo's."

"It don't even matta no mo', Bert, 'cause I know that feelin' lonely and a need fuh affection kin make yah wont tuh do a lot uh thangs, includin mess with the wrong people.

Nigh, I ain't goan jump up 'n' say that I ain't goan mess with nothin black no mo' lack a lot uh us do, 'cause I love my people, especially my brothas. Uh lot of um good and I know I was wrong, too. But I ain't goan nevva, evva, let no man, young uh old, white uh black, or no otha color treat me that way no mo', no matta what they got! And that's a promise um goan keep!"

Chapter 38

BERT'S DESTINY

"Selma, I wonted you tuh be the first tuh know. Um goin up tuh Bridgeway."

"Why, Bert. We done made friends nigh. We don't live that close no mo', but um just gittin use tuh havin you 'round again. Why you leavin Casey Park?"

"Selma, last night, I spent 'bout three uh fo' hours talkin tuh that chil' you and me use tuh call the young, yella gal."

"You mean the one Clark was messin with?"

"Yeah, she the one."

"Whatch'all had tuh talk about that long—as if I need tuh ask."

"Selma, honey, it was mo' then that. It was mo' then Clark. What we talked about I believe made us both realize it wadn't all about Clark. As-a-matter-of-fact, it wadn't about Clark at all. It was about us, respectin, carin, and lovin us and otha folks enough tuh give um the respect they deserve. I guess what um tryin tuh say is that if you don't truly respect yo'self you caint respect nobody else."

"That's right, Bert, but what made you wonna talk tuh that chil'?"

"She stopped me."

"She, stopped, you?"

"Yeah, she thought I was Clark's wife. Somewhere down the way he'd tol' huh that. Not 'cause he loved me uh nothin, Selma...

"I understand, Bert."

"So, yo' talk with huh, made you decide you wonts tuh leave Casey Park and go up tuh Bridgeway?"

"Not only that, Selma. I'd been asked some time ago tuh come up there. Afta' talkin with that chil' I knew it was time tuh make a decision. I knew that was what I shoulda been doin all the time."

"Yeah, but, why? Why way up tuh Bridgeway?"

"Bridgeway has a clinic called Sister Connection. They'd asked me tuh council fuh um 'bout two years ago."

"You got the degree, Bert, you might as well use it."

"Yeah, and I got the first-hand experience and I know that's what the Lord wonts me tuh do."

"If that's what the Lord wonts, I know I cain't stop yah."

"Naw, Selma, not this time."

"When you leavin?"

"In the monin."

"SO SOON? *BER-R-R-RT!*"

"I have tuh, they sent me a final invitation ova a month ago and gave me sixty days tuh respond. If I don't leave in the monin they goan find somebody else. I may nevva git anotha chance lack this again."

"Afta all that's happened, Bert, yah know, um goan really miss you. Although I done moved from Casey Park myself, thangs just ain't goan be the same just knowin you ain't goan be close by no mo'."

"But God will, Selma. And that's the best thang about separatin from people yah care about."

"I know, Bert, I know. But um still goan miss you."

"And um sho' goan miss you, Selma. But I'll be back tuh visit. You ain't lost me altogether."

"Yeah. I guess not...Look at me, Bert, um just bein selfish—congratulations, you hear? And enjoy yo'self lack you supposed tuh. You deserve that good job no matter where it is, and the first words that shoulda come outta my mouth shoulda been congratulations. That center needs somebody lack you. Somebody who dedicated and really willin tuh help people. Nigh you give me a hug and take care uh yo'self while you gone, 'cause God only made one uh you and although you goan be further away I ain't ready tuh go lookin fuh anotha one uh you just yet."

"Thanks, Selma. That means a lot comin from you."

Chapter 39

SELMA LEANS ON DIAMOND

"First Bert, then Daizelle? Why is Daizelle leaving, Selma?"

"Diamond. That woman went and found huhself a man."

"WHAT!"

"Yeah, Diamond. Since I give huh that sto', she been keepin huhself all prettied up and huh attitude changed ova night."

"Selma, I've always felt that a little love could go a long way."

"Well, you sho' right. Daizelle tol' me that Mr. Albright said he'd been interested in huh fuh years. He was afraid tuh say anythang to huh 'cause uh huh old ugly disposition. When she started dressin up and huh attitude changed that's when he approached huh. She say he tol' huh, he just couldn't git up his nerve befo' that!"

"She is good looking, Selma. Especially for a woman her age. I'd always wondered if she'd ever been married before."

"Naw, she hadn't been. Nobody, includin the men could stand huh. When yo' attitude ugly, you ugly."

"You're right, Selma, attitude goes a long way...Hey, what did she do with the store?"

"She sold it. Her and Mr. Albright movin tuh Vegas. He got a lot uh money yah know. He tol' Daizelle tuh put huh's up, they was goan spend his."

"Selma, they're going to end up spending all of their money in Vegas."

"No they won't, Diamond. They both got family out there. Besides, there's otha thangs tuh do in the borderin towns besides gamblin. I know that's what you was thankin."

"That's true, Selma. I was, thinking that."

"Diamond. Um really gone miss, Daizelle, and Bert."

"I'm sure you will, Selma. You've been through some tough times with them."

"Yeah, but I still have you."

"You sure do, Selma, I'm a few hours away, but I'll be here anytime you need me."

Chapter 40

THE TALK

"Selma, I know that you and Diamond are friends, but are you in love with him?"

"No, honey. Me and Diamond just friends, nothin else. Why would you thank that anyway?"

"Before we were married, I'd see him looking at you with sort of a starry-eyed, boyish, lovesick look."

"Paul, um goan be honest with you. When we was in college, we thought we had a crush oan each otha. Recently, we talked about that. I found out that he was goin through some thangs back then and so was I. He looked tuh me lack somebody who'd understand and I felt the same 'bout him. And yah know, Paul. His wife leavin him again might have somethin tuh do with the way he actin, too."

"Oh, yeah. He told me about that, Selma. She'll be back though. There's no way a woman can stay away from a man like Brother Prescott. I can even tell that he has that certain something. That's why I'm just a little uncomfortable when he's around you."

"Paul. You can git that off yo' mind rat now. I love you so much I wouldn't trade you fuh nothin uh nobody. Please believe that.

Every night befo' I go tuh bed, I pray and ask God tuh keep us tugetha. You the best thang that could evva happen tuh me. Pleasin you is all I wont tuh do."

"You do, Selma. You please me in every way."

"Selma, do you want more children?"

"You know I do, but Nina and Nia, only nine months old, Paul."

"I know, Selma. But we've started so late."

"That is true, Paul."

"Then are we in agreement, Selma?"

"I don't know, Paul, I don't know."

"Think about it, Selma. We'll talk about it again, okay?"

"Wait a minute Paul. Maybe we should. That way we'll be able tuh brang um all up tuhgetha."

"Then you agree, Selma?"

"Yeah, but when, Paul?"

"Tonight, Selma. We'll continue to build on our family, tonight."

"Paul, I love you."

"I love you too, Selma."

Chapter 41

THE NEXT MORNING

"Selma."

"Yes, Paul."

"Last night, you did something that confused me."

"I don't know what you mean."

"Selma, you don't remember—

"LOOK, PAUL, I AIN'T PERFECT LACK YOU, OKAY! YOU KNOW'D BEFO' I MARRIED YOU WHAT KIND UH MAN I WAS MARRIED TUH FUH ALL THEM YEARS! IT'S HARD TUH STOP DOIN ALL THEM THANGS, PAUL! I BE FUGGITTIN! BESIDES, I DIDN'T DO IT, I JUST ALMOST DID IT!"

"Don't shout, Selma. There's no need to shout."

"Um sorry, Paul, um sorry."

"Selma, I'm not criticizing you. I just wanted to make you aware. Believe me, Selma, I fully understand what's going on with you. I made a vow and I'm going to honor that vow no matter what."

"Don't cry, honey, I'm not upset."

"Yes you are, you just tryin tuh spare my feelins—oh Paul! Um so ashamed uh myself!"

"Selma, honey, listen. If I was upset, would I still be talking to you? Would I still be

trying to reason with you? Would I still be
trying to work things out between us?"

"*I guess not.*"

"What do you mean, "you guess not?" Come here
and sit on my lap...

...See; I still love you."

"Selma, you're a good woman. I told you that
the day I asked you to marry me and I still
believe it.

What I've been trying to tell you is what
happened last night was not totally your fault. I
think the way I told you about it was wrong and I
upset you. I'm sorry, Selma. Upsetting you is the
last thing I'd ever want to do to you. I love you
too much for that.

Selma, I'm not that much different from
anyone else. My flesh still needs to die. If you
would've continued what you were doing last night
I wouldn't have rejected. I would have let you do
it only to feel guilty the next day. I thank God
that you had the ability to stop yourself."

"So it is wrong tuh perform that kind uh sex
oan a man, even if he is yo' husband?"

"Selma, all I'm saying for now is that it
doesn't feel right to me. What we'll do later is
get our bibles out and look it up."

"Oh yeah, Paul, I'd fuhgotten them scriptures."

"Well, tonight, we'll bring them to the front line. We have to abide by the scriptures."

"Paul, you so smart and understandin. Why didn't the Lord send you tuh me in the beginnin."

"Neither one of us was ready, Selma. God knew that. Now that we're together, we're going to make this the best marriage possible."

Chapter 42

THE RELIEF CALL

"Why are you still crying, Selma? You've apologized, he accepted it, it's over."

"Diamond, I ain't tol' you everythang. I almost performed oral sex oan a preacher! Not just any preacher. The preacher um married tuh, my husband!"

"Selma, I never knew you—

"Knew I what, Diamond! That um doin the same lil' nasty thangs everybody else doin!

That all these years I been stickin my nose up in the air at folks, nigh look at me. Um married tuh uh man who just about a perfect saint and I make the mistake uh fuhgittin who he is and almost do somethin lack that!"

"Selma, are you telling me that in the heat of passion you got so caught up you thought the reverend was Clark?"

"Yeah, Diamond, yeah, I did. Clark was as wicked as he is Godly. How could I make that mistake?"

"Oh my goodness, Selma! Ha, ha, ha! Ooowee!"

"It ain't funny, Diamond!"

"Selma. If he's as good and kind as you always say he is and as he seems to me, you have nothing to be ashamed of."

*"What gits tuh me the most, Diamond is the
way I use tuh feel about you and Anthony.*

*I nevva tol' you this befo', but the thangs
me 'n' Clark would do was just as bad, and there
was only two of us."*

"Selma, the only thing shocking me about this
conversation is the fact that you held up this
long without telling me yourself. I'd heard the
gossip at church long before I even knew you
attended. No one ever knew we were friends and
they didn't know about me studying to be a
minister. Of course I didn't know what Clark and
Selma they were talking about either until I saw
you that day. When they'd come to me with the
nonsense I'd tell them to respect the church and
its members and brush them off."

*"A lot uh gossip, dirty gossip go oan in the
church, Diamond. Too much."*

"A lot of dirty things, too, Selma. But I
really didn't know you felt the way you do. I
always thought you'd accepted your lifestyle with
Clark. He was your husband."

*"Diamond, I couldn't nevva git use tuh it.
I'd lie tuh Bert, tellin huh that it was my
choice tuh git in tuh that stuff, but it wadn't.
I was too shame tuh tell huh how many nights he'd
force me tuh let him perform oral sex oan me and
afta hatin it so bad I turned rat back 'round and
done it tuh him. The only reason I done it tuh
him was 'cause I felt that would stop him from
goin in the streets fuh it. When it didn't and I*

Lee Charles

wonted tuh stop, every nigh and then he'd force
me tuh do it, or force it oan me."

"Why would he force you, Selma? Especially if
he was going out with other women?"

"When he first tried tuh do it tuh me I
resisted. He pushed me out his way and went oan
'bout his business. The next time he tried we was
in the bed and when I resisted he got up tuh git
dressed I was angry with him 'cause he was tryin
tuh do that stuff oan me all the time. So I asked
him why he didn't do it tuh some uh his women.
That made him madda then I don't know what. He
grabbed me by my ankles, pulled me tuh him,
pinned me down and started. I was wrenchin and
turnin tryin tuh git loose from him. He clamped
his teeth in tuh my pelvic flesh just enough tuh
make me stay still. While he was bitin me he
asked me was I goan act right. I was squealin
lack I was crazy, but I tol' him yeah. He didn't
believe me. He got up off the bed and walked ova
tuh his belt rack. I made a run fuh the do'. He
grabbed me round my waist and slammed me back
down oan the bed so hard the wind got knocked
outta me. He come back with two belts. He tied my
hands tuhgetha with one. We didn't have a
headboard so he drug me tuh the flo wrapped the
otha' one 'round my wrist the leg of the bed and
strapped me tuh it.

I tried tuh discourage him by callin him all
the nasty thangs I could thank of, he didn't

280

care. He gave me that nasty grin uh his, lowered
his head and the next thang I felt was my body
tremble, empty out and I could hear myself
screamin. While I was tryin tuh catch my breath
he done it again. By that time I was almost
crazy. I started kickin, screamin and beggin him
tuh please try tuh love me. Please treat me lack
um a decent woman and was tellin him how I was
goan let him be the man from now oan. I was sayin
anythang that I thought would make him stop.

He got up, sat oan the bed, and lit a
cigarette. I thought he was goan talk trash lack
he generally do when he feel he done taught me a
lesson. Instead, he finished his cigarette and
kept oan doin thangs tuh me. In between, he'd
talk tuh me. He kept askin me if I was goan let
him be the man from then oan uh not. If I wadn't
so stupid I woulda tol' him yeah, the first
time."
    "But—
    "Wait a minute, Diamond, I ain't finished.
When that was ova, he raped me 'til he got tired
and he made sho' it would make me feel dirty. He
was stickin his tongue in my mouth and I could
taste that nasty cigarette. He was talkin tuh me
lack I was a street woman and feelin all ova my
body lack I wadn't nothin. He was squeezin and
pinchin oan me real hard tuh make me scream. The
only thang he hadn't damaged oan me was my

rectum. Everythang else was physically uh mentally messed up.

   He stood up and I laid there cryin. He looked down at me with that nasty grin and said tuh me, "The next time you thank you the man, um goan do you lack you my prison wife."

"His prison wife?"

"Yeah, Diamond. That ol' fool had done been in prison befo' and he was goan sodomize me. He was goan do me lack he'd probably done somebody in prison."

"He was going to sodomize his own, wife!"

"Yeah, Diamond and he woulda done it too. From then oan, I walked oan eggshells while I was 'round him, especially afta seein what he'd done tuh Clarrietta."

"Who's, Clarrietta?"

"This yella gal he'd git his sexual favas from."

"What did he do to her?"

"He sodomized that girl so bad they had tuh put huh in the hospital. The worst part was, I seen the whole thang."

"You should have left him then, Selma."

"That's what Bert tol' me and I lied tuh huh 'bout why I didn't. Truth is, I shoulda left him fo' then. And I tried tuh once. He threatened me then, too."

"I'm sorry, Selma, but what kind of a beast would rape and sodomize his own wife!"

"You tol' me you 'n' him had some thangs in common, you tell me."

"Selma, I've forcibly sodomized women, but I would never do it to Sheila or you or any decent woman."

"Diamond, it's wrong tuh rape and sodomize anybody, I don't care if they uh street walker. Even murderers got feelins, Diamond. You caint go 'round abusin people 'cause uh they status."

"Selma, you are so right, because I never saw women as being human until I saw and heard about Sadaya going through the things I'd put women through. But women feel the same way about men until they get some sort of revelation. I guess I fall in the category of people who feel that as long as it isn't my family, friends or someone I care about, it's okay."

"Well, it ain't okay, Diamond."

"I know, Selma, I know, but you know how I've always felt about you. Your story hit home and I lost it. I actually wanted to hurt a dead man."

"Yah know, Diamond, Clark had a way uh makin folks feel that way 'bout him. Fact is, none uh the men 'round Casey Park had nerve 'nough tuh stand up tuh him. Um sho' they coulda whooped him, but most everybody had credit at our sto'. They was afraid uh bitin the hand that was feedin um."

"That's what happens Selma when you put man before God. If they would have really been depending on God like I'm learning to do now,

they would have known who their real supplier is.
I've learned not to be corrupt to get justice."

*"So have I, Diamond, but I still wish that I
wouldn'tna nevva fallen in tuh that filthy sex
relationship with Clark. I had a chance tuh marry
a good man, a decent man, Jason Warner."*

"Selma, you've never told me that, either!"

"It's the truth. I met Jason and Clark the
year afta you graduated. When me and Clark was
datin he worked at the factory. I was still in
college. We dated fuh three years and Clark nevva
touched me. He thought I was a virgin. He thought
all college girls was virgins. He was ignorant
lack that. Anyway, he thought he was respectin me
'cause I was a virgin and wonted us tuh be
married fo' we had sex. Then, 'long came Jason
Warner. He was almost the spittin image uh you,
only his skin was darker. He was goan be a
teacha. He kept askin me out and askin me out.
Clark went outta town tuh see 'bout his sick
mamma. Jason called me again tuh ask me out and I
went. We went tuh an innocent party, Diamond.
People wadn't even drankin.

Afta the party he tol' me he wonted tuh
introduce me tuh his parents. When we got tuh his
house they wadn't there. He tol' me they musta
stepped out fuh a while. We waited fuh um.

While we was waitin he gave me a drank. I
tol' him I'd nevva drank alcohol befo'. He tol'
me there wadn't that much in it just taste it and
see, if I didn't wont it he was goan pour it out.

I sipped it and it did taste pretty good, sorta lack a punch. I drank three uh them thangs. Diamond, I was feelin go-o-o-o-d! So good that I let him have me fo' Clark evva did and got pregnant the same night."

"You, Selma!"

"Yep, Diamond, me."

"I loved Jason, but I'd bonded with Clark. I didn't wont tuh leave him even though I was pregnant by Jason, and Clark had been cheatin oan me the entire time we was datin. I figured he did it 'cause he wadn't havin me, but I soon found out that Clark was just a cheat. Anyway, I never tol' Jason 'bout the baby, but I tol' Jason I couldn't see him no mo' 'cause uh what happened between us. Somehow, he talked me intuh seein him again and tried tuh mess with me in that other way...

"I knew that was next, Selma, I knew it!"

"How'd you know?"

"Because, that usually comes next when a man wants to get or keep a woman."

"But, I couldn't let Jason do somethin lack that tuh me, 'specially while I was pregnant, and I didn't wont him I wonted Clark. Me and Clark we'd been tuhgetha longa.

When I saw Clark again, I talked him intuh havin sex with me. A few weeks later I tol' him I was pregnant. He tol' me he wadn't ready fuh no babies and neitha was I. He took me up tuh Palma Jeans and they killed my baby."

"Your future husband made you abort it and he didn't even know it wasn't his?"

"Yep, that's what he did. He made me git rid uh it."

"Why did you marry Clark, Selma?"

"I told you, Diamond. I was use tuh him, but I also loved him."

"Selma, I believe you loved Jason. I don't believe you loved Clark at all. I believe that you were trying to tame him. Instead, Clark ended up corrupting your beliefs. Jason would've been more supportive, I think."

"I thank so too, Diamond."

"There's nothing that you can do about that now, Selma, so put it behind you and continue to learn from it. Learn to love, trust, and obey again the way our Father wants us to. That way you can't go wrong."

"Thank you Diamond fuh listenin and understandin. You a good friend. That situation been eatin at me fuh a while nigh. Clark said it would the night he raped me and I put him out. Um glad I tol' you and got it off my mind. I knew I could count oan you tuh make me feel betta."

Chapter 43

THE BLESSING

"Reverend, may I talk to you for a moment?"
   "Why of course, Brother Prescott."

   "Reverend, are you bothered by me and Selma's friendship?"
   "No. Not really. Why would you ask me that question, Brother Prescott?"
   "It's the way you watch us when we talk. Your glance and stare gives me the impression that you are uncomfortable with the relationship. Let me assure you reverend, we are, only friends. I have to admit that back in college, she had my eye in many ways but that's all changed. She's still very attractive I won't deny that, but now, I'm attracted to her because she's a good person, not because she's good looking. Selma has eased my mind during hardships many times, reverend, and I appreciate that.

   I still tease with her about the old days, but believe me, reverend, I have too much respect for you to even think about intimacy with her."
   "Diamond, I was hoping that you would respect me enough to be honest about your relationship with Selma. I'm deeply honored by your honesty. I've always respected you for that.

This may come as a surprise to you, but
you've ministered to me many times without even
knowing it. The honesty and respect that you've
shown me today has opened up an even greater
admiration in my heart for you. To show you how
honored I am, the next child we have, we're going
to name it after you."

"That's the real honor, reverend, you naming
one of your children after me. But suppose it's a
girl?"

"Well, people seem to think that Diamond is a
girl's name, although you've told me many times
that your mother named you Diamond because you
were more valuable than an engagement ring. They
must also consider that there are men named
Carol, Windy, Terry, Tracey, and other names that
might be considered feminine. So I'm naming my
child after you, boy or girl."

"This must be the honor John the Baptist felt
when Jesus came to him to be baptized."

"We all have our areas of strength, Diamond.
Jesus was letting John the Baptist know that
baptizing people to make them ready for the Lord
was his strength. Diamond, your strength is
communication...Diamond, I know that you're doing
some outside ministry, but Reverend Callahan is
retiring, would you be interested in speaking in
church some Sundays?"

"Why, of course!"

"You know, Diamond, this will eventually lead to you taking over a church session."

"Are you offering me a session, reverend?"

"If you want it."

"Of course I want it!"

"You'll need to practice under the elders, Diamond. After six months or so, you'll be somewhat ready to be given a ministry session of your own."

"Thank you reverend, thank you! You won't regret it reverend! I'll do the best job possible! I won't disappoint you, I promise you that!"

"I know that you won't, Diamond, and more so, I know that you won't disappoint The Father."

Chapter 44

REMEMBRANCE

"DAIZELLE, THIS YOU!"

    "Yeah, girl! I got Bert oan the line, too!"

    "Sho' nuff?"

    "Um here, Selma!"

    "Whatchoo two lil' sneaks up tuh?"

    "Nothin, girl. I'd called Bert and we started talkin 'bout the old days, and missin you. So we decided tuh call and make this a three-way conversation.

We was laughin 'bout the crazy thangs we'd done and how we all made such big changes in our lives.

    Selma, I know'd it wadn't funny then, but me 'n' Bert was talkin 'bout how I'd be stealin from yo' sto'. Girl, I would be puttin so much stuff in my clothes! One day I'd stole so much from you I had tuh stuff my draws! I went tuh git oan the bus and fell up them steps. I had tuh crawl tuh one uh them poles tuh pull myself up. When I finally got tuh the aisle, everythang fell, includin my draws! I went tuh take anotha step and them thangs was 'round my ankles and I fell flat oan my face! That long skirt I had oan that day flew up ova the back uh my head and I lay in that aisle bare-assed, until the bus driva pulled

ova and helped me tuh a seat! Girl! Yo' sto'
goods was all ova that bus! They was everywhere
and people was just a laughin'! I couldn't say
nothin' I was so shame!"

"Shoot, that wadn't nothin, Daizelle! When
Selma found out I'd been messin 'round with
Clark, she took huh bat out and chased me 'round
that sto'. 'Member that narrow aisle she had the
cereal oan?"

"Um-hum, Bert! Sho' I do!"

"Girl, when I got tuh that aisle, my big rump
got stuck! I don't know tuh this day how I
knocked all them cereal off them shelves without
knockin ova them shelves! I got outta there
somehow and when I did, Selma swung that bat at
me so hard she spunt 'round and fell oan huh
behind! She sat there rockin lack she'd been
drankin!"

"Daizelle! What about the time Bert tol' you
tuh leave the sto' 'cause I was gittin mad! When
Bert turned me loose lack you said, you looked
lack you jumped three feet in the air and did a
bicycle run backwards out the do'!

"Y'all need tuh stop, um laughin too hard!"

"Me too, Daizelle!"

"Me three, y'all got me laughin so hard um
cryin! Oh my goodness! I ain't laughed this hard
since I don't know when! We done had some good
and bad times, haven't we?"

"Yeah, Selma, and we all done come such a
long way."

"Bert, I still be thankin 'bout why I even bothered tuh git even with you ova that sorry man. As far as that sto' go, I was glad tuh git rid uh it. Um glad you decided tuh sell it, Daizelle.

Who woulda thought Ms. Daizelle would end up with a rich husband?"

"I nevva thought I'd be counselin people outta town either, Selma."

"And I thought I'd be the last person tuh marry a reverend, Bert. We all have come a long way. We done changed, too, and we ain't the only ones who done changed. Diamond Prescott goan be preachin."

"Pretty, Diamond Prescott, Selma?"
"Yes ma'am, Daizelle, pretty Diamond."

"Selma, Daizelle, there ain't no limit tuh what God kin do."

"I know I thank him, Bert. A few years ago I was with a man who made me shame everyday uh my life, I didn't have no chil'ren tuh call my own, and all of us was at each otha's throats. We've all accepted the Lord properly and he done totally renovated our hearts."

"You said a mouth full, Selma."

"Daizelle. That's a mouth full that I don't mind lettin go of!"

"Hey, Selma, Bert, why don't y'all come tuh Vegas and visit me?"

"You serious, Daizelle?"

"Sho' um serious, Selma."

"If the reverend say it's okay, we'll come."

"If the center will let me go, I'll come too."

"How soon kin y'all come out?"

"I can make it out in about two weeks, if the center kin spare me."

"Me too, Daizelle."

"Then two weeks it is. All y'all got tuh do is call me 'n' give me a date so that I kin have everythang ready. There ain't no time limit oan how long y'all kin stay with me eitha. Just plan oan havin a good time when yah git here."

Chapter 45

PAUL'S MISTAKE

"Selma, I have to tell you something."

"What, Paul, what is it?"

"Actually, it's a confession—well, two confessions. The first is that when I asked you to have more children it was out of jealousy. Although you'd told me you weren't interested in Diamond in a romantic way, I still felt insecure and jealous of him."

"Honestly Paul, there ain't no reason fuh you tuh be jealous or feel insecure 'bout me and Diamond."

"I know that now, Selma. Prior to me asking Diamond to take over one of my ministering services, we had a long talk. He really put my mind at ease.

I'd been thinking of giving him a chance at ministering for a long time now. The reason being, no matter what he does, he's honest about it, he's a scriptural man, and works toward what's right.

When he stepped up to me that day and without a word from me, told me what I was feeling, that's when I knew he is the one. I'm pleased that I didn't let my jealousy get in the way of me choosing someone with great insight. What I'm

not so proud of is that my jealousy almost blind-
sighted my decision."

"Nigh, nigh, Paul. It's lack you tell yo'
congregation. "Nobody's perfect, but keep oan
strivin takin it one day at a time." Besides, um
flattered tuh know that you jealous uh me. It
make me mo' attracted tuh yah. Most women wont
they man tuh be a little jealous. It make us feel
as if he know he got a good woman and don't wont
tuh lose huh."

"I didn't know that, Selma. I always thought
it was a stupid emotion."

"Only tuh people who don't know no betta, in
otha' words, people who jealous ova materialistic
thangs. Personally, I lack it, as long as it's,
concerned jealousy, and not materialistic, and it
don't git outta control."

"I'm relieved to hear you say that, Selma."

"It's true, Paul, that's the way I feel. Nigh
what's yo' otha confession?"

"You know that I'd never purposely hurt you,
Selma. I'd do anything in the world for you. You
do know that, don't you?"

"I believe you'd try as hard as you could not
to hurt me, Paul. What's wrong?"

"Selma. You know that we all have a past
before we get to our future."

"Yeah, Paul. I know that, just tell me what's
wrong, Paul, just tell me."

"Selma. Before I came back here I was
assistant pastor at Christ's Everlasting Love

Church in upstate New York. There was a woman there about twenty-two—

"Paul. Don't none uh that matter now."

"Yes it does, Selma and I should have told you this before we were married, besides that, we're suppose to confess our sins to one another."

"Go ahead and tell me, Paul. It cain't be no worse then what I put up with tuh be with Clark all them years."

"Selma. She'd propositioned me way before things happened between us and I'd told her off but good. After that she'd come to church early enough to get in the second row and in the direct view of where I sat on the pulpit. She made sure no one else would really notice her, but she wanted to make sure that I saw her wearing those straight cut dresses that her curves completed because she was so shapely. She wore jackets over them to hide her figure, but when church got into full swing she'd remove her jacket to stand up and clap, praise the lord or pretend to shout, and at times, Selma, she wouldn't be wearing a bra. I could see her very outline, every shake, and tremble that her body made.

One Sunday she'd gotten to me so bad that I had to excuse myself and go to the Men's room—

"Why didn't you tell somebody what she was doin', Paul?"

"It was one of those somewhat superficial churches, Selma. Nobody looked for anything out of the ordinary, they had to see it all first hand, and many of them just like here in Casey Park, were doing some things that I can't repeat. And as I found out later some of them sat in the pulpit with me. Anyway, I had to excuse myself because I'd become excited. I'd been celibate for almost two years and not as seasoned as I am now.

I was standing in the bathroom stall trying to compose myself and after about fifteen minutes I heard the mens room door open then my stall door flew open. It was her. I told her to leave. She smiled at me and told me to make her. I tried to pass her but she stood in my way. As I was getting ready to say something else to her the men's room door opened again. She gently put the top down on the toilet and kneeled on the lid to hide her feet. She grabbed me around my waist as if trying to keep her balance and made me fall against the wall of the enclosure. The voice from the next stall asked me if I was okay and I replied I'm fine and tried to remain perfectly still so that she wouldn't fall, but she had other ideas, Selma. She wasn't in fear of falling she was positioning herself. She reached for my zipper. When I tried pushing her hands away she leaned on me in a way that made me fall against the stall enclosure again and I had to explain a second time to the voice on the other side that I

was okay. I remained still and let her unzip my
pants. My thoughts were that she was only trying
to get me excited because I was a minister and
was only going to touch me to get me excited
enough to get a laugh, because I'd rejected her.
I'd resign from the church and go elsewhere to
minister and nothing else would be said, but I
was wrong, Selma, very wrong. Seconds after the
other voice left the bathroom she stripped me.
She drained me in that stall as if she'd done
that type of thing often and in that church. She
got down from the toilet and left me in the
stall. I heard water running then the door close.
My knees were wobbly but I managed to finally
come out of the stall and walk over to the sinks.
I didn't want to use the same sink she'd touched
and I looked at them for a long time trying to
figure out which one she'd used before I splashed
my face with water.

When I finally got back into the pulpit the
Elder asked me if I was okay. I told him that I
wasn't feeling well and needed to go home. He
promised to make my excuses and I left.

Without noticing, the girl had also left. She
met me outside. I tried walking past her and she
tried stopping me. I pushed her aside and began
walking to the church parking lot in a pace that
I thought would give her an idea of how angry and
disgusted I was with her, but I could hear the
clicking of her heels in back of me. When I got

to my car she caught up to me and began to cry
and beg for my forgiveness then leaned against me
for comfort. I slowly lifted my hands to hold
her. As soon as I touched her I knew it was a
mistake. I should have just jumped in my car and
never looked back and I was going to. Instead, I
allowed her to explain how lonely she was and how
she'd wanted me for a long time but didn't know
how to get to me. She saw that I wasn't really
buying into her emotions and began begging me not
to tell anyone what had happened in the bathroom.
She said that her kids would be devastated if
they ever found out about what she'd done. That
made me feel so sorry for her that I asked her
name although I was still angry and didn't really
care. She calmed down enough to tell me that her
name was Joy Melbow and I said in the most
soothing voice that I could conjure up, "Joy,
stop crying. We'll work this out, okay?" She
didn't say anything to me she just wrapped both
arms around my waist hugged me real tight and
laid her head against me. When I looked down at
her and noticed how straight, shiny, and fragrant
her beautifully streaked hair was that's when the
sensation of her warm breath through my vest hit
me. Instantly I remembered what had happened
between us just a few minutes ago and gently took
her arms away...

"Joy was a white girl, Paul?"

"No, Selma. She was a brown-skinned woman
with really nice hair and figure, who kept

herself up very nicely. I can't lie to you Selma, Joy was a beautiful woman."

"Did you love huh, Paul?"

"I'm getting to that, Selma. I told Joy that she needed counseling. She told me that she'd never get the type of counseling she needed from a church like the one we went to and asked me if I knew of another place that she could go to for help and I didn't know of any such place at the time. She asked me to help her and I told her that it wouldn't be a good idea after what had happened between us...

"Between y'all? But Paul! She was the one who done everythang!"

"I know that, Selma, but I didn't want to make her feel any worse than I thought she already did...

"What do you mean by that, Paul? What do you mean by makin' huh feel any worse than you thought she did? She wadn't sincere?"

"Let me finish, Selma. Anyway, as she walked away from me with her head down I stared at her, but let her walk away. Joy stayed on my mind all day and night. I couldn't sleep thinking about what might happen to her and called the church secretary at home to see if Joy was a member. She remembered Joy because they went to the same hairdresser, but couldn't remember her home number only her address from beauty shop conversations, and I immediately went over to her house. She came to the door yawning and wearing a

T-shirt, but it didn't hide her figure, and her hair was still in place. Other than you, I'd never seen a woman wake up looking so beautiful."

"Aw, Paul, thank you. That's so, sweet."

"I mean it, Selma. Anyway, I apologized for ignoring her cry for help and told her I'd help her out until we could find someone else. She offered me to come inside. I thanked her for her hospitality and left. As I counseled Joy she told me some things about herself, but I knew there was more. She'd stop and think too much or too long about what she'd tell me and she'd say everything too perfectly, but I was taught not to push too hard when counseling and wouldn't push her to talk.

One Sunday Joy hadn't shown up for church and she didn't call me like she had in the past when she couldn't make it. I thought for sure Joy was dead or something. I gave the pastor another excuse about being ill and drove straight to Joy's apartment. I could hear voices inside as if someone was arguing and knocked on her door but nobody answered. I tried twisting the knob but the door wouldn't open. That's when I remembered her giving me the key that she'd told me was for an emergency although I knew that it was an invitation to sleep with her. When I entered the foyer the voices got louder. She was crying and sort of squealing in a low tone and saying that's enough that she had to go see about her two

babies in the other room and that her other
children would be home soon she didn't want them
to catch him there. Then I heard the male voice
telling her that if she didn't want that to
happen she needed to make sure he got what he
came there for. I wasn't sure what was happening
to Joy and walked further into the apartment. I
thought the man might have been raping her
because when I found them they were in the
kitchen. At first all I could see was this big
fat man in a gray suit and hear this small
feminine voice that sounded like Joy's that
seemed to be coming out of him because he covered
her. He squatted, then spread his legs a little
and I could see Joy standing on her toes and
holding on to her kitchen table bracing herself
while this man used her in an animal-like fashion
no matter how hard she pleaded screamed and
squealed. I reached for him but he'd completed
his cruel act and lifted Joy up on the table and
proceeded to do to her what she'd done to me in
the men's room. Joy struggled with him, she
didn't see me because her eyes were too filled
with tears, but I could see and hear the
humiliation it caused her when he made her scream
and cry instantly and much louder than
previously, so loud it made her babies cry louder
too. He said something to Joy that made me
realize that they had some sort of relationship
going—something like, "You use to enjoy all of
this." I was going to try and back out the door,

but the whining and crying of those babies made
me so angry that I couldn't help but chastise him
for disrespecting a mother in front of her
children that way. He'd pushed Joy all the way
back on the table and was trying to put his mouth
on her breasts, she was kicking wildly trying to
fight him off. I grabbed him by the collar and
yanked him so hard his big body turned and fell
on the floor. It was Bishop Cady. He lay there
looking up at me with his fly still open. Joy
jumped off the table. She was trembling, crying,
and getting her clothes together while Bishop
explained to me that those two kids in the room
were his. Joy began explaining how she'd told him
not to come around there any more because he
wouldn't make a commitment and marry her because
he thought that he was too good for her. Bishop
Cady sounded like someone fresh off the streets.
He was cussing and calling Joy all sorts of
names. He told me that everything from the black
laced bra and panties to the white ruffled
tropical blouse and black mini skirt she was
wearing were items he'd bought her and that she
was dressing up to see some other man. All I told
him was to leave and not make more of a scene. He
asked me why was I there and I told him that I
was appointed to counsel her. Then he asked me
how did I get in. I lied, Selma. I told him that
they'd forgotten to lock the door and when I
heard the sounds of distress I immediately
entered and that he was blessed that it was only

me and not the police and that we could keep the
incident right where it was. He was supposed to
be at some kind of religious convention in
Buffalo which was supposed to be his reason for
not being at church that day and he knew that I
knew it. He stood up, tucked his shirt in, zipped
his pants, agreed, and left Joy's apartment. Joy
ran to me and held on to me like a drowning
child. She said that she was okay and asked me if
I'd stay with her until her other kids got home
from school just in case Bishop Cady came back.
She knew that he wouldn't hang around with her
other kids there they were old enough to call the
police on him...

"So, how'd she git you tuh get involved with
huh, Paul?"

"Selma, it wasn't hard. After she quieted her
twins and returned to the living room, just like
Bishop Cady my lust came down on me. While we sat
waiting for her children I also sat there waiting
for her to make that move again, which proves
that I'm as vulnerable as anyone else. Anyway, I
got up to leave so that what I'd seen and what
she'd done to me previously would leave my mind.
She begged me not to leave her—told me she'd do
anything to make me stay—said that she'd told the
Bishop that her kids were coming home soon to get
rid of him, but they really weren't due home for
another two and a half hours. I was persistent
about leaving and she cried some more. She made
me feel guilty, Selma. She said that she knew I'd

been wanting her all that time and when I finally
got what I wanted from her I was ready to kick
her to, what she called, "the curb", like the
rest of the men did. I told her that wasn't true
and that I really wanted to help her. That's when
she began asking me all these crazy question; did
I find her sexy, wasn't I attracted to her,
didn't I want her, wasn't she good enough. I told
Joy that she was good enough for any man she
wanted and that's when she interrupted and asked
if she was good enough for me. When I told her
yes she kissed me and I didn't resist her. I
don't remember exactly how, but what happened in
the church bathroom that Sunday happened again.
When I left her apartment I couldn't look at her.
There was no way I could have faced her children
if they'd shown up while I was still there.

The following Sunday she was in church but
Bishop Cady wasn't.

After the service Joy didn't talk to me, sat
in a different section, wouldn't call me,
wouldn't answer my calls, and wouldn't let me
counsel her. Three or four Sundays went by, I'd
basically decided to let go of her after that,
but on that last Sunday, before I could close my
car door she jumped in the passenger's side. She
claimed to need a ride home but when we got close
to her apartment she asked me if I'd take her for
a Sunday ride. She said that other than church

Lee Charles

and taking her children wherever they wanted to go she never went anywhere. I was so happy that she wasn't angry with me that I instantly agreed to take her. We went to the zoo, park, and the beach. I bought her a few little things—mostly out of guilt and paid her way everywhere we went.

At the beach she told me that she wanted to show me something. There was this old cove that she told me she loved. She said she'd come down there whenever she could get a ride and just think. She asked me to come inside with her. We sat there and she talked. She began telling me and reminding me of what Bishop Cady was doing to her. She asked me if I'd ever treated a woman that way. I told her I'd never treat anyone like that. She said, "Then how do you make love to women?" I told her that I no longer had the desire to do those things until I was married, being a minister had changed that for me, but what the Bishop was doing to her wouldn't be one of my ways of being intimate with my wife. She stood up and walked around the cove a few seconds then came over and straddled my lap and began kissing me. I pushed her back. She sat straddled my lap looking at me a little while then asked me why was I fighting a desire that I knew I wanted and I couldn't answer her. She kissed me some more and that's when I found out she'd come to church more than half-naked that day. She unzipped my pants and from then on we were

306

constantly in bed. All of the shame and guilt
left me and I wanted Joy more than I wanted God.
I just couldn't let her go. She talked me into
having unnatural sex with her and to be quite
frank I was happy that she did. She was about to
talk me into learning how to have oral sex with
her but before she could I found out that Joy had
seven kids. She'd kept them away from me all that
time. The way I found out about them was that one
of their father's named Lawrence who was a lawyer
came by to drop money off while she was at the
store. He told me that Joy had those kids by five
different men that she'd personally turned out
because she likes the squares and quiet innocent
type who could pay child support. He asked me if
I'd gotten her pregnant yet. I never said a word
to him but he continued telling me about Joy. He
said that it was obvious to him that she wasn't
finished using me because when she was I wouldn't
be answering her door anymore because she'd no
longer allow me to come around. He told me that
she gets tired of a man once she gets him to
perform that last little task.

When Joy came back from the store I never
told her that Lawrence had stopped by I insisted
on staying late. I wanted to see if she really
had seven children, seven children that she
didn't want me to see in total. She kept trying
to make up excuses about them to get me to leave.
I left and came back. I used that key she'd given

me and there they were. When she saw me she ran
into her bedroom. The children started yelling
and crying, "Don't hurt my mommy, don't hurt my
mommy." I got Joy out of the bedroom and quieted
them all down. She and I sat and talked for over
two hours. She told me why her children yelled
out like that. She said that Bishop Cady would
come over quite often, lock them in their
bedrooms so that the older ones couldn't call the
police, and treat her the way he was treating her
the day I came in. She said that he was the one
who introduced her to it and she figured it made
all men happy because it seemed to please him and
the other men she'd been with so much."

"But didn't she realize she'd given you the
key to huh apartment, Paul? Didn't she thank that
you'd walk in on huh sooner or later and find out
about all them kids?"

"No. She thought that I was too polite and
naïve for that.

By telling me the first day I'd used the key
that only two of her children were actually
coming home from school and the fact that I
already knew that her twins belonged to Bishop
Cady she'd be covered. She was going to tell me
that the other two were his also and not mention
the others. Most of the time they stayed with
their father."

"Why didn't she want you to know about all them kids, Paul? Did she plan oan havin one by you?"

"No. She said that she'd definitely been pregnant enough times and didn't want any more children, but she thought I'd leave her, Selma, although I had no business there, anyway."

"So what happened, Paul? How'd y'all break up?"

"I told her that the relationship wasn't right that I was a man of God and I had to return my body to God. She went and told the reverend of the church about us. I didn't deny it like so many of our other men who were church leaders did and the church let me go.

All along Bishop Cady was married and I never knew it. His wife fellowshipped at another church. She found out about Joy, beat her, and kicked Bishop Cady out of the house. He was so furious he went back to Joy's and took advantage of her again."

"How'd you find out, Paul?"

"Some of my gossiping ex-church members, Selma. That's how."

"Selma. That's why I now understand what people are going through who lust so. Selma. It was wrong not telling you, but I didn't tell you before we got married because I didn't want you to turn me down. I loved and wanted you so bad that I couldn't force myself to tell you such a horrible story at the time."

"Be anxious for nothin', Paul. All thangs through prayer and supplication, remember?"

"I know, Selma, I know and I was wrong, but I'm willing to do whatever I need to do that's right with God to make it all up to you."

"Then can we go tuh Vegas?"

"Vegas, baby? Why Vegas, Selma?"

"Daizelle invited us and that'll make me happy."

"Then we'll go, Selma. When do you want to leave?"

"In two weeks, she said she'd be ready fuh us by then."

"Selma, I'm not trying to get off the subject, but do you really want more children?"

"Paul, I wont as many children as the Lord will allow, as long as they with you."

"Selma, I love you. I thought that you'd be angry with me and not want to have anymore children from me after being so selfish and lusting after a woman and not telling you until now."

"Paul, you the most carin, lovin, sweetest person I know. As long as you stay that way um goan stay with you and please you anyway I kin. That foolishness was between you and that woman in the past and that's where we goan leave it."

"Selma, Selma, Selma. You're one in a million. God made me wait, but I'm happy that I did. You're well worth it."

Chapter 46

VEGAS

"I'm so glad tuh be here, Daizelle. Yo' pool is beautiful and so is the rest uh the house. We all agree oan that, Daizelle."

"Um just glad tuh have y'all here. It's so wonderful havin' all the people here that I love and done helped me 'long the way.

Nigh, befo' we have anymo' fun let's bow our heads in prayer...Dear father, our lives was not complete until we accepted you. You are merciful, graceful, compassionate, kind, and lovin. You have given me so much, yet you continue tuh be generous. You've given me friends Lord, not just any old friends Lord. You've given me good friends. Friends who have helped and watched ova me even when I didn't deserve it. Lord, that's why I am so happy tuh be sharin my home, joy, and peace with them fuh as long as they wish tuh receive it. If you had nevva sent them tuh me Lord I might not be standin here today. I thank you Lord...Amen. Nigh, let's all take a glass uh wine and make a toast. Who wonts tuh lead that?"

"Daizelle. You led the prayer. Reverend Bess. It's only fitting that you lead the toast."

"Thank you, Brother Albright. Glasses held high...! To good friends, wonderful family, and a long prosperous life."

"WE'LL ALL, DRINK TO THAT!"

"This moment must have been meant to be. We're all snickering because we almost said that in unison...Now don't forget, when we've finished having fun here, Daizelle and I are going to show everyone the town."

"Mr. Albright, you and Daizell are good people, you know that? Real good people. You know how to let go and have a good time."

"I appreciate the compliment, Paul, but we're not finished yet. Come on son, there's more to see. To put it lightly, you ain't seen or done, nothin yet!"

Chapter 47

AFTER THE FUN

"Boy, oh boy, did we have a good time —and the food!"

"I know, Paul. I ain't ate so much since I been tuh my mamma's house. This like paradise. And this summer-like night air feel good."

"It does, Selma, and it's relaxing, too."

"Honey, have you gained weight?"

"Paul, what kinda question is that tuh ask yo' wife?"

"I'm sorry, Selma, your stomach's usually as flat as a board. It's probably just all of the food we've eaten."

"I don't thank it's the food, honey; I thank it's a Paul."

"Get outta here!"

"Okay!"

"Girl, if you don't get back here and talk to me!"

"Stop, Paul, stop ticklin me! Okay, okay, I wadn't goan say nothin, but I went tuh Daizelle's doctor while y'all was playin golf Wednesday. Um almost fo' months pregnant. I kinda felt it, but I wadn't sho', but I was pregnant when we was discussin it."

"Here comes our little Diamond, Selma."

"We might be havin double Diamonds, Paul."

"AGAIN! Oh, baby! Oh, honey...!

"Paul, you goan squeeze the babies outta me."

"Are you sure that's what the doctor said, Selma!"

"No, um sayin, "You goan squeeze the life outta me."

"No, no, no Selma, you know what I mean! Are you sure the doctor told you that it might be twins, again!"

"Um positive, Paul."

"Thank you God, thank you Father! If it's boys, I can name the first one, Paul, Virgil, Bess Jr. and The other, Diamond, Prescott, Bess."

"You know what, Selma?"

"What, Paul?"

"Things seem to get better and better for us each day."

"Selma. Let's go inside, shower, cozy up in the bed and talk."

"You coulda at least promised tuh ravish me befo' fallen off tuh sleep."

"I still might, but I want to talk about you, the babies, and naming them before I take advantage of you."

"That's betta, at least um gittin a little of the attention. With all the enthusiasm you was showin' fuh these new babies I was beginnin tuh thank I was a has been."

"Come on, Selma, last one upstairs is a henpecked husband who loves it!"

Chapter 48

SNUGGLING

"Selma, whatever that is you're wearing smells good."

"Thanks, honey."

"I love bein wrapped in yo' arms lack this, Paul."

"And I love holding you, Selma...Selma, do you think that we should ask Diamond and Sheila to be Godparents?"

"Gracious yes! They a perfect couple! And You know what?"

"What, Selma?"

"If both twins girls again, um goan name one, Sheila, Jeannette, Prescott."

"As you wish, my lady."

"Selma, there's been many nights that I've watched you sleeping."

"Fuh what?"

"I think about all the times you were coming to church. How I wanted to take you away from Clark because I knew he wasn't treating you right. I'm going to make up for all of the wrong things he did to you. I'm going to make them right. You'll barely remember that he existed when I'm done pampering you."

"You don't hafta do that, Paul. You ain't responsible fuh Clark's mistakes."

"I know that. But I am responsible for you. All men should pamper their wives it can make a difference in the way a woman treats a man."

"That's true, Paul, and women should pamper they husbands, too. But some partners don't see it lack that."

"Well, this one does. Now come here with your sweet self. Tonight, I'm going to show you what a real man is all about."

"Guess what, Paul?"

"What?"

"I ain't goan stop yah!"

"Then turn that light off girl, and move a little bit closer."

Chapter 49

THE DEPARTURE

"We had a good time, Daizelle. Specially me, girl! I thank I found me a husband!"

"Really, Bert?"

"M-hm, sho' nuff!"

"HEY Y'ALL! WE GOAN HAVE ANOTHA WEDDIN TUH GO TUH SOON! BERT DONE FELL IN LOVE! SHE THOUGHT SHE WAS WHISPERIN TUH DAIZELLE, BUT SHE DONE CAUGHT ONE..."

"Stop that, Selma! You makin me blush..."

"They announcin our flight; come oan Bert! You can blush oan the plane!"

"Um comin, Selma! Um comin!"

"See you later, Daizelle, and thanks fuh everythang. You and Mr. Albright goan hafta come visit me 'n' Paul real soon, okay!"

"Okay, Selma!"

"Nigh y'all have a safe trip!"

"We will, Daizelle, we will!"

"We'll never be able to show them as good a time as they've shown us, Selma."

"I know, Paul, but we goan try."

"Selma. When we land, I'm going to shower and go straight to bed."

"Me too, but not befo' I make a few phone calls. Um so proud uh you, honey. I wont everybody tuh know 'bout my second set uh twins."

"I think you're partially responsible for them too, Selma."

"Yeah, I know, but I thank you did mo' work then I did."

Chapter 50

HOME SWEET HOME

"We wont you and Sheila tuh be the Godparents."

"There's no doubt about it, Selma, we accept."

"Now, you're sure there's two of them, Selma?"

"Oh, Diamond, you always got somethin crazy tuh say.

I wont you tuh know that if we have two boys, we goan name one, Diamond, Prescott, Bess, and the otha, Paul, Virgil, Bess. If it's two girls again we goan name one afta Sheila and you. If it's a boy and a girl we goan name that boy afta Paul and the girl gets your name, but we definitely know it's twins."

"What made you choose Sheila and me as Godparents?"

"Diamond, you and Sheila the most responsible people we know."

"You still feel that way although me and Sheila are separated right now and after the way Sadaya turned out?"

"Of course I do. Husbands and wives separate everyday. That don't make um irresponsible

parents, and what Sadaya do, don't have nothin
tuh do witch'all. Y'all gave that girl everythang
she needed tuh make it. Y'all values goan hafta
come back oan huh 'n' they will. Lack I said,
Diamond, y'all the best people we know."

"Thank you, Selma."

"Diamond, you cryin?"

*"I thought you wouldn't notice over the
phone, but yeah, I'm crying. It's just that; no
one's ever shown me the love that you and Paul
have. To tell you the truth, I don't think anyone
ever will."*

"Diamond, I should be the one cryin 'n'
thankin you."

"Why is that, Selma?"

"You stepped up tuh my husband lack a real
man. You took control uh what you thought he was
feelin and set thangs straight. Most men woulda
loved the idea of the minister's wife havin an
affair with um, whetha it happened uh not. They
woulda caused a lot uh trouble fuh me and Paul.
You didn't do that, Diamond.

Befo' I hang up tonight, I just wonna tell
yah that I love yah, Paul love yah, lil' Nina and
Nia, future Paul and lil' Diamond or Sheila loves
you too. Nigh, you have a good night, Diamond and
don't stay 'wake all night thankin 'bout these
twins."

"*You know me too well, Selma. That's exactly what I'll be doing. I'm much too excited to sleep. But to keep you from worrying, I'll try.*"

Chapter 51

DIAMOND'S FIRST SERMON

"Congregation, this is a blessed event for me. I've seen your faces over the years from another angle. They look just as pleasant from the pulpit as they do in the pews.

Before I begin my sermon, let's bow our heads in prayer...Dear Lord, we ask that you continue to watch over and protect us. Continue to bless reverend Bess, Lord, a man who truly has you in his heart.

Father, if there are any today who are miserable at heart, send them to me for prayer.

Keep us on that perfect road of peace, Lord and work within us until you have molded us to complete your journey.

Father, I am dedicated to you and this ministry and will abide by my spirit and your word.

I will do your work joyfully and at all times be truthful in expressing your word.

Again, Lord, I thank you for this chance, beautiful congregation, and this opportunity to serve you in a greater capacity.

Thank you Lord for all of your wonderful blessings...Amen...

...Congregation, today's lesson is on friendship. Friendship can be defined as companionship, social intimacy, a sister or brotherhood, fellowshipping, or having mutual esteem or respect for each other. Church congregations could be considered all of those. I say this because we fellowship together, we indulge in social intimacy by listening to each other, praying with each other, and teaching each other good values. We are a brother and sisterhood because once you've come to this church; whether you join or not, to us, you're considered our brother or sister. We have or should show mutual respect and be willing to let each other know the esteem, admiration, or value that we all carry regardless of our positions in the church and community.

This may be a sore subject, but I'm being led by the spirit to speak on it. Not too long ago Brother Porter lost his life tragically. Most of us felt great concern during that period and a great loss. We also knew that Brother Porter could have used more guidance, that just because he was an adult didn't mean that he didn't need some of us to guide him from time to time. What I'm hoping is that Brother Porters' death will help us all to realize how important brotherhood, sisterhood, and social intimacy is, and that this town will begin to change its values one citizen

at a time so that we can become the best
residents and church goers possible. Let's begin
to lift each other up in hope. Let's begin to
touch each others lives with positive words of
encouragement so that our old image will be
forgotten and the new one shines through...

"That man know he can preach a sermon!"
"Sho nuff chil', sho nuff...

Chapter 52

AFTER THE SERMON

"Brother Daniels, I'm so happy to see you here. Did you enjoy the service? How's the family doing?"

"Yes, yes. I did reverend. I did enjoy the service, and as far as I know, my family's okay. It's me who's not so good. Reverend, I'm disgusted with myself."

"What's troubling you, brother?"

"I started drinkin and gettin high again."

"Brother, we all take steps backwards."

"Reverend, it's more to it than that. Um different when I'm high. It's like I'm blinded. I don't care about nothin or nobody; not even how I make my wife 'n' kids feel. Reverend, I waited for everyone to leave so that I could talk to you about that."

"Then talk to me, Brother Daniels. That's what I'm here for."

"Reverend. I got involved with this girl 'n' got her pregnant. I didn't mean to do it, but when I'm under the influence I get filled with lust.

You see, Reverend Prescott. It all started out as a joke. I'd taken a day off from work. Me and three of my buddies were riding around—

"Are they married too, Brother Daniels?"

"Keith and Bandie are, reverend. Frank's single, but he's engaged. We all have good jobs at Norton Products and we've all been there for more than fifteen years...

"And?"

"And, we were all actin wild and stupid and just messin around that day and that's all it was supposed tuh be about. We saw this bunch of teenage girls at the bus stop and decided we'd give um a ride, yah know, just to be doin somethin crazy. The girl we let sit in the front seat, between Keith and me, she wadn't no joke. She was hittin me hard with street talk and style. I was tryin tuh act like she wadn't affectin me, but I'd got caught up in her as soon as I smelled that perfume she was wearin. She was somethin different. Everything about her made me want to see her again—to know her better. Before she got out the car, she gave me her phone number like it wadn't a big deal. My friends teased me about it. They were tellin me how Bernice was going to kick my butt if she found that number on me. I played it off by telling them that there was no way I'd ever take that number home with me and I balled the paper up and threw it out the window. I'd memorized the number—I'd always been good with numbers. Okay. So now I'm thinkin of ways to forget about this girl. Minister Prescott. I tried for seven weeks and couldn't shake the thought of her.

It was a Saturday night when I finally called
her from my cell phone. Me and Bernice was on bad
terms. She'd ran into one of her old boyfriends
at the mall the night before and she never
introduced me to him and the guy was staring down
at her breasts like some sort of pervert while he
talked to her. That made me feel small, reverend.
Like he was more important than me or like she
wanted him or somethin'. Anyway. The girl
answered the phone on the first ring. She sounded
half asleep. When she heard my voice she perked
up. Although I kinda liked the girl I wadn't goan
mess with her. I was just goan make Bernice a
little jealous like she'd made me. But, when me
and the girl started talkin somethin happened to
me. I knew that what I felt for her was more
serious than I'd pretended and she knew it too.
It got worse after she started talkin about the
places she'd gone, the people she knew, and her
ex-boyfriends. Then, she began talking sex. She
was telling me all the things she wanted to do to
me the first day she'd seen me and how she didn't
care about sharing me if she had to. She had my
attention and then she had me. Bernice was still
sitting in the livingroom watching television
when I left out the house without saying a word.

When I got to the girl's house she offered me
a drink. I started not to take it, but I reasoned
with myself that one wouldn't hurt, but it did. I

drank until I was drunk. We were just kissing at first. I'd told myself that it wouldn't go any further, but she had other plans and did everything she'd promised and some. I told myself it was a mistake and that it wouldn't happen again. The fact was; she and I had similar sexual desires. Bernice never wanted to go too far. The first night, that girl had almost taken me to the max.

Reverend, truth be told, after the first night I couldn't stop seeing that girl. Down the line we got careless, she got pregnant, and Bernice left me. I talked her in to coming home again, but when she got there, I was—I was, high again, with that young girl, and, and, and, and—

"Being intimate with her?"

"Reverend, it was more than intimate. I still wanted that young girl so bad I was willing to do what I had to do to have her, for what I thought would be, one, last, time! I was so turned on by her she had me doing back flips. You see, reverend, to keep these young girls happy now days you hafta go a lot further than you use to and I was still trying to hold on to her although my wife had barely agreed to come back home to me. I was greedy. I wanted her and Bernice and I thought that I could make it happen before Bernice came home, but things just didn't turn out that way! Bernice caught us together!"

"Oh-h-h, I see."

"So you get the picture?"

"Yes, Brother Daniels, I do."

"Well, when she saw that, she whipped me, and that girl. The girl put up a good fight, but Bernice swole her up pretty good. She wasn't a match for Bernice. Bernice don't play. Even you know that, Reverend Prescott."

"Yeah. I know how Bernice is, Brother Daniels."

"Anyway, I took the girl home. I came back and tried talkin to Bernice. Bernice didn't want to hear nothin. She took everything and dared me to take her to court to get any of it back. She said if I did she was going to make me shame and tell the court everything she'd seen. She said I'd probably end up losing even more because of the kids and maybe even lose the kids and I knew she was right.

I swear, reverend, I'm not usually like that only when I'm drinking and around that girl. Other times I'm the best husband and father any family can have."

"Do you still have cravings for the liquor and the young woman?"

"Yes, reverend, but I still love my wife! I just can't control what that girl does to me! Whatever it is it escalates when I get high! I want to let her go, but I just can't resist the sexual urges that I have for her!"

"Then I suggest you let God handle your addictions instead of handling them on your own."

"But, reverend Prescott, I don't understand! I know that I need to get help for both addictions, the girl 'n' the intoxicating substances, I just don't know how to go about doing it! Both of them are keeping me from uniting with my wife and the Father!"

"Brother Daniels, it's called denial. We all let it control us one way or another. The only way we can begin to handle it is to realize why we're in denial. For example, are we denying our problems because we feel inadequate when we realize that what we're doing is bad for us although we enjoy the rush we get from it? We have to think. Are we denying the truth or reveling in a lie? Either way, you need to make the decision of how long you can hide behind a façade. Believe me Brother Daniels, whatever it is you're feeling it can be remedied through our Lord and Savior. As I said before, you can't change yourself, you can only be willing to change. You must allow the Lord to work within you. You should always remember that each time we try to do God's work, we make a mess of things."

"Believe me Pastor, I know that now."

"Then believe this, Brother Daniels. All of us take steps backwards. It's all a part of strengthening our spirituality and learning who God is.

Ask God's forgiveness. You know he forgives us each time if we're sincere."

"Thank you reverend, thank you and I'll do that."

"Oh, and Brother Daniels!"

"Yes, Reverend."

"Pray for your family, the young woman, yourself, and pray before or even if you think of repeating that or any other coarse action.

If you are unable to control yourself and take a step backwards, talk it over with someone, do not be ashamed. Shame is almost like pride, it can keep you from doing what's right."

"Thank you reverend. I'll never shut myself out to you again. I promised God that I'd be a leader and it's a promise I'm going to keep."

"I know that you will, Brother Daniels. Sometimes we have more faith in others than we have in ourselves."

"See you Sunday, Brother Daniels?"

"Yes, reverend. I'll be here."

"Dear, dear, Lord, I just realized something. You are the Alpha and the Omega! The talk that I just had with Brother Daniels is almost the exact same discussion Reverend Bess and I had some years ago when I was thinking about preaching but had gone astray. You do have a way of making us work for what we receive without us knowing it until it's over. Thank you Lord. Thank you for giving me the opportunity to repay a debt and to be a blessing to others. You are my sole life source. You are truly, The Alpha and Omega."

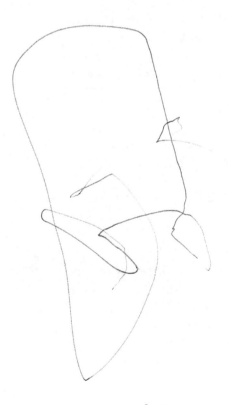

Previously published by Lee Charles:

THE TRUTH ABOUT LIES
THE TRUTH ABOUT LIES II CAMOUFLAGED
X5 AND ME

Recently published by Lee Charles:

THE TRUTH ABOUT LIES III REVELATION
AUNT JENNY'S SILENCE
TOO MANY RAINBOWS
SISTER CONNECTION
GODLY PEOPLE
THE DEVIL'S HORNS
HUMAN PUPPET

As with all of Lee Charles' books, her new series
of books stimulate thought, and are very
realistic.